PUBLIC UTILITY ECONOMICS

Public Utility Economics

Michael A. Crew

and

Paul R. Kleindorfer

St. Martin's Press   New York

Library of Congress Cataloging in Publication Data

Crew, Michael.
    Public utility economics.

    Bibliography: p.
    Includes index.
    1. Public utilities. I. Kleindorfer, Paul R.,
joint author. II. Title.
HD2763.C7 1979   338.4'3   78–24611
ISBN 0–312–65569–X

Contents

Preface and Acknowledgements

The growth in public utilities and public enterprise over the last thirty years has prompted an increasing interest by economists, management scientists, administrators and politicians in the problems of public utility economics. This book aims to provide an analytical basis for those who wish to study, manage or prescribe policies for public utilities. Its approach is primarily theoretical and research-orientated, with applications provided for purposes of illustration.

The level of the analysis is within the capabilities of graduate students who have completed courses in microeconomic theory, and those who have done the now commonplace courses in calculus, linear algebra and optimisation. However, in an attempt to be comprehensive and rigorous, a number of appendixes have been provided which furnish detailed proofs of certain propositions and which review some of the more specialised techniques used. In addition numerical exercises, some with fully worked answers, are provided. These, it is hoped, will prove valuable to serious students in assessing their grasp of the theory.

The idea of the book arose out of a long research collaboration which began in 1969 at Carnegie–Mellon University. Since then, except for 1977, the collaboration has taken place mostly at an average distance of 3000 miles, with occasional trips by both authors across the Atlantic. All of what is contained here, with the exception of Chapter 7, arises out of our joint published work. On Chapter 7 however, we collaborated with Hong-Chang Chang, a Ph.D. candidate of the University of Pennsylvania. We are pleased to acknowledge his participation as a co-author of Chapter 7 and his comments on the rest of the text.

We are especially grateful to Roger Sherman of the University of Virginia who acted as reader for the publisher. His comments made us think carefully about our ideas and strive for clarity of exposition, and went far beyond the normal duties of reader with the result that we were able to improve and extend our original manuscript in a number of important respects.

We would also like to acknowledge comments and discussion with many colleagues over the years that gave us insights into our work, especially Walter Goldberg, Howard Kunreuther, Bridger Mitchell, Fred Sudit and Sidney Weintraub, who are not to be blamed for any remaining errors, however.

We would like to thank Shelley Bauer, Naomi Coyle, Lenore Rutz and Diane Weinstock for typing assistance.

Finally, we are most grateful to our wives for their support and uncommon patience in the ten-year wait for the fruits of this endeavour.

M. A. C.
P. R. K.

Part One

Setting the Scene

1 Introduction

In this book we are concerned with some of the important issues of theory and policy in the economics of public utilities. Our approach is different from most previous texts on public utilities which have aimed to be comprehensive in their treatment of the field. Given the rapid growth of the literature on public utilities in recent times we have preferred to follow a more eclectic approach, treating a few vital issues at length and with some rigour. In this chapter we start by examining briefly the nature of public utility economics and by sketching the contents of the rest of the book.

Public utilities are easily recognised. Gas, electricity, telephones and water are the traditional examples, followed more recently by cable television. The question of whether a company is a public utility is essentially technical, though there is a body of legal and historical precedent to support the view that an industry must be of some public or social significance to be considered a public utility. The technical features defining a public utility are those giving rise to economies of scale in public utilities and their resulting 'natural monopoly' position.[1] The point is intuitively obvious. There are definite cost savings in having only one water main in the street, and similarly with the other utilities. Such economies of scale give rise to the fundamental problem of public utility economics: how to establish 'benevolent monopolies' which will take advantage of these economies of scale, but will not engage in monopolistic excesses in the process. We are slowly learning that there are no complete answers to this problem.

Practical solutions to the problem of public utilities have traditionally opted either for nationalising such monopolies or for regulating them by a commission set up to guard the public interest. Neither solution has been a stellar success, either from the point of view of benevolence or that of efficiency, and this has led in the past decade to a re-examination of the foundations of public utility economics. The main outlines of this reassessment might be classified as follows:

(i) the *historical–legal perspective*, which attempts to understand what forces brought regulation or nationalisation into existence and which groups benefited thereby,

(ii) the *theoretical perspective*, which has attempted to understand the institutional design issues involved in regulation and has also extended earlier welfare analyses to deal with time-varying demand and uncertainty,

(iii) the *practical perspective*, which has recently come to the fore in attempting to provide a basis for implementing some of the more compelling reforms arising from economic theory, e.g. peak-load pricing.

Although this book spans all the above recent developments, we have placed our main emphasis on theory. In particular we present a thorough examination of the peak-load problem, which is a persuasive problem of public utilities producing a commodity (or service) which is economically non-storable and for which demand fluctuates over time. In such a situation the trade-offs between social welfare, pricing policy and investment requirements (e.g. to meet peak demand) are critical. A major aim of this book is to examine these trade-offs and to relate them to institutional design problems arising from regulation or nationalisation.

We have divided the book into four parts. Part One provides our introduction to the nature of public utilities and underlying welfare considerations. Chapter 2 deals with the theoretical foundations of our welfare framework. As our analysis is normative we set out here the foundations for our analysis of policy alternatives. These include the value judgements in the social-welfare function employed, which is the traditional measure using the excess of consumers' surplus and total revenue over total cost.

In Part Two we provide a comprehensive statement of the theory of peak-load pricing. In Chapter 3 we introduce the familiar solutions to the peak-load problem of Steiner and Boiteux. In Chapter 4 we discuss extensions of the traditional peak-load problem to take into account the existence of multiple-plant types. In Chapter 5 we examine the effects of random demand on the peak-load model, while Chapter 6 illustrates the previous chapters with some numerical examples. Chapter 7 examines some extensions to the peak-load model by means of a dynamic analysis.

In Part Three we examine the methods of utility regulation in the U.S. and the U.K. Chapter 8 is mainly concerned with the descriptive, legal and institutional background to regulation in the U.S. and the U.K. Chapter 9 discusses the theory of regulation by commission, particularly the theory of rate-of-return regulation, including its traditional implications as well as extensions to include stochastic demand and managerial discretion.

Part Four examines the case study of electricity supply – Chapter 10 – and the role of peak-load pricing in energy conservation – Chapter 11. Finally, as well as providing a brief summary and conclusion, we present in Chapter 12 our personal postscript, giving our views as to the desirable directions of research and public policy in the field of public utilities.

2 Welfare Economic Foundations

Our purpose in this book is to provide a normative basis for public utility pricing and investment decisions. Accordingly we begin with a discussion of the welfare economic foundations of public policy decisions. A vast literature[1] in welfare economics and cost–benefit analysis underlies these issues, but we aspire here only to a brief overview of the traditional welfare analysis of public utility problems. This traditional view holds that the net social worth of a particular policy may be represented as the sum of consumers' and producers' surpluses generated by the policy in question – i.e. the excess of consumers' total 'willingness to pay', net of the actual price paid, plus producers' profits.

The use of consumers' and producers' surplus as a measure of welfare was apparently first proposed by Jules Dupuit (1844) in connection with the evaluation of public-works projects. Alfred Marshall (1890) developed and extended the concept, and Hotelling (1932, 1938) used it as a basis for his proposals on public utility pricing. Although there have been detractors,[2] the use of consumers' and producers' surplus is now broadly accepted as appropriate for welfare analysis in public utility economics. The rationale for this will be explored in the following section. Thereafter, we will address the related issue of marginal-cost pricing and optimal departures from it when minimum revenue (or other institutional) constraints make marginal-cost pricing infeasible.

2.1 THE SOCIAL-WELFARE FUNCTION

As indicated above, the traditional measure of welfare employed in evaluating public utility policies has been the following:

$$W = TR + S - TC, \tag{2.1}$$

where W = net social benefit, TR = total revenue, S = consumers' surplus, and TC = total costs.

In the case of a single product the net benefits in (2.1) accruing at a given output level x may be expressed as:[3]

$$W = \int_0^x P(y)dy - C(x), \tag{2.2}$$

where $P(x)$ is the (inverse) demand function and $C(x)$ is the total cost function. The integral (2.2), which we refer to as 'gross surplus', encompasses both total revenue, $TR(x) = P(x) \cdot x$, as well as consumers' surplus S. In this case S is just the area of the Marshallian triangle (i.e. the shaded area in Figure 2.1):

$$S(x) = \int_0^x [P(y) - P(x)]\, dy. \tag{2.3}$$

$TR - TC$ includes any profit (or loss) by the producer. This means that benefits to the producer and the consumer are valued equally in the social-welfare function.

In the case where the price of more than one commodity changes the definition of gross surplus is somewhat more complicated.[4] Let a typical commodity bundle be represented by $x = (x_1, \ldots, x_n)$. (We use

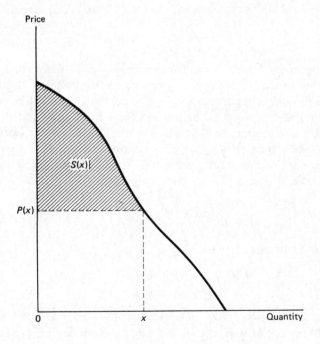

Fig. 2.1

bold-face type to denote vectors and vector functions.) Let $X(p) = (X_1(p), \ldots, X_n(p))$ be the n demand functions for x, and let $P(x) = (P_1(x), \ldots, P_n(x))$ be the inverse demand functions for these commodities, i.e. $P(X(p)) = p$ for all price vectors p. When, for each commodity, $P_i(x) = P_i(x_i)$ – i.e. the demand for commodity i is unaffected by price changes of other commodities – we have the case of independent demands. In this case the natural extension of (2.2) to encompass the multiproduct case would simply sum the gross surpluses of each of the n commodities. The resulting net social benefits at the vector of outputs $x = (x_1, \ldots, x_n)$ would be:

$$W = \sum_{i=1}^{n} \int_0^{x_i} P_i(y_i) dy_i - C(x). \tag{2.4}$$

In general, of course, one would expect P_i to depend on the entire output vector x and not just on x_i. In this general case Hotelling (1932) suggested that the appropriate analogue to (2.2) and (2.3) should be:

$$W = \oint_{F(o, x)} \left(\sum_{i=1}^{n} P_i(y) dy_i \right) - C(x), \tag{2.5}$$

where gross surplus is represented as a line integral[5] along some curve $F(o, x)$ connecting the origin (of n-space) and the vector x. Thus gross surplus in (2.5) is measured, just as in (2.2), as the total willingness to pay, integrated along some adjustment curve from o to x. As it turns out,[6] the line integral in (2.5) will generally depend on the particular path $F(o, x)$ along which this gross surplus is measured. However, as the appendix to this chapter points out, W in (2.5) will depend only on x and not on the path $F(o, x)$ provided that:

$$\frac{\partial P_i}{\partial x_j} = \frac{\partial P_j}{\partial x_i} \quad \text{for all } i, j, \tag{2.6}$$

or equivalently (see Exercise 2.1):

$$\frac{\partial X_i}{\partial p_j} = \frac{\partial X_j}{\partial p_i} \quad \text{for all } i, j. \tag{2.7}$$

Conditions (2.6)–(2.7) are called 'integrability conditions'. When they hold W in (2.5) is well-defined and may be rewritten, independent of $F(o, x)$, as:

$$W = \oint_0^x \left(\sum_{i=1}^{n} P_i(y) dy_i \right) - C(x), \tag{2.8}$$

a function of x alone. Moreover, if (2.7) holds, the partial derivatives of gross surplus exist and satisfy:

$$\frac{\partial}{\partial x_i} \oint_0^x \left(\sum_{i=1}^n P_i(y) dy_i \right) = P_i(x),\tag{2.9}$$

so that the first-order conditions, $\partial W/\partial x_i = 0$, for maximising W again here lead to marginal-cost pricing.

We will generally assume the integrability conditions (2.6) or (2.7) to hold whenever we use the traditional welfare function W. These conditions clearly hold when $P_i(x) = P_i(x_i)$, the independent demand case, since for this case $\partial P_i/\partial x_j = 0$ whenever $i \neq j$. Hotelling (1932, 1935) also showed that the integrability conditions hold if each consumer, in determining his joint demand for the commodities $x_1, \ldots, x_n$, assumes that his budget constraint need not be met exactly.[7] This and other economic rationale for (2.6)–(2.7) are discussed further in Pressman (1970).

Before leaving this section it is interesting to illustrate briefly the relationship of the welfare function W to a simple two-period peak-load pricing problem. In this case a non-storable product is supplied in two equal-length periods. Output in these periods is denoted $x = (x_1, x_2)$. We assume prices and outputs of all other commodities are fixed and denote the demand functions for the product in question for the two periods as $X_1(p)$ and $X_2(p)$, with inverse demand functions $P_1(x)$ and $P_2(x)$. Then the above analysis suggests the following formulation for choosing capacity and prices so as to maximise net social benefits:

$$\text{Max } \oint_0^x (P_1(y) dy_1 + P_2(y) dy_2) - C(x, q),\tag{2.10}$$

subject to $0 \leqslant x_i \leqslant q, i = 1, \ldots, n$, where $\overline{q}$ represents installed capacity and $C(x, q)$ is the long-run cost function. We will have much more to say about problems of the form (2.10) below.

2.2 JUSTIFICATION OF THE TRADITIONAL WELFARE FUNCTION

A central issue, which this section addresses, is when the welfare function W of (2.1) is a justifiable measure of social benefits. Our discussion will follow closely the recent work of Willig (1973, 1976).

We begin by considering a single consumer whose preferences for n commodities, denoted $x_1, \ldots, x_n$, are assumed to be represented by a strictly increasing, strictly quasi-concave,[8] twice continuously differentiable utility function $U(x_1, \ldots, x_n)$. His indirect utility function $L(\mathbf{p}, m)$ in response to the price vector $\mathbf{p} = p_1, \ldots, p_n$ for $\mathbf{x} = x_1, \ldots, x_n$ and the budget m, is defined as:

$$L(\mathbf{p}, m) = \text{Max}\left\{U(\mathbf{x})|\mathbf{x} \geqslant 0; \sum_{i=1}^{n} p_i x_i \leqslant m .\right\} \tag{2.11}$$

L can be shown (see Katzner, 1970) to be decreasing (increasing) in $\mathbf{p}$ (in m), strictly quasi-convex and, provided the maximising $\mathbf{x}$ in (2.11) is positive), twice continuously differentiable at the corresponding $(\mathbf{p}, m)$.

Suppose we are interested in evaluating the desirability to our consumer of two policies yielding price vectors $\mathbf{p}'$ and $\mathbf{p}''$ and incomes m' and m''. Our approach to this evaluation will be through the Hicksian measures of compensating and equivalent variations which we now define (as in Hicks, 1956).

Let $\mathbf{p}'$ and $\mathbf{p}''$ be two price vectors, of which we will interpret $\mathbf{p}'$ as the status quo. The *compensating variation* is the sum of money required to make the consumer indifferent between prices $\mathbf{p}'$ and $\mathbf{p}''$ when his current budget is m'. Thus C(= *compensating variation*) is defined through:

$$L(\mathbf{p}', m') = L(\mathbf{p}'', m' + C). \tag{2.12}$$

Similarly equivalent variation is defined as the sum of money which the consumer would be willing to pay to keep the present price structure $\mathbf{p}'$ in preference to the alternative $\mathbf{p}''$. Thus E(= *equivalent variation*) is defined through:

$$L(\mathbf{p}', m' - E) = L(\mathbf{p}'', m'). \tag{2.13}$$

When income changes are also envisaged, as in comparing price-income pairs $(\mathbf{p}', m')$ and $(\mathbf{p}'', m'')$, it is clear from (2.12)–(2.13) that $(\mathbf{p}'', m'')$ is preferred to $(\mathbf{p}', m')$ if and only if $C < m'' - m'$. Similarly if E is the equivalent variation with respect to moving from $(\mathbf{p}', m')$ to $(\mathbf{p}'', m')$, then $(\mathbf{p}'', m')$ is preferred to $(\mathbf{p}', m'')$ if and only if $E > m' - m''$. Thus C and E are sufficient for evaluating the benefits of price changes from the point of view of the individual.

Restricting attention for the moment to single price changes under fixed income we note the following link between consumers' surplus and the C and E measures just given.

FUNDAMENTAL APPROXIMATE RESULT (WILLIG, 1976). Consider a single consumer with fixed income m' and faced with prices p' and p'' for some commodity. Let the consumer's demand function for the commodity be denoted $X(p, m)$, where m is his income level. If $|\bar{\eta}S/2m'| \leqslant 0.05$ and $|S/m'| \leqslant 0.9$, then the following bounds obtain:[9]

$$\frac{\bar{\eta}|S|}{2m'} \leqslant \frac{C - S}{|S|} \leqslant \frac{\bar{\eta}|S|}{2m'} \tag{2.14}$$

$$\frac{\eta|S|}{2m'} \leqslant \frac{S - E}{|S|} \leqslant \frac{\bar{\eta}|S|}{2m'}, \tag{2.15}$$

where $S = \int_{p'}^{p''}, X(p, m')dp$ = the consumer's surplus increase (if $p'' \geqslant p'$), or decrease (if $p'' \leqslant p'$) associated with the price p' to p''; C and E are defined above through (2.12)–(2.13); $\bar{\eta}$ and η are upper and lower bounds on the income elasticity of demand, $\eta = (\partial X(p, m)/(\partial m) \cdot (m/X(p, m))$ for $m = m'$ and p between p' and p''.

Since one may expect the ratio S/m' to be quite small for realistic price changes, and since income elasticities are usually near unity, we see that the hypotheses of the above proposition are mild. As a result of Willig's analysis we can indicate the extent to which consumer's surplus is a good approximator of both compensating and equivalent variations, dependent only on the size of income effects of price changes and the proportion of the consumer's income accounted for by the compensating or equivalent variations.

Although the above results assume only a single price change, analogous results are proved in Willig (1973) for multiple price changes, i.e. for the case involving n commodities and a general price change from the price vector $\mathbf{p}'$ to $\mathbf{p}''$. These results are identical in form to (2.14)–(2.15) above except that η and $\bar{\eta}$ must be understood as the minimum (respectively, maximum) of the income elasticities of demand for the several commodities over all price vectors in a suitable region encompassing the possible paths of adjustment of prices from the status quo $\mathbf{p}'$ to the new price vector $\mathbf{p}''$.

We see from the above that compensating and equivalent variations are appropriate for evaluating the monetary worth of price and income changes for a single consumer. Because we can aggregate these measures over all consumers and use them to compare the net social benefits derivable from alternative price structures, i.e. such aggregates can serve as a social-welfare function, we find these results useful in the development of our analysis. However, before doing this we examine as background their use in the two classical 'compensation principles' of Kaldor–Hicks and Scitovsky,[10] which were two of the forerunners to the Bergson (1938) social-welfare function which we employ. These classical welfare criteria will then be shown to be expressible in terms of aggregates of compensating and equivalent variations. We are interested in comparing the social desirability of pairs $(\mathbf{p}, \mathbf{m})$, where $\mathbf{p}$ is a price vector and $\mathbf{m} = (m_1, m_2, \ldots, m_n)$ an income distribution resulting from some policy, where m is the income of individual i.

Kaldor–Hicks. The state $(\mathbf{p}'', \mathbf{m}'')$ is preferred to the state $(\mathbf{p}', \mathbf{m}')$ if it is possible to redistribute $\mathbf{m}''$, with resulting income distribution $\mathbf{m}$ so that everyone prefers $(\mathbf{p}'', \mathbf{m})$ to $(\mathbf{p}', \mathbf{m}')$.

Scitovsky. The state $(\mathbf{p}'', \mathbf{m}'')$ is not preferred to $(\mathbf{p}', \mathbf{m}')$ unless it is not possible to redistribute $\mathbf{m}'$, with resulting income distribution $\mathbf{m}$, such that $(\mathbf{p}', \mathbf{m})$ is preferred by everyone to $(\mathbf{p}'', \mathbf{m}'')$.

Stated loosely the Kaldor–Hicks criterion indicates that one social state is preferred to another if those gaining from the changed social state can compensate the losers sufficiently to still their woes. Scitovsky argued that additionally, one should require that these same losers will not suffer sufficient loss from the change so that they would be willing and able to bribe the gainers not to make the change. Both criteria are directed at discovering potential Pareto improvements over the status quo. Achieving these potential improvements in Pareto fashion would of course require the actual implementation of the income transfers mentioned in these criteria. Interestingly, as Baumol (1972, p. 403) has noted, if arbitrary income redistributions are possible, then a Pareto criterion (with lump-sum transfers) could be applied directly. Note, however, that the above criteria will not lead us astray in the sense that whenever Pareto improvement is possible (with or without lump-sum transfers of income) both criteria will be satisfied.

To illustrate the use of compensating and equivalent variations with welfare criteria, we note that the Kaldor-Hicks criterion is equivalent to:

$$(\mathbf{p}'', \mathbf{m}'') \text{ is preferred to } (p', m') \text{ if } \sum_i C_i < \sum_i (m_i'' - m_i'), \qquad (2.16)$$

where C_i is the ith individual's compensating variation in going from $(\mathbf{p}', m_i')$ to $\mathbf{p}''$, i.e., $L_i(\mathbf{p}', m_i') = L_i(\mathbf{p}'', m_i' + C_i)$ as in (2.12). To see that (2.16) is equivalent to the Kaldor–Hicks criterion, note first that $\mathbf{m}$ is a redistribution of $\mathbf{m}''$ means:

$$\sum_i m_i = \sum_i m_i'' \qquad (2.17)$$

Thus there exists a redistribution $\mathbf{m}$ of $\mathbf{m}''$ such that everyone prefers $(\mathbf{p}'', \mathbf{m})$ precisely when (2.17) holds and $L_i(\mathbf{p}'', m_i) > L_i(\mathbf{p}', m_i')$ for every individual i. Since $L_i(\mathbf{p}'', m_i' + C_i)$, by definition of C_i, this last means that $m_i > m_i' + C_i$. Summing over i and using (2.17) yields (2.16).

A similar reasoning establishes that the Scitovsky criterion is equivalent to:

$$(\mathbf{p}'', \mathbf{m}'') \text{ is not preferred to } (\mathbf{p}', \mathbf{m}') \text{ unless } \sum_i E_i < \sum_i (m_i'' - m_i'), \qquad (2.18)$$

where E_i is the equivalent variation defined in (2.13). When incomes are unchanged and we are comparing only prices $\mathbf{p}'$ and $\mathbf{p}''$, we see that the above welfare criteria reduce to $C(\mathbf{p}', \mathbf{p}'', \mathbf{m}') = \sum C_i < 0$ and $E(\mathbf{p}', \mathbf{p}'', \mathbf{m}'') = \sum E_i < 0$.

Now returning to consumers' surplus, Willig's *fundamental approximation result* implies, when extrapolated to aggregate compensating and equivalent variations, that as long as each consumer satisfies the requirements of this proposition then the bounds in (2.14)-(2.15) also hold for, aggregate surplus and C and E measures (see also Exercise 2.3). Thus for single price changes consumers' surplus serves as a close approximation of C and E. As Willig (1973) and Zajac (1977) show, similar results obtain for multiple price changes as well.

If, in the context of microeconomic policy, we are prepared to separate distributional from allocative issues, then the aggregate of consumers' surplus as a measure of consumers' benefit is even more acceptable to the extent that it avoids the problem of non-payment of compensation implicit in the Kaldor-Hicks and Scitovsky criteria. In the same spirit we introduce the producer(s) into the welfare analysis by adding their 'surplus', i.e. profits, to that of the consumers in obtaining total welfare. Doing so, in fact, yields the traditional welfare function W in (2.1).

Summarising, the traditional welfare function employing an equally weighted[11] sum of consumers' and producers' surpluses, particularly when coupled with a suitable mechanism for compensation to be paid, is an appropriate measure of social benefits whenever income effects are not too large and the policy variations under consideration are not too drastic. We shall assume this to be the case throughout, departing only occasionally from this framework in discussing distributional and equity issues.

2.3 MARGINAL-COST PRICING

As indicated in Section 2.1 the traditional social-welfare function W leads to a marginal-cost pricing solution. This is certainly reassuring since marginal-cost pricing is one of the corner-stones of economic efficiency. The general theory of marginal-cost pricing holds that under perfectly competitive conditions setting the price of every commodity equal to its marginal cost is required for efficiency.[12] The familiar logic of this requirement is that if the price of some commodity is not equal to its marginal cost, then this price would not reflect accurately the social cost of increasing (or curtailing) output of the commodity by an additional unit and would thus fail to give out the appropriate signal to purchase the optimal quantity. If, for example, price is above marginal cost, some consumers will not consume something for which they would have gladly paid the cost of production.

Thus marginal-cost pricing has strong arguments in its favour. There are also significant problems with marginal-cost pricing. First, if any of the various conditions for a competitive equilibrium are violated elsewhere in the economy, the price–marginal-cost equality may be violated in these other sectors. Such departures from marginal-cost pricing then raise the question of the optimality of marginal-cost pricing in the remaining sectors. Problems of this sort resulting from a breakdown of price–marginal-cost equality are termed 'second-best-problems'. Some of the early contributions on second-best, Lipsey and Lancaster (1956) for example, argued that there were just no general rules for optimality in second-best situations. Each case had its own peculiar second-best solution. Recent developments, however, have been more positive. For example, Davis and Whinston (1965) indicate that where there is little or no interdependence between sectors, enforcing competitive prices in the competitive sector may be appropriate. Textbooks on industrial organisation, like Scherer (1970) and Sherman (1974), have also begun to reflect a more positive attitude towards second-best problems. When faced with the impossibility of having an economy operate on quasi-competitive lines (maintaining the price–marginal-cost equality in all sectors) there still may be a presumption in favour of competition, as Scherer (1970, p. 26) argues: 'On the positive side, if we have absolutely no prior information concerning the direction in which second-best solutions lie, eliminating avoidable monopoly power is as likely statistically to improve welfare as to reduce it.'

Other arguments may be put forward in support of competitive solutions in second-best situations. The 'X-efficiency' hypothesis, originated by Harvey Leibenstein (1966), offers support for such solutions. Leibenstein argued that another inefficiency, likely to be at least as great as the allocative inefficiency which results from a price–marginal-cost divergence, is the inefficiency which arises from a failure to combine resources effectively in production. This he calls 'X-inefficiency' and is, he argues, more likely to arise under monopolistic situations. In a competitive product market firms that fail to achieve X-efficiency are unlikely to obtain sufficient return to stay in business. However, a monopoly, with the cushion of monopoly profits, does not need to minimise costs to survive. For a monopoly there is only the discipline of the capital market operating externally to make it X-efficient. Thus there may be an additional welfare loss from monopoly arising from X-efficiency,[13] and considerations of X-efficiency may well strengthen the presumption in favour of competitive solutions, like the marginal-cost pricing solutions discussed here.

Supposing for the moment that we lean in the direction of marginal-cost pricing for public utilities, there remains the critical problem of decreasing costs.[14] If, as in the traditional view of most public utilities, average costs are declining, then they are necessarily greater than marginal costs.[15] Thus declining average costs lead to deficits under marginal-cost pricing, presenting a number of problems. Although these deficits may be covered by tax revenues, significant allocative distortions may be caused by the tax levies themselves, perhaps more severe than the distortions which would be caused by pricing the public utility's output at average cost in the first place.[16] There are also serious managerial incentive problems with allowing a utility to operate at a deficit while guaranteeing that its losses will be covered. Finally, if public utilities must compete for investment resources in a capital market, these problems become further compounded with stockholder liability and ownerhsip issues.

The two alternatives which have served as the focus for discussing the issue of decreasing costs have been fair rate-of-return regulation and welfare optimal break-even analysis. Let us consider these two approaches briefly.

Consider first a profit-maximising monopolist producing the two commodities $\mathbf{x} = (x_1, x_2)$, with total costs $C(\mathbf{x})$ and faced with 'willingness to pay' (i.e. inverse demand) functions $P_1(\mathbf{x}), P_2(\mathbf{x})$. Such a monopolist would set price and output so as to:

$$\text{Max} \sum_{i=1}^{2} x_i P_i(\mathbf{x}) - C(\mathbf{x}).\quad\quad (2.19)$$
$$\mathbf{x} \geq 0$$

This leads to the familiar solution that marginal revenue should be equated to marginal cost, i.e. $\partial \text{Rev}(\mathbf{x})/\partial x_i = \partial C(\mathbf{x})/\partial x_i$, or from (2.19):

$$x_i \frac{\partial P_i}{\partial x_i} + x_j \frac{\partial P_j}{\partial x_i} + P_i(\mathbf{x}) = \frac{\partial C(\mathbf{x})}{\partial x_i},\quad\quad (2.20)$$

where $j \neq i, i, j = 1, 2$. Depending on the sign of $\partial P_j/\partial x_i$ various possibilities result, but the usual presumption is that own effects dominate cross effects so that the first term in (2.20), which is negative since $\partial P_i/\partial x_i < 0$, dominates the second, leading to higher prices $P_i(\mathbf{x})$ and lower output $\mathbf{x}$ than would obtain under marginal-cost pricing.

In order to limit these welfare losses due to monopoly pricing one might attempt to regulate the level of profits to some 'fair' level, say high enough to pay competitive rates to the various factors used in producing $\mathbf{x}$, including capital. This approach presumes that some form of regulatory commission will be set up to adjudicate what the competitive rates for various productive factors are and also to monitor how much of each regulated factor is used in the production process. As we show in detail in Chapters 8 and 9, welfare gains can materialise from such a system which is administered properly, though there are many complications. The critical difficulty with this approach is that it creates an incentive for the profit-maximiser to inflate his use of or claimed use of those productive factors which are regulated in an attempt to limit profits.

A second approach, which owes much to Boiteux (1956) and the recent synthesis by Baumol and Bradford (1970), is to deal directly with the problem of deficits that would follow marginal-cost pricing above marginal cost in order to break even and avoid a deficit. The best departures from marginal-cost pricing can be found by optimising some welfare function subject to an explicit break-even constraint. Using the traditional welfare function in the present case leads to the following in place of (2.19):

$$\text{Max}\ W(\mathbf{x}) = \oint_0^x \sum_{i=1}^{2} P_i(\mathbf{x}) dx_i - C(\mathbf{x}),\quad\quad (2.21)$$
$$\mathbf{x} \geq 0$$

subject to:

$$\pi(\mathbf{x}) = \sum_{i=1}^{2} x_i P_i(\mathbf{x}) - C(\mathbf{x}) \geqslant \pi_0, \qquad (2.22)$$

where π_0 is the required profit level. Associating the Lagrange multiplier μ with (2.22), we form the Lagrangian:[17]

$$L(\mathbf{x}, \mu) = W(\mathbf{x}) + \mu(\sum_{i=1}^{2} x_i P_i(\mathbf{x}) - C(\mathbf{x}) - \pi_0), \qquad (2.23)$$

and consider the first-order conditions $\partial L/\partial x_i = 0$ (assuming $x_i > 0$) and $\partial L/\partial \mu = 0$ (assuming (2.22) holds as an equality at optimum). This yields $\pi(\mathbf{x}) = \pi_0$ and:

$$P_i(\mathbf{x}) - MC_i(\mathbf{x}) + \mu(MR_i(\mathbf{x}) - MC_i(\mathbf{x})) = 0, i = 1, 2, \qquad (2.24)$$

where $MR_i = \partial \text{Rev}/\partial x_i$, $MC_i = \partial C/\partial x_i$. From (2.24), then, deviations $(p_i - MC_i)$ of price from marginal cost should be proportional to the difference between marginal revenue and marginal cost. In the case of independent demands $P_i(\mathbf{x}) = P_i(x_i)$, and (2.24) may be rewritten as:

$$\frac{P_i(x_i) - MC_i(\mathbf{x})}{P_i(x_i)} = \left(\frac{\mu}{1 + \mu}\right)\frac{1}{E_i}, i = 1, 2, \qquad (2.25)$$

where $E_i = -[P_i(x_i)/x_i](1/P_i'(x_i))$ is the price elasticity of demand. This last is the so-called *inverse elasticity rule*; it says that the percentage deviation of price from marginal cost should be inversely proportional to elasticity. The intuitive rationale for this rule is that in achieving a required level of profit in a welfare optimal fashion those prices ought to be raised the most which will least distort the resulting output pattern from the socially efficient pattern obtainable through marginal-cost pricing.[18] This suggests that contributions toward covering the deficit should be extracted more from products with inelastic demands than from those which are more price sensitive.

We may summarise the above discussion of decreasing costs as follows. If decreasing costs are handled through rate-of-return regulation, then X-inefficiency may result because there are incentives to distort (reported) use of regulated factors. The other approach is to turn control of the public utilities directly over to the government, in the hope that the responsible government agency would implement the just-described welfare optimal break-even solution. This second approach is also likely to have problems of X-inefficiency, however, as the growing literature on bureaucracy indicates – (see, for example, Niskanen, 1973); we will discuss this in Chapters 8 and 9.

Our approach to these problems will be to examine extensively in Part Two the nature of welfare optimal (i.e. marginal-cost) pricing and capacity decisions under various environmental and technological conditions. This will provide an ideal reference point against which to compare alternatives which may seem more practicable in light of the above discussion. Alternatives will then be investigated further in the last half of the book.

EXERCISES

2.1   Verify that conditions (2.6) and (2.7) are equivalent.

2.2   Assume the following utility function for an individual for two commodities: $U(x_1, x_2) = x_1^{\alpha} x_2^{\beta}$, where $x_1, x_2 \geq 0$, $\alpha, \beta > 0$, $\alpha + \beta \leq 1$. Let p_1, p_2 be the prices for x_1, x_2 and show that his indirect utility function is:

$$L(p_1, p_2) = \left(\frac{\alpha}{p_1}\right)^{\alpha} \left(\frac{\beta}{p_2}\right)^{\beta} \left(\frac{m}{\alpha + \beta}\right)^{\alpha + \beta}$$

and that his demand function for x_1 is (independently of $p_2 > 0$):

$$X_1'(p_1) = \frac{\alpha m}{(\alpha + \beta)p_1}.$$

Show that, for price pairs $\overline{p}'$, $\overline{p}''$, compensating and equivalent variations are given by $C = E = (R - 1)m$, where:

$$R = \left(\frac{\overline{p}_1''}{\overline{p}_1'}\right)^{\frac{\alpha}{\alpha + \beta}} \left(\frac{\overline{p}_2''}{\overline{p}_2'}\right)^{\frac{\alpha}{\alpha + \beta}}.$$

Verify that income elasticity of demand (η) is unity here and verify Willig's bounds for this case.

2.3   Verify that if (2.14)–(2.15) hold for each of m individuals (with the same bounds on income elasticity), then these same bounds hold for the aggregate measures:

$$C = \sum_{i=1}^{m} C_i, \quad E = \sum_{i=1}^{m} E_i, \quad S = \sum_{i=1}^{m} S_i.$$

2.4 The social-welfare function employed here exhibits the same formal marginal-cost-price equality as is derived more usually from general-equilibirum models. Such models derive the result that for all consumers the marginal rate of substitution between all pairs of goods is equal to the respective marginal rate of transformation. It is readily derivable that the marginal rate of transformation is none other than the ratio of marginal costs. From this and the equalities of *MRS* and *MRT* the price–marginal-cost rate follows (see, for example, Bator, 1957). To see this for a simple case, assume an economy of two persons and two goods and consider a general social-welfare function of the form $W = W(u^1, u^2)$, where $u^1 = u^1(x^1{}_1, x^1{}_2)$ is individual 1's utility function for goods x_1 and x_2. The boundary of the social transformation set is assumed given by the function $F(y_1, y_2) = 0$, where y_1, y_2 represent the quantities of goods 1 and 2 produced. We assume that

$$y_i = x_i = \sum_{j=1}^{2} x_i{}^j$$

for $i = 1, 2$, so that everything that is produced is consumed.

(i) Set up the Lagrangian to maximise W.

(ii) Derive the equality of *MRS* and *MRT*.

(iii) Derive the marginal-cost pricing rule.

APPENDIX ON LINE INTEGRALS

This appendix provides a brief introduction to consumers' surplus for the case of multiple products. In this case, Hotelling [1932] argued that the appropriate measure of welfare is the line integral (2.5). We therefore first discuss the meaning of line integrals in general.

Let R^n denote n-dimensional Euclidian space and let R^n_+ be the non-negative orthant of R^n. Let $[a, b] \subset R$ be an interval in the real line and let $\phi[a, b] \rightarrow R^n_+$ be a mapping which associates with each $t \in [a, b]$ a point $\phi(t)$ in R^n_+.

We define a (*smooth*) *curve* $F(\mathbf{x}, \mathbf{x}')$ in R^n between two points $\mathbf{x}$

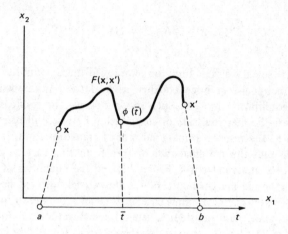

Fig. 2.2

and $\mathbf{x}'$ in R^n as the set of points traced out by a continuous (continuously differentiable) function $\phi[a, b] \to R^n$, where $\phi(a) = \mathbf{x}$ and $\phi(b) = \mathbf{x}'$. Thus a curve in R^n is just a vector function $[\phi_1(t), \ldots, \phi_n(t)]$, where t takes values in some interval $[a, b]$. Intuitively a curve can be thought of as a piece of string connecting the end-points ($\mathbf{x}$ and $\mathbf{x}'$). A curve in 2-space is shown in Figure 2.2. Note that if $C(\mathbf{x}, \mathbf{x}')$ is defined through the functions $[\phi_1(t), \ldots, \phi_n(t)]$, $t \in [a, b]$, and if $t = \psi(\tau)$ with $\tau \in [\alpha, \beta]$, $\psi(\alpha) = a$, $\psi(\beta) = b$, then the curve $C'(\mathbf{x}, \mathbf{x}') \doteq [\phi_1(\psi(\tau)), \ldots, \phi_n(\psi(\tau))]$, $\tau \in [\alpha, \beta]$ is identical to $C(\mathbf{x}, \mathbf{x}')$. Thus the same curve can have several parametric representations.

Example. Let $C(\mathbf{x}, \mathbf{x}')$ be the straight line going:

$\mathbf{x} = (0, 0)$ to $\mathbf{x}' = (1, 1)$ in R^2, whose parametric representation is $\phi_1(t) = \phi_2(t) = t$, $t \in [0, 1]$. Clearly a different parametric representation of the same curve is $\phi_1(\tau) = \tau^2 = \phi_2(\tau)$, $\tau \in [0, 1]$.

Now let $\mathbf{P}(\mathbf{x}) = (P_1(\mathbf{x}), \ldots, P_n(\mathbf{x}))$, where $\mathbf{x} = (x_1, \ldots, x_n)$, be n functions such that $P_1, \ldots, P_n$ and $\partial P_i / \partial x_j$ are continuous on R_+^n. Let $F(\mathbf{x}, \mathbf{x}')$ be a smooth curve with parametric representation $[\phi_1(t), \ldots, \phi_n(t)]$. The *line integral* of $\mathbf{P}$ along $F(\mathbf{x}, \mathbf{x}')$ is written:

$$\oint_{F(\mathbf{x}, \mathbf{x}')} [P_1 dx_1 + P_2 dx_2 + \ldots + P_n dx_n], \tag{A1}$$

and is defined as the simple (one-dimensional) integral:

$$\int_a^b \sum_{i=1}^n P_i(x_1(t), \ldots, x_n(t)) \frac{dx_i(t)}{dt}\, dt, \tag{A2}$$

where $dx_i(t)$ in (A1) is the change in x_i along $F(\mathbf{x}, \mathbf{x'})$, i.e. $dx_i(t)/dt = d\phi_i(t)/dt$.

Example. Let $P_1(x_1, x_2) = x_1 - x_2$, $P_2(x_1, x_2) = x_1 + x_2$. Let $\hat{F}(\mathbf{x}, \mathbf{x'})$ be the straight line going from $\mathbf{x} = (0, 0)$ to $\mathbf{x} = (1, 1)$ in R^2 whose parametric representation is $\phi_1(t) = x_1(t) = t = x_2(t) = \phi_2 = (t)$, $t\epsilon(0, 1)$. Then, from above:

$$\oint[P_1 dx_1 + P_2 dx_2] = \int_0^1 [P_1(x_1(t), x_2(t)] \frac{dx_1}{dt}$$

$$+ P_2(x_1(t), x_2(t), \frac{dx_2}{dt})\, dt = \int_0^1 ([x_1(t) - x_2(t)] \cdot 1$$

$$+ [x_1(t) + x_2(t)] \cdot 1)\, dt = \int_0^1 2t\, dt = 1. \tag{A3}$$

Using elementary integration theory it is easy to show that the line integral is well-defined and that different parametric representations of the same curve $F(\mathbf{x}, \mathbf{x'})$ lead to identical values of the line integral.

Example (continued). In the example above let $x_1(t) = t^2 = x_2(t)$, $t\epsilon[0, 1]$. This is a different parametric representation of $\hat{F}(\mathbf{x}, \mathbf{x'})$. The reader can check that this representation leads to the same value of the line integral (A3) along $\hat{F}$.

A second point to note about the line integral in (A1)–(A2) is that in general its value depends not just on the end-points $(\mathbf{x}, \mathbf{x'})$ but also on the particular curve $F(\mathbf{x}, \mathbf{x'})$ along which the line integral is evaluated.

Example (continued). The curve $\bar{F}(\mathbf{x}, \mathbf{x'})$, defined by $x_1(t) = t^2$, $x_2(t) = t$, $t\epsilon[0, 1]$, is a smooth curve connecting $(0, 0)$ to $(1, 1)$. However, as the reader may check:

$$\oint_{\bar{F}(\mathbf{x}, \mathbf{x'})}(P_1 dx_1 + P_2 dx_2) = 2/3 \neq \oint_{\hat{F}(\mathbf{x}, \mathbf{x'})} (P_1 dx_1 + P_2 dx_2). \tag{A4}$$

The above example shows that, in general, the line integral in (2.5) depends on the path connecting $\mathbf{x}$ and $\mathbf{x'}$. According to Stokes's celebrated theorem, however, the line integral depends only on $\mathbf{x}$ and $\mathbf{x'}$ and not on the particular path $F(\mathbf{x}, \mathbf{x'})$ along which the integration is taken, provided only that:

$$\frac{\partial P_i}{\partial x_j} = \frac{\partial P_j}{\partial x_i}, \text{ for all } i,j. \tag{A5}$$

These are just the conditions (2.6) mentioned above. If these hold, then the line integral (A7) may be expressed unambiguously as:

$$\oint_x^{x'} \sum_{i=1}^{n} P_i(x)dx_i, \tag{A6}$$

where the path of integration between x and x' is immaterial.

Example (continued). The reader may verify that if $P_1(x) = x_1 + x_2 = P_2(x)$, then the line integral of P along both $\hat{F}$ and $\bar{F}$ has the same value. This is because (A5) is satisfied here but not when $P_1(x) = x_1 - x_2$, as was the case in the previous example.

If we specialise the above considerations to the traditional social-welfare function in (2.5), we see that the conditions (2.6), or (2.7), are sufficient to ensure independence of W from the particular path along which surplus is evaluated. Moreover, using (A2) and (2.6) the derivatives of the line integral (A1) can be shown to be:

$$\frac{\partial}{\partial x_i} \left(\oint_{F(o, x)} [P_1 dx_1 + \ldots + P_n dx_n] \right) = P_i(x), \tag{A7}$$

so that the first-order conditions for maximising (2.5) are simply that $P_i(x_i) = p_i = \partial C(x)/\partial x_i$, i.e. marginal-cost pricing.

Example (concluded). Verify (A7) for several curves connecting x, x' when $P_1(x) = x_1 + x_2 = P_2(x)$.

Part Two

A General and Comprehensive Analysis of Peak-load Pricing

3 Introduction to the Theory of Peak-load Pricing

Part Two deals with various types of peak-load pricing problems faced by public utilities. Such problems arise when a utility's product is economically non-storable and demand fluctuates over time. Under these circumstances non-uniform utilisation of capacity can result. Thus using a 'peak-load pricing' policy to discourage consumption in peak periods and encourage off-peak consumption can improve such utilisation. The evaluation of the trade-off between utilisation gains and consumer welfare is the central issue of peak-load pricing theory.

In this chapter we set out the basic peak-load model as originated by Boiteux (1949) and Steiner (1957), and developed by Hirshleifer (1958) and Williamson (1966). In Section 3.1 we present the Boiteux–Steiner–Hirshleifer contributions for the simplest cases of equal-length periods and independent demands. In Section 3.2 we show how to deal with the complications of unequal-length periods. We will employ graphical analysis throughout.

3.1 THE BOITEUX–STEINER MODEL

Boiteux (1949) and Steiner (1957) arrived at solutions to the peak-load problem independently and their approach has become the basis for further work in this area. Boiteux's contribution, published in French, had little or no impact on the Anglo-American literature until Steiner had published his own contribution, which set off a growing literature in the Anglo-American journals. By contrast Boiteux's impact in France, and especially in the *Electricité de France* (see later), was substantial.

Steiner adopted the conventional welfare maximising approach discussed in Chapter 2, namely setting prices to achieve 'the maxim[is]ation of the excess of expressed consumer satisfaction over the cost of resources devoted to production' (Steiner, 1957, p. 485). He assumes a typical 'day' divided into two equal-length periods, each governed by its own independent demand curve, denoted $D_1(p)$, $D_2(p)$ below. The peak-load problem here results from the assumption that one of these two demand curves lies everywhere above the other. The demands are independent, in the sense that the price charged in one period has no effect on the quantity demanded in the other priod. Costs are assumed linear: b is operating cost per unit per period; β is the cost of providing a unit of capacity. Thus a unit demanded in a period will cost b if the capacity already exists to supply it, and b plus β if additional capacity has to be installed. Once a unit of capacity is installed (at cost β) it is available for meeting demands in both periods. It is assumed in Steiner's analysis that sufficient capacity will be installed to meet demand.

The solution to the two-period problem is given in Figure 3.1, in which the demand curves D_1 and D_2 are drawn. Figure 3.1(a) illustrates the 'firm-peak case' and involves pricing at $p_2 = b + \beta$ and $p_1 = b$, with period outputs $x_2 > x_1$ as indicated and with capacity $q = x_2$.

To illustrate why this solution is optimal, consider prices p_2' and p_1' slightly higher than the given p_2, p_1. We will sum and compare the areas

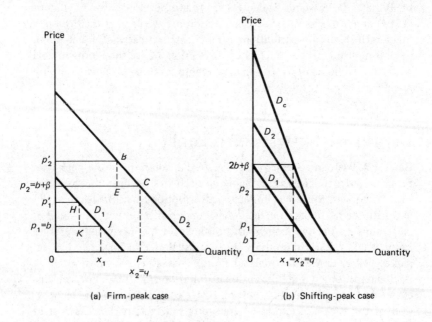

(a) Firm-peak case   (b) Shifting-peak case

Fig. 3.1

of net revenue and consumers' surplus for each case. For the peak period, net revenue corresponding to p'_2 will be increased by $p'_2 BEF$, but consumers' surplus will be reduced by $p'_2 BCEF$, a net loss in welfare of BEC. Similarly, under p'_1 a welfare loss of HJK results. For other permutations of p_1, p_2, similar losses in welfare occur. (See also Exercise 3.1 in this regard.) Optimal capacity will be $q = \max (x_1, x_2)$ because of the fact that at the optimal prices quantity demanded cannot exceed capacity.

Note that in the firm-peak case, the peak-period revenue $(p_2 x_2)$ covers the clearly identifiable peak-period costs, both capacity (βq) and running costs (bx_1); and the off-peak period revenue $(p_1 x_1)$ only covers running costs. Since it follows directly from our welfare function that no price less than b nor greater than $b + \beta$ is warranted, charging the highest feasible price in the peak period and the lowest feasible price in the off-peak period is something of a polar case. Steiner's analysis implies that as long as these prices can be charged while still leaving spare capacity $q - x_1 > 0$ in the off-peak period, such prices are in fact optimal.

By contrast if the prices $(b + \beta, b)$ are charged in the 'shifting-peak case', quantities of $x'_2 < x'_1$ result. The peak has apparently 'shifted' in that what was the off-peak demand (x_1) has now become the larger quantity demanded, and thus the determinant of the amount of capacity required. This solution appears odd and, in fact, fails to maximise welfare. The correct solution is obtained by adding vertically the two demand curves D_1 and D_2 to get D_c. (The reader may verify this solution by an analogous argument, comparing areas, to that which we just employed for the firm-peak case.) Where D_c cuts the horizontal line drawn at $2b + \beta$ gives optimal capacity q, allowing prices to be read off as p_1 and p_2, which, as in the firm-peak case, satisfy $p_1 + p_2 = 2b + \beta$.

Note, in the shifting-peak case, that peak users pay a higher price than off-peak users even though the quantity supplied is identical in both periods. This supplies some of the rationale of Steiner's (1957) convention that welfare-optimal peak-load pricing may involve price discrimination.

In the shifting-peak case both demands contribute to capacity cost (β), and capacity is fully utilised in both periods. Note that there is no precise rule for allocating capacity costs between peak and off-peak; it depends on the relative strength of these demands. Thus, if peak demand increases relative to off-peak demand, optimality would require that the peak demand pays relatively more of the capacity cost of β. It is not just the relationship between the demands that determine whether it is a firm or a shifting peak; the size of capacity costs relative to demands is also important. Thus in Figure 3.1(b), if β were to fall, this case would become a firm peak; and if β were to rise in Figure 3.1(a), this would become a shifting peak.[1] Intuitively it is apparent why this happens. If capacity costs are relatively large, any failure (as in a firm-peak case) to utilise capacity fully is expensive, and encourages better utilisation or a switch-over to a shifting peak. Note that in both the shifting-peak and the firm-peak case profit equals zero, a consequence of our welfare function and the assumed constant returns to scale.

Before completing our analysis of the two-period case we would like to note an interesting graphical device employed by Steiner to summarise both the firm-peak and shifting-peak cases on the same diagram. In Figure 3.2 we have redrawn the demand curves of Figure 3.1; this time, however, using (O, b) as the origin of the diagram instead of (O, O). However, the capacity costs on the price scale continue to be measured in absolute terms so that the distance $b\beta$ in Figure 3.2 equals β, i.e. the point β represents the price $b + \beta$. Then the above discussion may be seen to imply the following for Figure 3.2. If capacity costs are greater than $\hat{\beta}$, a shifting peak occurs; otherwise a firm peak obtains. In the former case (e.g. β') period outputs and prices may be read along the vertical line drawn at $D_c(\beta')$ (e.g. $x'_1 = x'_2 = q'$, as shown). In the firm-peak case (e.g. β) prices are $p_2 = b + \beta$, $p_1 = b$, with corresponding quantities.

This device is particularly valuable when it comes to extending the peak-load geometry to more than two periods, in that it makes simple addition of the demand curves possible, as in Figure 3.3, where we illustrate a three-period case.[2] By changing the level of capacity cost we can note the three possibilities:

shifting peak in all three periods;
shifting peak in periods 1 and 2; and
firm peak in period 1.

The three regions of capacity cost corresponding to these possibilities are labelled (i), (ii), (iii) in the diagram. The capacity cost β is in region (i), and this implies a shifting peak in all periods with $q = x_1 = x_2 = x_3$, and corresponding prices. For β' a shifting peak in periods 1 and 2 obtains with resulting prices p'_2 and capacity q', as shown. Finally, if capa-

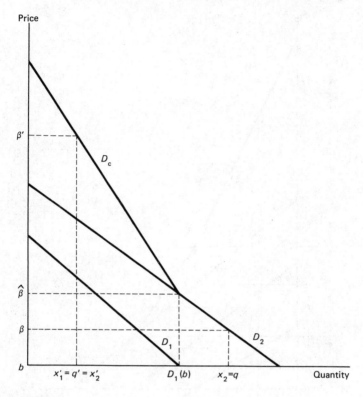

Fig. 3.2

city cost is β'', period 1 is a firm peak and $q'' = x_3 > x_2 > x_1$, with prices $p_3'' = b + \beta''$, $p_2'' = p_1'' = b$. In all cases it can be verified that $p_1 + p_2 + p_3 = 3b + \beta$, and that profits equal zero. The case where only periods 2 and 3 present a shifting-peak situation (in the sense that their period outputs are equal at optimum) never arises as long as their demand curves are non-intersecting, so that the above three cases are exhaustive. Of course, if the assumption that demand curves do not intersect is abandoned, other possibilities may arise.

The extension to n periods is analogous, and there too we find the sum of the n-period prices equals $nb + \beta$ and that there are exactly n possibilities, each of which corresponds to the case where, for some $j \leqslant n$, periods $1, \ldots, j$ all have output equal to capacity, with remaining periods all priced at marginal running costs (b).

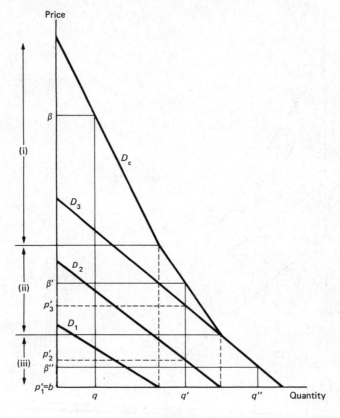

Fig. 3.3

3.2 UNEQUAL-LENGTH PERIODS

It is not necessary for peak and off-peak periods to be of exactly the same duration (as was assumed in the previous section). When they are of unequal length, however, some care must be exercised in specifying the dimensions of cost and demand. Williamson (1966) developed an interesting approach to this problem which we review in this section and relate to the Steiner-Hirshleifer approach.

We start by noting that the non-storability character of demand implies that demands must be indexed by their location in time, for example by their starting time and duration. We will follow the usual procedure in assuming that a finite number of periods are given, that all demands within a period are constant over time, and that the units of demand are expressed in terms of capacity and time. Thus in electricity supply the units of capacity are kilowatts (kW) and the units of demand are kW-hrs. When we speak of a demand of, say, 20 kW-hrs in a period of length 4 hours, then we assume that a steady demand of 5 kW-hrs per hour obtains throughout the period. Similarly in telephone service the units of demand may be expressed as call-hrs, representing the fact that capacity consists of a finite number of circuits on to which calls of specific duration are loaded.

Keeping the above discussion in mind suppose there are two periods with independent demands $D_i(p_i)$ and with lengths L_1, L_2, where $L_1 + L_2 = L$, L being the length of the cycle. $D_i(p_i)$ is to be understood as the total number of units demanded in period i at price p_i, where each such unit has dimensions of capacity and time (e. g. kW-hrs). Then period demands of $D_1(p_1)$, $D_2(p_2)$ represent instantaneous demands on capacity of $D_1(p_1)/L_1$ and $D_2(p_2)/L_2$ respectively (e.g. a total demand of 1000 six-minute calls in a ten-hour period represents an average instantaneous demand on capacity of $(1000 \times 6) \div (10 \times 60) = 10$ calls). From this we see that capacity required when prices p_1, p_2 are charged is $q = \max\ [D_1(p_2)/L_1,\ D_2(p_2)/L_2]$. In the previous section we assumed that $L_1 = L_2 = 1$, i.e. each sub-period lasts one time-unit, and therefore $q = \max\ [D_1(p_1), D_2(p_2)]$.

Now let b and β be as before, but in compatible units to demand.[3] Then we note the following identity characterising the optimal solution:

$$(p_1 - b)L_1 + (p_2 - b)L_2 = \beta. \tag{3.1}$$

The left-hand side of (3.1) represents the incremental benefits above operating costs of an added unit of capacity. If capacity is greater than demand in period i, then $p_i = b = SRMC$, and no benefits occur to period i consumers from additional capacity. If capacity is equal to demand in period i, then incremental benefits from additional capacity would be $(p_i - b)$ for each of the L_i additional units of demand which an incremental unit of capacity could service in period i. As the right side of (3.1) is the cost of an additional unit, clearly equality must prevail. Another view of (3.1), as Williamson (1966) points out, is that it represents the zero net revenue requirement which necessarily holds in long-run equilibrium for constant returns to scale and completely divisible plant (as assumed here).

Let us now examine the main features of Williamson's approach. Amongst other things it makes possible the use of conventional neo-

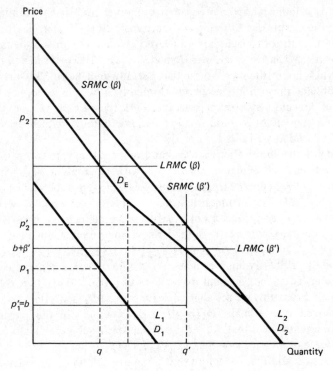

Fig. 3.4

classical terminology of short-run and long-run marginal cost which is
not readily transferable to the Steiner–Hirshleifer analysis. If we assume
that capacity is the 'fixed' factor, then we can characterise *LRMC* as
consisting of operating costs plus capacity costs, $b + \beta$. Short-run costs
can be regarded as equal to operating costs (b) until capacity is reached
and indefinite at capacity. It is thus possible, as in Figure 3.4, to represent *LRMC* by a horizontal straight line $b + \beta$, and *SRMC* by a line
which is horizontal up to capacity (q) and then vertical.[4]

Given (3.1) we may easily solve graphically for the optimal prices. In
Figure 3.4 we show Williamson's solution which assumes that units are
chosen so that $L = 1$. Thus the units of b are in £ per unit of capacity
over the entire cycle (e.g. £/kW-day). The demand curves $D_i^{L,i}$ shown
are *not* period demand curves. Rather, they exhibit for each price the
demand which would obtain if period demands $D_i(p)$ were to prevail

over the entire cycle. Thus $D_i^{L\,i}(p) = (L/L_i) \cdot D_i(p)$. Finally, the curve D_E, which is the effective demand for capacity, is obtained by vertically adding to b the difference between $D_i^{L\,i}$ and b - i.e. D_E is just the left-hand side of (3.1) plus b. Where this cuts *LRMC*, (3.1) is solved and we have optimal capacity. Optimal prices are derived as in the Steiner model, where the vertical line at optimal capacity cuts *SRMC*. Optimal-period outputs are obtained by deflating cycle-equivalent demands. In Figure 3.4 the case where capacity cost is β leads to a shifting peak with prices p_1 and p_2, capacity q and period outputs of $x_1 = L_1 q, x_2 = L_2 q$. With β' a firm peak obtains and period outputs are $x_1 = D_1(p_1') = L_1 D_1^{L_1}(p_1'), x_2 = L_2 q$.

To illustrate the above procedure consider the following example:

$$L = 1, L_1 = 1/3, L_2 = 2/3, b = 1, \beta = 1$$

$$D_1(p_1) = \tfrac{2}{3}(3 - p_1), D_1^{L_1}(p_1) = 2(3 - p_1)$$

$$D_2(p_2) = \tfrac{7}{6}(5 - p_2), D_2^{L_2}(p_2) = \tfrac{7}{4}(5 - p_2) \tag{3.2}$$

where $D_1(p_1)$, $D_2(p_2)$ are the period demands and $D_1^{L_1}(p_1)$ and $D_2^{L_2}(p_2)$ are the demands if $D_i(p)$ were to prevail over the whole cycle. The above procedure applied here leads to a firm-peak case with optimal solution:[5]

$$p_1 = 1, p_2 = 2.5, x_1 = \tfrac{4}{3}, x_2 = 2\tfrac{11}{12}, q = 4\tfrac{3}{8}. \tag{3.3}$$

Interestingly we can obtain the same solution from the Steiner framework. To do so we simply split period 2 into two equal length sub-periods, called periods 2a, 2b, of length 1/3 and with demands $D_{2a}(p) = D_{2b} = \tfrac{1}{2}D_2(p)$. This yields a problem with three equal-length periods and with problem data:

$$L = 1, L_1 = L_{2a} = L_{2b} = 1/3, b = 1, \beta = 1$$

$$D_1(p) = \tfrac{2}{3}(3 - p); D_{2a}(p) = D_{2b}(p) = \tfrac{7}{12}(5 - p). \tag{3.4}$$

One final change is required to apply the Steiner procedure. We must convert the above problem into an equivalent one for which $L_i = 1$ for all i and $L = 3$, i.e. for which b is the cost of supplying a unit for one period. This is done easily and leads to the following equivalent problem data:

$$\hat{L} = 3, \hat{L}_1 = \hat{L}_{2a} = \hat{L}_{2b} = 1, \hat{b} = 1/3, \hat{\beta} = 1$$

$$\hat{D}_1(\hat{p}) = 6(1 - \hat{p}), \hat{D}_2(\hat{p}) = \hat{D}_{2b}(\hat{p}) = \tfrac{7}{4}(5 - 3\hat{p}). \tag{3.5}$$

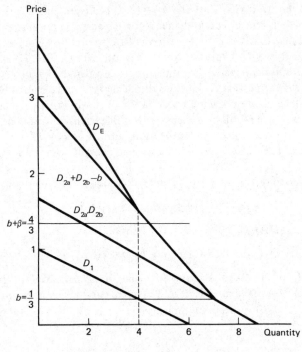

Fig. 3.5

Thus, if the units of demand in (3.4) are kW-days, the units in (3.5) are kW-1/3 days. Prices and outputs are adjusted[6] correspondingly to obtain (3.5). Applying the Steiner procedure of the previous section we obtain (see Figure 3.5):

$$\hat{p}_1 = 1/3, \hat{p}_{2a} = \hat{p}_{2b} = 5/6, \hat{x}_1 = 4, \hat{x}_{2a} = \hat{x}_{2b} = q = 4\tfrac{3}{8}, \quad (3.6)$$

which is identical to (3.3) when the change in units is accounted for. Thus the Steiner and Williamson approaches may be seen to lead to identical results when units are dealt with properly. One must only convert the underlying problem into one having equal-length periods with period-based costs to use the Steiner approach.

Williamson (1966) also treats problems of indivisibility and pricing under fixed capacity. The latter implies pricing at the intersection of the *SRMC* and the demand curve, while the former can be solved by a comparative area analysis at each of the possible levels of plant size, prices at each level determined optimally via the *SRMC* rule just indicated.

In concluding this brief review of the early contributions to peak-load pricing it is worth stressing that the basic solution of pricing at *SRMC* while setting capacity through *LRMC* is perfectly general. The problem is only to determine *SRMC* and *LRMC* under more general demand and technology conditions than the very simple ones assumed here. We start our investigation of this in the next chapter.

EXERCISES

3.1 A peak-load problem exists where demand is represented by two equal-length period demand curves:

$$p_1 = 9 - \tfrac{6}{7}x_1$$
$$p_2 = 3 - \tfrac{1}{2}x_2$$

(i) Draw a diagram and derive optimal prices and quantities for the cases where (a) $b = 1, \beta = 3$; and (b) $b = 1, \beta = 5$. Which is the firm-peak case?

(ii) Verify that profit is zero for (a) and (b) in (i).

3.2 Suppose $L = 24$ hrs, $b = £1/\text{cap-hr}$ ('cap' being the unit of capacity), $\beta = £10/\text{cap}$, with two periods of length $L_1 = 18$ hrs, $L_2 = 6$ hrs, and demand curves $D_1(p) = D_2(p) = 30(4 - p)$. Using both the Steiner and Williamson procedures, determine the optimal prices and capacity.

4 Peak-load Pricing Models under Certainty

The classical models of peak-load pricing analysed in the previous chapter embody strong simplifying assumptions concerning demand and technology. In this chapter we begin our inquiry into the implcations of relaxing one or other of the assumptions of the traditional theory. We continue to maintain the assumption that demand curves are known with certainty. Since a number of generalisations of the traditional theory have been presented during the past decade for this deterministic demand case, a brief historical sketch of these developments may be useful at the start.

The first major extension to the traditional model was presented by Pressman (1970), who synthesised earlier works by Hotelling and the marginal-cost pricing school[1] in providing a model of peak-load pricing incorporating demands with time interdependencies (e.g. the peak-period price affects off-peak demand) as well as a more general specification of technology. This contrasts sharply with the traditional models of the previous chapter which assume proportional costs and time-independent demands.

A further theoretical generalisation appeared in the present authors' papers, starting with Crew and Kleindorfer (1971), which investigated the implications for pricing and capacity decisions of a diverse technology where more than one type of 'plant' is available to meet demand.[2] Such cases are typical for public utilities and present interesting new trade-offs. For example, in the firm-peak case discussed in Chapter 3 it may be economical to employ an additional plant type to help meet peak-period demand. Such a 'peaking plant' would typically have lower construction costs and higher operating costs relative to existing plants, thus offering cost advantages in meeting a peak demand of short duration.

Returning to our historical sketch, two additional recent developments deserve attention. Panzar (1976) presented a reformulation of the peak-load problem in which technology is specified through a neo classical production function. Dansby (1976) used the same technology specification as Crew and Kleindorfer (1975a) but allowed demand

36

to vary continuously with time, while still maintaining only a finite number of pricing periods. Thus, within each pricing period, demand was allowed to vary with time.

The above approaches share many common features, and it is important to understand these, inasmuch as we shall analyse only the Crew and Kleindorfer model in detail. To illustrate the similarities in these approaches, consider first the following n-period peak-load pricing problem, similar to Pressman (1970);

$$\text{Max } W = \oint_0^x \left\{ \sum_{i=1}^n P_i(y) dy_i \right\} - C(\mathbf{x}, z)$$

$$\text{subject to } x_i \leqslant z, x_i \geqslant 0, z \geqslant 0, i = 1, \ldots, n, \tag{4.1}$$

where $\mathbf{x} = (x_1, \ldots, x_n)$, x_i is demand in period i, $P_i(\mathbf{x})$ is the inverse demand function, z is installed capacity, and $C(\mathbf{x}, z)$ represents total costs. Notice that demands are allowed to be interdependent ($P_i(\mathbf{x}) = P_i(x_1, x_2, \ldots, x_n)$), so that a line-integral formulation of gross surplus is used in (4.1), and the integrability conditions (2.6) are assumed as usual.

For comparison consider the n-period model from Crew and Kleindorfer (1975a), where technology is specified explicitly through m types of capacity, indexed $l = 1, \ldots, m$, having constant marginal operating cost b_l and marginal capacity cost β_l. With this specification of technology the corresponding problem to (4.1) is:

$$\text{Max } W = \oint_0^x \left\{ \sum_{i=1}^n P_i(y) dy_i \right\} - \sum_{i=1}^n \sum_{l=1}^m b_l q_{li} - \sum_{l=1}^m \beta_l q_l, \tag{4.2}$$

subject to:

$$\sum_{l=1}^m q_{li} = x_i, \text{ for all } i \tag{4.3}$$

$$q_l - q_{li} \geqslant 0, \text{ for all } i, l \tag{4.4}$$

$$x_i \geqslant 0, q_l \geqslant 0, q_{li} \geqslant 0, \text{ for all } i, l, \tag{4.5}$$

where x_i is demand in period i, q_l is capacity of type (or plant) l, and q_{li} is output from plant l in period i. Constraint (4.3) specifies that demand be met in each period, while (4.4) requires output from plant l in each period to not exceed capacity of plant l. Similarly, the first term in W in gross surplus, the second term represents total operating costs, and the third represents capacity costs. It is assumed at the start that different prices $(P_i(\mathbf{x}))$ may be charged in each of the n sub-periods comprising the basic cycle of interest. This assumption is relaxed below (pp. 50–3). Equal-length periods are assumed with corresponding units for demand and capacity, as discussed in Chapter 3. Note, in particular, that the marginal capacity cost is a cost for the entire cycle (no matter into how many periods it may be sub-divided, i.e. regardless of n).[3]

Now the above two formulations are closely related. Indeed, starting with (4.2) one could define the cost function in (4.1) aş:

$$C(\mathbf{x}, z) = \text{Min} \left[\sum_{i=1}^{n} \sum_{l=1}^{m} b_l q_{li} - \sum_{l=1}^{m} \beta_l q_l \right], \tag{4.6}$$

subject to:

$$\sum_{l=1}^{m} q_{li} = x_i, \text{ for all } i \tag{4.7}$$

$$\sum_{l=1}^{m} q_l = z; q_{li}, q_l \geqslant 0, \text{ for all } l, i, \tag{4.8}$$

where $\mathbf{x}, z$ in (4.6)–(4.8) are given. Thus $C(\mathbf{x}, z)$ in (4.6) is the minimal cost of providing period outputs $\mathbf{x} = (x_1, \ldots, x_n)$ and total capacity when available technology is specified as in (4.2)–(4.5). The reader should convince himself that the solutions to (4.1), with $C(\mathbf{x}, z)$ as defined in (4.6), will be precisely the same solution as the solutions to (4.2)–(4.5).[4] This equivalence amounts simply to the assertion that the welfare maximisation (4.2) implies the cost minimisation (4.6) at the optimal output levels of x_i. A similar transformation would of course work if more general (non-proportional) cost functions were assumed for the m available capacity types. Thus the main difference between (4.1) and (4.2)–(4.5) is that the latter treat technology choice explicitly.

Similarly the use of a neoclassical production function to express technological possibilities, as in Panzar (1976), can be viewed as an alternative representation of (4.1) or (4.2)–(4.5). Just as in (4.1)–(4.5) the welfare-optimal solution here would involve cost minimisation, i.e. minimising factor costs at the optimal output levels. Thus, given the familiar conditions for optimal factor substitution, the neoclassical specification of technology again leads to essentially the same insights as (4.1) or (4.2)–(4.5).

The thrust of the above discussion is that the major recent reformulations of the peak-load pricing problem may be viewed as close substitutes for one another in a welfare-maximising framework.[5] For this reason, and in order to present a unified discussion of technology choice and pricing policy, we shall concentrate mostly on the more detailed representation (4.2)–(4.5).

4.1 MULTI-PERIOD PRICING WITH A DIVERSE TECHNOLOGY

We start our analysis with the problem represented by (4.2)–(4.5) which assumes that different prices can be charged in each of the equal-length supply periods $i = 1, \ldots, n$. Our first task in solving the problem will be to derive first-order conditions for it via the Kuhn–Tucker theory. First form the Lagrangian, L:

$$L = W + \sum_{i=1}^{n} \lambda_i \left(\sum_{l=1}^{m} q_{li} - x_i \right) + \sum_{i=1}^{n} \sum_{l=1}^{m} \mu_{li}(q_l - q_{li}). \tag{4.9}$$

Assuming strictly positive output, i.e. $x_i > 0$, at the optimal solution, the Kuhn–Tucker conditions for (4.2)–(4.5) are then:

$$P_i(\mathbf{x}) = \lambda_i, \text{for all } i \tag{4.10}$$

$$\sum_{i=1}^{n} \mu_{li} \leqslant \beta_l, q_l \left(\sum_{i=1}^{n} \mu_{li} - \beta_l \right) = 0, \text{for all } l \tag{4.11}$$

$$\lambda_i - \mu_{li} \leqslant b_l, q_{li}(\lambda_i - \mu_{li} - b_l) = 0, \text{for all } l, i \tag{4.12}$$

$$\mu_{li} \geqslant 0, \mu_{li}(q_l - q_{li}) = 0, \text{for all } l, i. \tag{4.13}$$

Before proceeding to an analysis of the general case we solve (4.9)–(4.13) for the case of two *independent* demands, and first one plant and then two plants. We assume that the demands satisfy $D_1(p) < D_2(p)$ for all p so that period 2 is the peak period. For these cases the analysis is simplified considerably because of the fact that for independent demands, (4.1) is strictly necessary and sufficient (see Exercise 4.5).

For the one-plant case $m = 1$, $n = 2$, the reader may verify the Steiner (firm-peak) result, i.e. assuming $D_1(b_1) < D_2(b_1 + \beta_1)$, so that a firm peak obtains, the following solves (4.9)–(4.13):

$$p_1 = b_1 = \lambda_1; \mu_{11} = 0 \qquad\qquad (4.14)$$

$$p_2 = b_1 + \beta_1 = \lambda_2; \mu_{12} = \beta_1, \qquad\qquad (4.15)$$

where $q_1 = q_{12} = x_2 > x_1 = q_{11}$.

For the two-plant case $m = 2 = n$, ahead of detailed considerations of optimal plant mix to follow in this section, we assume plant 1 has the cheaper marginal running cost ($b_1 < b_2$) and that both plants will be used at the optimum. Then, by a simple process of elimination, while assuming $x_1, x_2, q_1, q_2 > 0$, we obtain the following solution to (4.9)–(4.13) (again for the firm-peak case, where at optimum $x_2 > x_1$):

$$p_1 = 2b_1 + \beta_1 - (b_2 + \beta_2) = \lambda_1; \mu_{11} = \lambda_1 - b_1, \mu_{21} = 0$$
$$(4.16)$$

$$p_2 = b_2 + \beta_2 = \lambda_2; \mu_{12} = \lambda_2 - b_1, \mu_{22} = \beta_2 \qquad (4.17)$$

$$q_1 = q_{11} = q_{12} = x_1 > 0, q_{21} = 0, q_2 = q_{22} = x_2 - x_1 > 0.$$
$$(4.18)$$

Let us understand (4.16)–(4.18) intuitively. Given $b_1 < b_2$, we must also have $\beta_1 > \beta_2$ if both types of capacity are to be used at optimum (otherwise, if $\beta_1 \leqslant \beta_2$, plant 2 would be both more expensive to build and to operate). Now, with an eye on (4.18), we see that $q_{11} = x_1$, so that off-peak demand is met by plant 1, which is more expensive to construct but cheaper to operate than plant 2. Note that plant 1 continues to supply $q_{12} = x_1$ units in the peak period, the additional peak requirements $x_2 - x_1 = q_{22}$ being met by plant 2. The use of the cheaper operating-cost plant in both periods is as expected, with the more expensive operating-cost plant used only to meet peak demand.

Since plant 2 is only used in the peak period at optimum, we must have:[6]

$$b_1 + \beta_1 > b_2 + \beta_2, \qquad\qquad (4.19)$$

which states that the marginal cost of supplying a unit of peak demand using type 2 capacity should be less than that of meeting this marginal unit with type 1 capacity. Similarly, since plant 1 is used to capacity in both periods, the cost of the marginal unit supplied by plant 1 is $2b_1 + \beta_1$, and the following must hold:

$$2b + \beta_1 < 2b_2 + \beta_2, \qquad\qquad (4.20)$$

since otherwise plant 1 would not be needed.

Regarding the optimal prices, a close look at (4.16)-(4.17) reveals the expected result that prices are set at marginal cost. For example, given (4.20) and the above discussion, the minimum cost of meeting an additional unit of demand in period 1 is to increase plant 1 capacity by 1 unit and decreasing plant 2 capacity by 1 unit, while maintaining the operating regime (4.18). The increased costs of meeting the additional unit of demand in period 1 are $b_1 + (\beta_1 - \beta_2)$, but note that the additional unit of plant 1 installed will also be used in period 2, since $b_1 < b_2$, with net savings in operating costs of $b_2 - b_1$. The total incremental cost of meeting the additional unit of demand in period 1 is therefore $b_1 + (\beta_1 - \beta_2) - (b_2 - b_1) = p_1$, as given in (4.16). A similar discussion serves to show that p_2 in (4.17) is the long-run marginal cost. of meeting an additional unit of demand in period 2. Finally, it is interesting to note from (4.16) and (4.19)-(4.20) that $b_1 < p_1 < b_2$. Thus (4.16)-(4.20) imply the following bounds:

$$b_1 < p_1 < b_2 < b_2 + \beta_2 = p_2 < b_1 + \beta_1. \tag{4.21}$$

Note from (4.14)-(4.15) that the introduction of a more diverse technology leads to lower peak-period prices and higher off-peak prices. The reader may verify, however, that costs are exactly covered at the optimal prices (4.16)-(4.17) just as they are in the one-plant case with prices (4.14)-(4.15).

Summarising the two-period, two-plant case, the cost conditions (4.19)-(4.20) must hold if both types of capacity are to be used at optimum. Given this and the fact that (once installed) plants with cheaper operating cost will always be used first, the usual rule of pricing at marginal cost emerges. Net profits are zero at optimum. We will see below that analogous cost conditions and pricing results obtain more generally.

OPTIMAL PLANT MIX. Before we can consider more general cases, we have to consider some of the features of the optimal plant mix. Before going any further, we can state one obvious category of plants that is not used, namely, any plant type whose b_l and β_l are both higher than some other available plant type. Thus, without loss of generality, we can assume that the m available technologies have been numbered so that the following cost conditions hold:

$$\beta_1 > \ldots > \beta_m > 0; \quad 0 < b_1 < \ldots < b_m. \tag{4.22}$$

Next we note that whatever (optimal) output vector $(x_1, \ldots, x_n)$ obtains, the optimal q_l, q_{li} must be solutions to the following capacity-planning problem:

Problem CP: For $\{x_i \geqslant 0 | 1 \leqslant i \leqslant n\}$ given,

$$\text{Min CQ} = \sum_{i=1}^{n} \sum_{l=1}^{m} b_l q_{li} + \sum_{l=1}^{m} \beta_l q_l \qquad (4.23)$$

subject to:

$$\sum_{l=1}^{m} q_{li} = x_i, \text{ for all } i \qquad (4.24)$$

$$0 \leqslant q_{li} \leqslant q_l, \text{ for all } i, l, \qquad (4.25)$$

where $Q = (q_{11}, q_{12}, \ldots, q_{1n}, q_{21}, \ldots, q_{m1}, \ldots, q_{mn}, q_1, \ldots, q_m)$ and where C is the corresponding cost vector in (4.23). In solving Problem CP, we assume, for convenience, that the $\{x_i\}_1^n$ are ordered as follows:

$$0 = x_0 < x_1 \leqslant x_2 \leqslant \ldots \leqslant x_n < x_{n+1}, \qquad (4.26)$$

where x_0 and x_{n+1} are added just for notational purposes. In solving Problem CP we will need the following lemma.

Lemma A: For any plant types $k, \hat{k}(k < \hat{k})$ the following must hold if both plants are to be used in the optimal solution:

$$\frac{\beta_k - \beta_{\hat{k}}}{n} < b_{\hat{k}} - b_k < \beta_k - \beta_{\hat{k}} \qquad (4.27)$$

If the left (respectively, right) inequality is violated, only plant $\hat{k}$ (respectively, k) need be used.

Proof: Suppose $b_{\hat{k}} - b_{\hat{k}} \geqslant \beta_k - \beta_{\hat{k}}$, and $q_k > 0$ is some solution Q to Problem CP. Define a new solution $\overline{Q}$ by shifting plant $\hat{k}$'s load to plant k:

$$\overline{q}_k = q_k + q_{\hat{k}}, \overline{q}_{\hat{k}} = 0; \overline{q}_l = q_l \text{ for } l \neq k, \hat{k} \qquad (4.28)$$

$$\overline{q}_{ki} = q_{ki} + q_{\hat{k}i}, \overline{q}_{\hat{k}i} = 0; \overline{q}_{li} = q_{li}, l \neq k, \hat{k}. \qquad (4.29)$$

Then the cost change between Q and $\overline{Q}$ is:

$$\text{CQ} - \text{C}\overline{\text{Q}} = (b_{\hat{k}} - b_k) \sum_{i=1}^{n} q_{\hat{k}i} + (\beta_{\hat{k}} - \beta_k)q_{\hat{k}}. \qquad (4.30)$$

Now note that in an optimal solution:

$$\sum_{i=1}^{n} q_{\hat{k}i} \geqslant q_{\hat{k}}, \tag{4.31}$$

because otherwise too much capacity of type $\hat{k}$ has been provided. But (4.31) coupled with (4.30) yields:

$$\mathbf{CQ} - \mathbf{C\bar{Q}} \geqslant [(b_{\hat{k}} - b_k) + (\beta_{\hat{k}} - \beta_k)] q_{\hat{k}}, \tag{4.32}$$

which by the hypothesis on the bracketed term yields $\mathbf{CQ} \geqslant \mathbf{C\bar{Q}}$, establishing the superiority of leaving plant $\hat{k}$ idle. Similarly, if $\beta_k - \beta_{\hat{k}} \geqslant n(b_{\hat{k}} - b_k)$ and $q_k > 0$, then increasing $q_{\hat{k}}$ to $\bar{q}_k = q_{\hat{k}} + q_k$ and decreasing q_k to zero improves the solution.

We henceforth assume, without loss of generality, that the plants $l = 1, \ldots, m$ satisfy (4.27) for all $k, \hat{k}$. The following proposition, in providing optimal values of q_l and q_{li}, gives a general solution to Problem **CP**.

Proposition A: Let the $x_i\{_0^{n+1}\}$ be ordered as in (4.26). Assume that all plant types satisfy (4.22) and (4.27) for $k, \hat{k}, \epsilon\{1, \ldots, m\}$. For each $i\epsilon\{0, \ldots, n\}$ let $\zeta(i)\{\epsilon 0, \ldots, n\}$ be determined by $x_{\zeta(i)} = x_i < x_{\zeta(i)+1}$.

Then an optimal plant mix $q = (q_1, \ldots, q_m) = q(\mathbf{x})$ solving Problem **CP** is given by:

$$q_l = \begin{cases} 0 & \text{if } n_{l-1} = n \\ x_{n_l} - x_{n_{l-1}} & \text{if } l < m \text{ and } n_{l-1} < n \\ x_n - x_{n_{l-1}} & \text{if } m = l, \end{cases} \tag{4.33}$$

where $n_l \; \epsilon\{0, 1, \ldots, n\}$ and $k_l \; \epsilon\{0, 1, \ldots, n\}$ are determined inductively by:

$$n_0 = 0 \tag{4.34}$$

$$\frac{\beta_l - \beta_{l+1}}{n - n_{l-1} - k_l + 1} \leqslant b_{l+1} - b_l < \frac{\beta_l - \beta_{l+1}}{n - n_{l-1} - k_l},$$

$$\text{for} \quad l = 1, \ldots, m - 1 \tag{4.35}$$

$$n_l = \text{Min}\,[n, \zeta(n_{l-1} + k_l)], l = 1, \ldots, m, \tag{4.36}$$

where the right-hand inequality in (4.35) is considered to hold always when $n - n_{l-1} - k_l = 0$. (*Note*: if $k_l = 0$ for some l, then $n_l = n_{l-1}$ and $q_l = 0$.) Furthermore, optimal $q_{li} = q_{li}(\mathbf{x}, \mathbf{q})$ are determined inductively (in the order $l = 1, i = 1, \ldots, n; \ldots$, setting **q** as in (4.33); $l = m$, $i = 1, \ldots, n$) by

$$q_{li}(\mathbf{x}, \mathbf{q}) = q_{li} = \text{Min}\,[x_i - \sum_{k=1}^{l-1} q_{ki}, q_l]\,, \text{ for all } l, i. \qquad (4.37)$$

As the rationale of (4.33)–(4.37) is not obvious, we are leaving the proof to an appendix at the end of this chapter. We shall concentrate here upon the intuitive background to our arguments, using mainly the numerical example given below. The quantities installed and operating regime of each plant (q_l and q_{li}) depend upon costs (β_l, b_l) and quantities demanded in all periods (x_i). The rationale of (4.37) derives from the fact that q_{li} cannot exceed q_l, but otherwise should be the difference between quantity demanded in period $i(x_i)$ and the amount provided by all the plants of lower running cost than plant l, i.e.

$$\sum_{k=1}^{l-1} q_{ki}.$$

This rule simply embodies the fact that, for a given capacity vector $(q_1, \ldots, q_m)$, costs are minimised by using first the plants with lowest running cost. Now for an example to illustrate the above proposition.

Consider the following cost and output data:

i	1	2	3	4	5	
x_i	4	7	2	1	4	$n = 5$

l	1	2	3	4	
β_l	13	9	4	1	$m = 4$
b_l	1	2	4	7	

Reorder x_is

x_i	0	1	2	4	4	7	20
i	0	1	2	3	4	5	6

Compute $\zeta(i)$

$\zeta(i)$	0	1	2	4	4	5	—

Compute n_l, k_l from (4.34)–(4.36)

l	0	1	2	3	4
n_l	0	2	4	5	5
k_l	—	2	1	1	0

Compute q_l from (4.33)

l	1	2	3	4
q_l	2	2	3	0

Compute q_{li}

from (4.37)

li	1	2	3	4	5
1	1	2	2	2	2
2	0	0	2	2	2
3	0	0	0	0	3

$$CQ = \sum_{i=1}^{n} \sum_{l=1}^{m} b_l q_{li} + \sum_{l=1}^{m} \beta_l q_l = 89.$$

We note that n_l represents the number of periods of demand covered by capacity up to type l. For example, $n_1 = 2$ and, indeed, q_1 supplies all output in periods 1 and 2 ($x_1 = 1, x_2 = 2$). The numbers k_l indicate the number of additional periods of demand (beyond n_{l-1}) covered by plant l. For example, $k_3 = 1$ above and plant 3 covers incremental demand in period 5 beyond that covered by plants 1 and 2 (note $n_2 = 4$). When a shifting peak occurs, as in periods 3 and 4, then meeting demands up through period 3 also entails meeting demand through period $\zeta(3) = 4$.

The heart of Proposition A is (4.35), which we illustrate for the case $m = 2$. For $m = 2$ Proposition A indicates that plant 1 should be used to meet all demand up through period k_1, determined by:

$$(n - k_1)(b_2 - b_1) < (\beta_1 - \beta_2) \leqslant (n - k_1 + 1)(b_2 - b_1),$$

$$(4.38)$$

with plant 2 filling the remaining demand. Assuming plant 1 is to meet all demand in the first k_1 periods, the cost on the left in (4.38) is the operating-cost savings from replacing a unit of plant 2 by a unit of plant 1. If this were done, the additional unit would be the first used in the remaining $n - k_1$ periods, since $b_1 < b_2$ -thus the savings indicated. The term on the right is similar but for $(n - k_1 + 1)$ periods. Of course, $\beta_1 - \beta_2$ is the increased capital cost of the substitution in question. Thus (4.35) indicates that k_1 must be chosen so that operating-cost savings are just balanced at the margin by increased capital costs. Similar conditions were derived by Wenders (1976) and elucidated by Joskow (1976). We will return to this in Chapter 10.

The interested reader may wish to check that the above proposition leads to (4.18) in the case $m = n = 2$, where $x_2 > x_1$. Note also that (4.27) is equivalent to (4.19)-(4.20) in the two-plant case, so that our earlier intuitive reasoning is validated by Lemma A. (Further insight into the meaning of conditions (4.34)-(4.36) may be obtained through Exercises 4.3 and 4.4.)

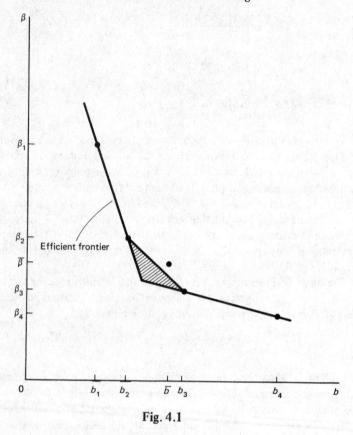

Fig. 4.1

Perhaps the most interesting implication of the above proposition for optimal plant mix is the following:

Corollary A: The efficient technological frontier is downward-sloping and convex in (b, β) space (as shown in Figure 4.1).

Proof: From (4.35) it follows for each $l \in \{1, \ldots, m-1\}$ that:

$$n - n_{l-1} - k_l < \frac{\beta_l - \beta_{l+1}}{b_{l+1} - b_l} \leqslant n - n_{l-1} - k_l + 1. \qquad (4.39)$$

If $k_l = 0$, then $q_l = 0$ and we may omit l from the set of efficient technologies. Otherwise, we note that $\zeta(i) \geqslant i$ so that if $k_l \geqslant 1$, (4.36) implies $n_{l-1} + k_l \geqslant n_{l-2} + k_{l-1} + 1$, or $n - n_{l-2} - k_{l-1} \geqslant n - n_{l-1} - k_l + 1$. Thus, using (4.39) at l and $l - 1$ we see that:

$$\frac{\beta_{l-1} - \beta_l}{b_l - b_{l-1}} > n - n_{l-2} - k_{l-1} \geqslant n - n_{l-1} - k_l + 1 \geqslant$$

$$\frac{\beta_l - \beta_{l+1}}{b_{l+1} - b_l}. \tag{4.40}$$

Thus (4.22) and (4.40) are equivalent to the asserted properties of the efficient technological frontier.[7]

The technological frontier is illustrated in Figure 4.1 for four plant types $(l = 1, \ldots, 4)$. Plant type $(\bar{b}, \bar{\beta})$ would be ruled out in this case as its addition to the existing plant mix would violate the required convexity of the technological frontier. In fact only plant types falling in the shaded area would be efficient additions to the current mix.

A further corollary to Proposition A, which we need below, is the following obvious consequence of (4.33)–(4.37).

Corollary B: Assuming (4.22) and (4.27) are satisfied, capacity is installed and operated in order of increasing operating cost. In particular plant 1 is used in every period $(q_{1i} > 0$ for all i).

OPTIMAL PRICING. Let us first note that equation (4.10) indicates that price is to be set to λ_i, the Lagrangian multiplier associated with constraint (4.3) at period i. This is none other than the long-run incremental cost of meeting an additional unit of demand in period i, i.e. $\lambda_i = LRMC_i$. (To establish this rigorously simply note from the theory of linear programming that the optimal solution to the dual linear programme to Problem CP is characterised by (4.11)–(4.13), and so we may interpret λ_i as the shadow price of constraint (4.24) at optimum. Clearly, the shadow price of (4.24) at optimum is the per unit incremental cost of increasing x_i marginally. Thus $\lambda_i = LRMC$.) Given this meaning for λ_i, we may begin a more specific analysis of optimal pricing.

From the just-stated result that $q_{1i} > 0$ for all i we see from (4.12) that $\lambda_i - \mu_{1i} = b_1$ for all i. Since plant 1 capacity q_1 is positive, (4.11) implies:

$$\sum_{i=1}^{n} \mu_{1i} = \beta_1, \tag{4.41}$$

so that from $\lambda_i = \mu_{1i} + b$ and (4.10):

$$\sum_{i=1}^n p_i = nb_1 + \beta_1. \tag{4.42}$$

From (4.11) and $\mu_{li} \geqslant 0$ we obtain $\mu_{li} \leqslant \beta_l$ for all i, l. Thus from (4.10) and (4.12):

$$\lambda_i = p_i \leqslant b_l + \mu_{li} \leqslant b_l + \beta_l, \text{ for all } i, l. \tag{4.43}$$

To obtain more stringent bounds on the optimal prices we note from Lemma A that $b_l + \beta_l < b_{l-1} + \beta_{l-1}, l = 2, \ldots, m$, for an efficient plant mix. Thus, assuming an efficient mix, the most stringent requirement in (4.43) is for $l = m$. Using (4.40) and $\mu_{li} \geqslant 0$ we therefore obtain the following bounds on prices:

$$b_1 \leqslant \lambda_i = p_i \leqslant b_m + \beta_m, \quad i = 1, \ldots, n. \tag{4.44}$$

If only plant 1 were available, (4.42) would still hold. Note, however, that the addition of further plant types has reduced the possible peak price from $b_1 + \beta_1$ to $b_m + \beta_m$. Equation (4.44) is the general analogue to the two-period, two-plant result (4.21).

Turning to specific cases the reader can now verify for the case $m = n = 2$ the previously given results (4.16)–(4.18), this time for the interdependent demand case. Simply note that if (4.19)–(4.20) hold and $x_2 > x_1$ at optimum (the firm-peak case), then Proposition A guarantees that (4.18) is the optimal solution to Problem **CP**. When (4.18) is coupled with the Kuhn–Tucker necessary conditions (4.10)–(4.13), we obtain (4.16)–(4.17) as the unique solution.

For the shifting-peak case and $m = n = 2$, where $x_1 = x_2 = x$ at optimum, we note from (4.42) that:

$$p_1 + p_2 = P_1(\mathbf{x}) + P_2(\mathbf{x}) = 2b_1 + \beta_1 \tag{4.45}$$

must obtain, where $\mathbf{x} = (x, x)$. This is then used to solve for x (and therefore also p_1, p_2). Note from Proposition A that only plant 1 is used in the two-period case where $x_1 = x_2 = x$, so that a less diverse optimal technology obtains under a shifting-peak case.

Mild regularity conditions assure that the shifting- and firm-peak cases are mutually exclusive and that the p_1, p_2 solving (4.45) satisfy $p_1 < p_2$. Thus, to solve the $m = n = 2$ case, one checks whether the prices (4.16)–(4.17) lead to $x_2 \geqslant x_1$. If so, a firm-peak solution obtains; otherwise the shifting-peak solution determined through (4.45) obtains. We see that the case $m = n = 2$ is solved completely.

For the case $n = 3$ we note that there are many possibilities (twelve, in fact) for ordering the outputs x_1, x_2, x_3 according to magnitude. Assuming, given our usual notation, that demand intensities go from low to high in going from period 1 to period 3, we need only consider the cases: $x_3 > x_2 > x_1$; $x_3 = x_2 > x_1$; $x_3 > x_2 = x_1$; and $x_3 = x_2 = x_1$. For each such assumed ordering, we would in theory have to solve the Kuhn–Tucker conditions (4.10)–(4.13) for p_1, p_2, p_3 and then check that at the prices so obtained the assumed initial ordering was valid. We illustrate this process below.

Let us first note the results of Proposition A when $x_1 < x_2 < \ldots < x_n$ and:

$$\frac{\beta_l - \beta_{l+1}}{n - l + 1} \leqslant b_{l+1} - b_l < \frac{\beta_l - \beta_{l+1}}{n - l}, l = 1, \ldots, m - 1, \quad (4.46)$$

where $n \geqslant m$. Assuming (4.46), an optimal solution to Problem **CP** is given by:

$$q_l = x_l - x_{l-1}, \quad l = 1, \ldots, m - 1 \quad (4.47)$$

$$q_m = x_n - x_{m-1}. \quad (4.48)$$

Using (4.46)–(4.48) and assuming $m = 3$, we can now illustrate the solution to (4.10)–(4.13) for the case where $x_3 > x_2 > x_1$. If $x_3 > x_2 > x_1$ holds at optimal and (4.46) holds for $l = 1, 2$, then by (4.47)–(4.48) $q_1 = x_1$, $q_2 = x_2 - x_1$, and $q_3 = x_3 - x_2$. Again, using Proposition A, by (4.40) $q_{32} = q_{31} = q_{21} = 0$, implying from (4.13) that $\mu_{32} = \mu_{31} = \mu_{21} = 0$; (4.11) holds as equality for all l, since $q_l > 0$ for all l. Moreover, (4.12) holds as equality for $(l, i) \epsilon \{(1, 1), (1, 2), (1, 3), (2, 2), (2, 3), (3, 3)\}$. These equalities are sufficient to solve for all remaining unknowns, and yield the following prices:

$$p_1 = 3b_1 + \beta_1 - (2b_2 + \beta_2) \quad (4.49)$$

$$p_2 = 2b_2 + \beta_2 - (b_3 + \beta_3) \quad (4.50)$$

$$p_3 = b_3 + \beta_3. \quad (4.51)$$

Finally, we must check that at these prices the assumed ordering $x_3 > x_2 > x_1$ holds. If so, a solution is at hand. The reader should also note that with prices determined by (4.49)–(4.51), $p_1 < p_2 < p_3$ will always hold.[8]

In a similar fashion to the above firm-peak case, one can use Proposition A and the Kuhn–Tucker conditions to derive the following shifting-peak result (again assuming (4.46) for $l = 1, 2$) for the case where at optimum $x_1 < x_2 = x_3$ (which case arises when the prices (4.49)–(4.51) lead to $x_1 < x_3 < x_2$):

$$p_1 = (3b_1 + \beta_1) - (2b_2 + \beta_2) \tag{4.52}$$

$$p_2 + p_3 = 2b_2 + \beta_2 \tag{4.53}$$

$$q_1 = x_1 = q_{1i}, \text{ for all } i; q_2 = x_2 - x_1 = q_{22} = q_{23}, q_{21} = 0, \tag{4.54}$$

where only plants 1 and 2 are now used. (Thus, just as in the case $m = n = 2$, so also here the shifting-peak case leads to a less diverse optimal technology as compared with the firm-peak case $x_3 > x_2 > x_1$.) Note that (4.53) is to be solved together with the requirement $x_2 = x_3$ here. Obviously this can be somewhat tricky in practice, with highly interdependent demands.

Other sub-cases of the three-period and n-period cases can be analysed similarly (see also the exercises to this chapter). The important point to realise is the strong interaction between optimal technology, as embodied in Proposition A, and optimal pricing. Basically, the more variable demand is between the periods $1, \ldots, n$, the more diverse will be the optimal technology, though optimal diversity interacts strongly with cost parameters as well. Looking at the same thing from the pricing side, the more diverse the available technology, the less will be the tendency to flatten demand through peak-load pricing, i.e. the flatter the optimal price schedule will be.

TIME-VARYING DEMAND AND UNEQUAL-LENGTH PERIODS. We have assumed up to this point that the pricing periods ($i = 1, 2, \ldots, n$ above) are of equal length and that within each such pricing period demand is constant over time. In this section, following Dansby (1976), we relax both assumptions. We assume the cycle of n periods is divided into a set of off-peak periods N_o and a set of peak periods N_p, where $N_o \cup N_p = \{1, 2, \ldots, n\}$, and where the prices p_o and p_p must prevail uniformly throughout the respective off-peak and peak periods. The following problem emerges:

$$\text{Max } W = \oint_0^x \left\{ \sum_{i=1}^n P_i(\mathbf{y}) dy_i \right\} - \sum_{i=1}^n \sum_{l=1}^m b_l q_{li} - \sum_{l=1}^m \beta_l q_l, \tag{4.55}$$

subject to:

$$\sum_{l=1}^{m} q_{li} = x_i, \text{ for all } i \tag{4.56}$$

$$q_l - q_{li} \geqslant 0, \text{ for all } i, l \tag{4.57}$$

$$P_i(\mathbf{x}) = p_o, i \in N_o; P_i(\mathbf{x}) = p_p, i \in N_p \tag{4.58}$$

$$x_i \geqslant 0, q_l \geqslant 0, q_{li} \geqslant 0, p_o, p_p \geqslant 0, \text{ for all } i, l, \tag{4.59}$$

where all variables other than p_o, p_p are as in (4.2)–(4.5). Note that the problem (4.55)–(4.59) is obtained from (4.2)–(4.5) by adding the constraints (4.58). The new problem formulation now allows for unequal-length periods and time-varying and interdependent demand.

To derive first-order conditions for (4.55)–(4.59) we associate multipliers η_i with constraints (4.58) and, differentiating the resulting Lagrangian as in (4.9), we obtain the following analogues to (4.10)–(4.13):

$$P_i(\mathbf{x}) = \lambda_i + \eta_i \sum_{j \in N_o} \frac{\partial P_j}{\partial x_i} = p_o, \quad i \in N_o \tag{4.60}$$

$$P_i(\mathbf{x}) = \lambda_i + \eta_i \sum_{j \in N_p} \frac{\partial P_j}{\partial x_i} = p_p, \quad i \in N_p \tag{4.61}$$

$$\sum_{i \in N_o} \eta_i = \sum_{i \in N_p} \eta_i = 0 \tag{4.62}$$

$$\sum_{i=1}^{n} \mu_{li} \leqslant \beta_l, q_l \left(\sum_{i=1}^{n} \mu_{li} - \beta_l \right) = 0, \text{ for all } l \tag{4.63}$$

$$\lambda_i - \mu_{li} \leqslant b_l, q_{li}(\lambda_i - \mu_{li} - b_l) = 0, \text{ for all } i, l \tag{4.64}$$

$$\mu_{li} \geqslant 0, \mu_{li}(q_l - q_{li}) = 0, \text{ for all } i, l. \tag{4.65}$$

Notice that (4.63)–(4.65) are the same as (4.11)–(4.13). This allows similar solution techniques to be applied here. In particular the multipliers λ_i have the same meaning here as in (4.10)–(4.13), namely λ_i is the long-run incremental cost of meeting an additional unit of demand in period i. We will concentrate on the independent demand case where $\partial P_i/\partial x_j = 0, i \neq j$. In solving for optimal prices for this case note from (4.60)–(4.62) that:

$$\sum_{i \in N_o} \frac{p_o - \lambda_i}{\partial P_i/\partial x_i} = \sum_{i \in N_o} \eta_i = 0 = \sum_{i \in N_p} \eta_i = \sum_{i \in N_p} \frac{p_p - \lambda_i}{\partial P_i/\partial x_i} \tag{4.66}$$

so that solving for p_o, p_p in (4.66) yields the following optimal prices when demands are independent:

$$p_o = \sum_{i \in N_o} \alpha_i \lambda_i, \quad \alpha_i = \frac{1}{\partial P_i / \partial x_i} \bigg/ \left(\sum_{j \in N_o} \frac{1}{\partial P_j / \partial x_j} \right) \tag{4.67}$$

$$p_p = \sum_{i \in N_p} \alpha_i \lambda_i, \quad \alpha_i = \frac{1}{\partial P_i / \partial x_i} \bigg/ \left(\sum_{j \in N_p} \frac{1}{\partial P_j / \partial x_j} \right) \tag{4.68}$$

Since clearly

$$\alpha_i \geqslant 0 \text{ and } \sum_{N_o} \alpha_i = \sum_{N_p} \alpha_i = 1,$$

we see that p_o and p_p are convex combinations of period long-run marginal costs in the respective off-peak and peak pricing periods. Thus, when a different price can be charged in each period, we have price = λ = *LRMC*, and when the constraints (4.58) are imposed, a weighted average of period-specific *LRMC*s results, with period weights determined by the slope of the period demand curve relative to the slope of other period demands in the pricing period, where the slopes are evaluated at the optimal solution x.

To illustrate, consider the case $m = 1$ and assume a firm peak where, for some period $k \in N_P$, $q_{1k} = q_1 > 0$ and where $0 < q_{1i} < q_1$ for all $i \neq k$. Then from (4.63) and (4.65) we have $\mu_{1k} = \beta_1$ and $\mu_{1i} = 0$ for $i \neq k$. From (4.64) $\lambda_i = \mu_{1i} + b_1$ so that $\lambda_k = b_1 + \beta_1$ and $\lambda_i = b_1$ for $i \neq k$. Thus from (4.67)–(4.68) we have:

$$p_o = b_1 \tag{4.69}$$

$$p_p = b_1 + \alpha_k \beta_1 \leqslant b_1 + \beta_1, \tag{4.70}$$

where α_k is given in (4.68). Thus we see that p_p never exceeds $b_1 + \beta_1$, which is the optimal price to charge in period k if different prices could be charged in each period i.[9] The above result reflects a trade-off between suppressing peak demand in period k and resulting welfare losses from pricing above b_1 in periods ($i \in N_p$) other than k. From the definition of α_k in (4.68), the greater the slope of demand in period k relative to other demands $i \in N_p$, the smaller will be the factor α_k and therefore the lower the price p_p.

To investigate the shifting-peak case where $m = 1$, suppose $x_i = q_{1i} =$

q_1 for $i \in \overline{N}$ and $q_{1i} < q_1$ for $i \notin \overline{N}$. Then, from (4.64)-(4.65), $\lambda_i = b_1 + \mu_{1i}$ for all i with $\mu_{1i} = 0$, $i \notin \overline{N}$, and:

$$\sum_{\overline{N}} \mu_{1i} = \beta_1. \tag{4.71}$$

Substituting the just-given λ_i in (4.67)-(4.68), we obtain the following prices:

$$p_o = b_1 + \sum_{\overline{N} \cap N_o} \alpha_i \mu_{1i} \tag{4.72}$$

$$p_p = b_1 + \sum_{\overline{N} \cap N_p} \alpha_i \mu_{1i}, \tag{4.73}$$

where the μ_{1i} in (4.72)-(4.73) are determined from (4.71) and the shifting-peak requirement that, at the prices (4.72)-(4.73), $x_i = q_1$ for all $i \in \overline{N}$.

Two examples may serve to illustrate the shifting-peak case. In the first, assume that $\overline{N} \subset N_p$ and that $\partial P_i / \partial x_i = \partial P_j / \partial x_j$ for all $i, j \in \overline{N}$. Then $p_o = b_1$ and $p_p = b_1 + \beta_1 (\overline{n}/n_p)$, where $\overline{n}$ and n_p are the number of periods in $\overline{N}$ and N_p respectively. Only when the peak is completely flat (i.e. $\overline{N} = N_p$) will $\overline{n} = n_p$ and $p_p = b_1 + \beta_1$.

As a second example, consider the case where $\overline{N} = (j, k)$, with $j \in N_o$ and $k \in N_p$. Then (4.72)-(4.73) imply:

$$p_o = b_1 + \alpha_j \mu_j \tag{4.74}$$

$$p_p = b_1 + \alpha_k \mu_k, \tag{4.75}$$

where μ_j and μ_k are determined through the requirements that $\mu_j + \mu_k = \beta_1$ and $x_j = x_k$ (at the prices (4.74)-(4.75)).

In the more general cases where $m > 1$, we must use Proposition A to determine q_{li} and q_l and therewith μ_{li} and λ_i. The bounds (4.44) of the previous section on λ_i continue to apply here as well, so that, in particular, $b_1 \leqslant \lambda_i \leqslant b_m + \beta_m$, from which also $b_1 \leqslant p_o, p_p \leqslant b_m + \beta_m$ follows from (4.67)-(4.68).

The reader may wish to test his understanding of these matters in the exercises. In any case, it should be noted that the essential ingredient in solving for optimal prices in this more complex setting continues to be the solution of Problem **CP** for the optimal investment and operating regime, and for the resulting long-run incremental costs λ_i.

4.2 PEAK-LOAD PRICING WITH STORAGE POSSIBILITIES

Feasible storage might be regarded as similar to the multiple-plant technology of Section 4.1, to the extent that it implies a relaxation of the peak-load conditions through technology. The storage case simply means that there is available a technology which permits storage at an economical cost, thus allowing demand in one period to be met through output produced in some other period. The problem has been solved apparently independently and simultaneously by Nguyen (1976) and Gravelle (1976). In this section we briefly state the problem and compare it with our results of Section 4.1.

To incorporate storage we must reformulate the social-welfare function (4.2) as follows:

$$\text{Max } W = \oint_o^x \left\{ \sum_{i=1}^n P_i(y)dy_i \right\} - \sum_{i=1}^n \left[\sum_{l=1}^m b_l \left(x_{li} - \sum_{\substack{k=1 \\ k \neq i}}^n y_{li}^k \right) \right]$$

$$- \sum_{i=1}^n \sum_{l=1}^m \sum_{\substack{k=1 \\ k \neq i}}^n c_i^k y_{li}^k - \sum_{l=1}^m \beta_l q_l, \tag{4.76}$$

where q_l is capacity installed of type l, x_{li} is output produced by plant l to meet demand in period i; y_{lk}^i is sales in period i of the output of plant l produced in period $k \neq i$. Thus, together,

$$x_{li} + \sum_{k \neq i} y_{lk}^i$$

represents total sales in period i of output from plant l in all periods. The per-unit cost of storing output produced in period i for use in period k is represented by c_i^k.

The problem is to maximise (4.76) subject to the following demand and combined storage/capacity constraints:

$$\sum_{l=1}^m \left(x_{li} + \sum_{\substack{k=1 \\ k \neq i}}^n y_{lk}^i \right) = x_i, \text{ for all } i \tag{4.77}$$

$$q_{li} = x_{li} + \sum_{\substack{k=1 \\ k \neq i}}^n y_{li}^k \leqslant q_l, \text{ for all } i, l. \tag{4.78}$$

Equation (4.78) replaces the usual capacity constraint and incorporates storage. Thus output produced from plant l for use in period $i(x_{li})$ and for storage

$$\left(\sum_{k \neq i} y_{li}^k \right)$$

cannot exceed capacity of plant $l(q_l)$.

Associating multipliers λ_i and μ_{li} with (4.77)–(4.78) and setting up the Lagrangian as usual, we obtain the following Kuhn–Tucker conditions:

$$P_i(\mathbf{x}) = \lambda_i, \text{ for all } i \tag{4.79}$$

$$\lambda_i - \mu_{li} \leqslant b_l, x_{li}(\lambda_i - \mu_{li} - b_l) = 0, \text{ for all } i, l \tag{4.80}$$

$$\lambda_k - \mu_{li} \leqslant b_l + c_i^k, y_{li}^k(\lambda_k - \mu_{li} - b_l - c_i^k), \text{ for all } i, k, l \tag{4.81}$$

$$\sum_{i=1}^n \mu_{li} \leqslant \beta_l, q_l \left(\sum_{i=1}^n \mu_{li} - \beta_l \right) = 0, \text{ for all } i \tag{4.82}$$

$$\mu_{li} \geqslant 0, \mu_{li}(x_{li} + \sum_{\substack{k=1 \\ k \neq i}}^n y_{li}^k - q_l) = 0, \text{ for all } i, k, l. \tag{4.83}$$

Again price is set to $LRMC(\lambda_i)$ in each period, though a somewhat more complicated version of Problem **CP** would have to be solved to determine the λ_i in this case. The general solution to this more complicated problem is not known at this point. Note, however, that if we define period i output from all plants as:

$$\bar{x}_i = \sum_{l=i}^m \left(x_{li} + \sum_{\substack{k=1 \\ k \neq i}}^n y_{li}^k \right), \tag{4.84}$$

then, if we know what the optimal levels $\bar{x}_i$ were, the solution to Problem **CP** with$\{\bar{x}_i\}$ substituted for$\{x_i\}$would be the optimal solution to the above problem. In particular the order of plant installation and utilisation and the cost characteristics of the technological frontier implied by Proposition A remain unchanged when storage is feasible.

Turning now to the solution of (4.76)–(4.78), we start by noting that if $y_{li}^k > 0$, then (4.81) implies $\lambda_k = \mu_{lk} + b_l + c_i^k$ and (4.80) implies

$\lambda_k \leqslant \mu_{lk} + b_l$, from which $\mu_{lk} > 0$ follows. Therefore, if plant l provides some output in period i to meet demand in period k (i.e. $y_{li}^k > 0$), then (4.83) (and $\mu_{lk} > 0$) imply that plant l is used to capacity in period k. In particular, if any output in period i is to be used to meet demand in period k, then total output must be greater in period k than in period i, i.e. the effect of storage is to smooth the supply schedule. Given the convex nature of costs here and the fact that marginal-cost pricing obtains at optimum, smoothing the supply schedule will also smooth period marginal costs, i.e. also the price schedule. The reader may also verify through the conditions (4.34)–(4.36) that a smoother supply schedule[10] will result in a less diverse optimal technology. This is essentially because storage acts as a substitute for peak-load plants (plants where $l > 1$).

We can illustrate the above remarks for the case $m = n = 2$. In the shifting-peak case $x_1 = \bar{x}_1 = \bar{x}_2 = x_2$, storage is not used and the solution characterised by (4.45) obtains. Consider, therefore, the firm-peak case $x_2 > x_1$. From the above discussion, $\bar{x}_2 \geqslant \bar{x}_1$ at optimum. From Proposition A, therefore, $q_1 = \bar{x}_1$, $q_2 = \bar{x}_2 - \bar{x}_1$, assuming (4.27) is satisfied (since otherwise only one plant need be used). We then have two cases:

(i) storage is used and $y_{11}^2 > 0$; and
(ii) storage is not used.

Note that $y_{21}^2 = 0$ since $q_1 = \bar{x}_1$. Also clearly storage only takes place in the off-peak period for use in the peak period, so $y_{l2}^1 = 0$ for $l = 1, 2$. To determine when case (i) obtains and when case (ii), we note that for storage to be used, the marginal unit met from plant 1 and storage must be cheaper than supplying this unit from plant 2. Constructing the additional unit of plant 1 and producing and storing a unit for period 2 entails costs $\beta_1 + b_1 + c_1^2$. The additional cost of plant 1 available also leads to savings of $b_2 - b_1$ in period 2, since this unit would be used to replace a marginal unit of the higher running cost plant 2. This leads to the following conditions for storage to be economical: $\beta_1 + b_1 + c_1^2 - (b_2 - b_1) < b_2 + \beta_2$, or:

$$c_1^2 < 2b_2 + \beta_2 - (2b_1 + \beta_1). \tag{4.85}$$

Clearly when (4.84) holds, storage will be substituted for plant 2 until $q_2 = 0$. Given this, optimal prices follow directly from (4.79)–(4.83) and are given by:

$$\bar{p}_1 = b_1 + \mu_{11} = b_1 + \frac{\beta_1 - c_1^2}{2},$$

$$\bar{p}_2 = b_1 + \mu_{12} = b_1 + \frac{\beta_1 + c_1^2}{2}, \tag{4.86}$$

or

$$\hat{p}_1 = 2b_1 + \beta_1 - (b_2 + \beta_2), \quad \hat{p}_2 = b_2 + \beta_2, \tag{4.87}$$

where (4.86) holds if storage is used (i.e. if (4.85) holds) and (4.86) obtains otherwise. As noted, when storage is used $q_2 = 0$. When storage is not used both plants are used (assuming, of course, that Lemma A continues to hold). Moreover, it can be shown that when (4.85) holds, $\bar{p}_1 > \hat{p}_1, \hat{p}_2 < \hat{p}_2$. Thus the use of storage, when economical, increases the off-peak price and decreases peak price compared to the case where two plants only are used. As the cost of storage decreases to the difference between peak and off-peak prices, the symptoms of the peak problem get less until, at the extreme where storage is a free good, both prices are equal at $b_1 + \beta_1/2$ (from (4.86)). Thus storage, like extra-plant types, reduces the differential between peak and off-peak prices. Storage is essentially a substitute for peak-load plants (plants where $l > 1$). Moreover, the presence of economical storage causes the optimal technology to be less diverse. Pricing continues to be at *LRMC*, of course.

4.3 PROFIT MAXIMISATION AND SECOND-BEST RESULTS

It is interesting to compare the above welfare-optimal results with those of a profit-maximising monopolist. As a change of pace we will investigate this issue using the Pressman formulation (4.1) instead of (4.2)–(4.5). We restrict attention to the two-period, firm-peak case (where at optimum $x_2 > x_1$) throughout this section. We first note that the solution to (4.1) for this case is easily found from Kuhn–Tucker theory to be:

$$P_1(x) = \frac{\partial C(x, z)}{\partial x_1}, P_2(x) = \frac{\partial C(x, z)}{\partial x_2} + \frac{\partial C(x, z)}{\partial z}, \tag{4.88}$$

i.e. long-run marginal-cost pricing as expected. We may reformulate (4.1) as follows for the profit-maximising case:

$$\text{Max } \Pi = \sum_{i=1}^{2} x_i P_i(\mathbf{x}) - C(\mathbf{x}, z), \tag{4.89}$$

subject to $x_i \leqslant z, x_i \geqslant 0, z \geqslant 0, i = 1, 2$.

Forming the Lagrangian for (4.89) and taking first-order conditions, we obtain:

$$\frac{\partial R(\mathbf{x})}{\partial x_i} = \frac{\partial C(\mathbf{x}, z)}{\partial x_i} + \mu_i, i = 1, 2 \tag{4.90}$$

$$\frac{\partial C(\mathbf{x}, z)}{\partial z} = \mu_1 + \mu_2 \tag{4.91}$$

$$\mu_i \geqslant 0, \mu_i(z - x_i) = 0, i = 1, 2, \tag{4.92}$$

where $R(\mathbf{x})$ = total revenue = $\Sigma x_i P_i(\mathbf{x})$ and μ_i is the multiplier associated with the constraint $x_i \leqslant z$. Since $x_1 < x_2$, we obtain the following profit-maximising result:

$$\frac{\partial R}{\partial x_1} = \frac{\partial C}{\partial x_1}, \frac{\partial R}{\partial x_2} = \frac{\partial C}{\partial x_2} + \frac{\partial C}{\partial z}, \tag{4.93}$$

which differs from (4.88) only in that marginal revenue, instead of price, is equated to marginal cost. This same result would obtain if profit-maximisation were carried out in (4.2)–(4.5) in place of welfare maximisation; the corresponding results for the profit-maximising case throughout the preceding analysis are then obtained by equating marginal revenue in period i to $LRMC_i = \lambda_i$, as determined via Proposition A. Under mild regularity conditions this leads to higher prices and lower outputs under monopoly pricing, as we now illustrate for the case where $C(\mathbf{x}, z)$ is given by (4.6)–(4.8) with $m = n = 2$. For this case we obtain the optimal solution by substituting $\partial R/\partial x_i$ for p_i in (4.16)–(4.17), that is:

$$\frac{\partial R}{\partial x_1} = 2b_1 + \beta_1 - (b_2 + \beta_2), \frac{\partial R}{\partial x_2} = b_2 + \beta_2. \tag{4.94}$$

Since $\partial R/\partial x_i = P_i(\mathbf{x}) + x_i \partial P_i/\partial x_i + x_j \partial P_j/\partial x_i$, $(j \neq i)$, we see that if cross-effects are not too large (so that $x_i \partial P_i/\partial x_i + x_j \partial P_j/\partial x_i < 0$), then $\partial R/\partial x_i < P_i(\mathbf{x})$ for $i = 1, 2$. Thus comparing (4.94) with (4.16)–(4.17) we see that, normally, prices will be everywhere higher and output everywhere lower under profit-maximising behaviour than under the corresponding welfare-optimal solution.[11]

When demands are independent, $\partial R/\partial x_i = P_i(x_i) + x_i dP_i/dx_i$, and we may write (4.93) as:

$$p_1 = \frac{\partial C/\partial x_1}{1 - \dfrac{1}{e_1}}, \quad p_2 = \frac{\partial C/\partial x_2 + \partial C/\partial z}{1 - \dfrac{1}{e_2}}, \tag{4.95}$$

where e_i = elasticity in period $i = -P_i(x_i)/(x_i dP_i/dx_i)$. Thus the more elastic demand is in period i, the lower will be the price in period i. In fact, as Bailey and White (1974) have pointed out, if e_1 is sufficiently small compared with e_2, then the peak-price may actually be lower than the off-peak price with profit maximisation.

The above analysis indicates that the translation and comparison of welfare-maximising and profit-maximising solutions is straightforward. The deleterious welfare consequences of the pure profit-maximising solution are evident here and have provided the rationale for state intervention and regulation of utilities. As we indicated in Chapter 2, and as we discuss more fully in Part Three, a critical issue for evaluating such public control is an understanding of second-best solutions which maximise welfare while providing a specified level of profit. Such a profit-constrained, welfare-maximising approach is especially important under increasing returns to scale ($\partial C^2/\partial z^2 < 0$ above) where deficits occur under marginal-cost pricing, the first-best solution. Two approaches have been suggested for dealing with this problem: (i) the determination of second-best prices by appending a minimum profit constraint to (4.1); and (ii) the use of multi-part tariffs. Let us consider each of these briefly.

Consider the first problem of maximising (4.1) subject to $\Pi \geqslant \Pi_0$, where Π is as in (4.89) and Π_0 is a pre-specified minimum profit level. Taking first-order conditions (while still assuming $n = 2$ and $x_2 > x_1$) we obtain the following:

$$P_1(x) + \xi \frac{\partial R}{\partial x_1} = \frac{\partial C}{\partial x_1} (1 + \xi) \tag{4.96}$$

$$P_2(x) + \xi \frac{\partial R}{\partial x_2} = \left(\frac{\partial C}{\partial x_2} + \frac{\partial C}{\partial z} \right)(1 + \xi) \tag{4.97}$$

$$\xi \geqslant 0, \xi(\Pi - \Pi_0) = 0, \tag{4.98}$$

where ξ is the multiplier associated with the constraint $\Pi \geqslant \Pi_0$. Again restricting attention to the case of independent demands, (4.96)–(4.97) may be written:

$$p_1 = P_1(x) = \frac{(1 + \xi)\partial C/\partial x_1}{1 + \xi\left(1 - \dfrac{1}{e_1}\right)} \tag{4.99}$$

$$p_2 = P_2(x) = \frac{(1 + \xi)(\partial C/\partial x_2 + \partial C/\partial z)}{1 + \xi\left(1 - \dfrac{1}{e_2}\right)}, \tag{4.100}$$

where ξ is determined from (4.98). Since $\xi > 0$ when the constraint $\Pi \geqslant \Pi_0$ is binding (i.e. when the unconstrained welfare-maximising solution yields $\Pi < \Pi_0$), we see that the second-best prices (4.99)–(4.100) are both higher with relative price increases proportional to demand inelasticity as with the inverse elasticity rule discussed in Chapter 2.

Following Bailey and White (1974) we summarise the above discussion in Table 4.1, which provides comparative results for the profit-maximising, welfare-maximising and second-best solutions for the case

Table 4.1

Objective	Peak price	Off-peak price
Maximise welfare	$b + \beta$	b
Maximise profits	$\dfrac{b + \beta}{1 - \dfrac{1}{e_2}}$	$\dfrac{b}{1 - \dfrac{1}{e_1}}$
Maximise welfare subject to $\Pi \geqslant \Pi_0$ (ξ determined by (4.98))	$\dfrac{(1 + \xi)(b + \beta)}{1 + \xi\left(1 - \dfrac{1}{e_2}\right)}$	$\dfrac{(1 + \xi)b}{1 + \xi\left(1 - \dfrac{1}{e_1}\right)}$

of a simple two-period, one-plant technology with costs b and β.

The second approach to second-best pricing is the use of multi-part tariffs, as explained by Oi (1971), Ng and Weisser (1974), and Leland and Meyer (1976). In the simplest case[12] a two-part tariff obtains where customers are first charged a licence fee (or connect charge) F. After paying the licence fee consumers may purchase additional units in period i at price p_i as usual.

Consider the case of a single period ($n = 1$). For a single consumer at a given price (p) consumer's surplus (S) is defined straightforwardly as previously. Now if F exceeds S, clearly the consumer will consume nothing at price p (since he would have to first pay F to do so, with the result that net surplus at price p would be negative). If $S \geqslant F$, of course, then the price pair (F, p) could be levied, and demand would be x for this consumer.

Turning to the problem of welfare-maximising (F, p) pairs, we may note that, neglecting income effects, the optimal solution is easily seen to be price equals marginal cost, providing that this allows a licence fee F to be collected at this price sufficiently high to satisfy $\Pi \geqslant \Pi_0$, and sufficiently low so that no consumer disconnects (because $F > S$). The problem of solving for optimal (F, p) pairs when marginal cost is not feasible is difficult since it must consider explicitly the set of subscribers implied by each (F, p) combination. For any given subset $\overline{V} \subset V$ of the total consumer population V, one can solve for second-best (F, p) pairs by appending to the problem ((4.1), subject to $\Pi \geqslant \Pi_0$) the additional constraint that only pairs (F, p) are considered for which the surplus at p exceeds F for every consumer in $\overline{V}$. By then considering all possible subsets of V which allow for the profit constraint to be met, the welfare-optimal subscriber set $\overline{V}^*$ and corresponding prices (F^*, p^*) can be obtained. Not surprisingly, distributional matters may play a role here, in determining (through F) the subscriber subset. Also not surprisingly, Pareto improvements over simple tariffs may be effected through the use of the more flexible two-part tariffs as a policy instrument in meeting budget constraints.

The above discussion underlines some of the difficulties one may encounter in attempting to interpret and implement marginal-cost pricing in practice. The important thing to bear in mind is the central position of long-run marginal-cost pricing as the basis for understanding the trade-offs which practical necessity may force on the policy-making process.

EXERCISES

4.1   Derive the optimal prices (4.88) to Pressman's problem. Relate these to the solution of (4.2)–(4.5) through (4.6)–(4.8) and the following discussion.

4.2   A peak-load problem has demands represented by $P_1(x_1) = 50 - x_1$ and $P_2(x_2) = 100 - x_2$.
   (i) Derive (max W) prices if costs are given by (a) $\beta_1 = 8, b_1 = 1$ (only plant available); (b) $\beta_1 = 8, b_1 = 1; \beta_2 = 3, b_2 = 5$ (two plants available).
   (ii) Calculate the value of W and optimal capacities for both parts of (i).

4.3   Refer to the example of p. 44 and answer the following:
   (i) Do all plants lie on a convex technological frontier?
   (ii) Is Lemma A satisfied for all l?
   (iii) If the same cycle were considered, but were cut into twice as many sub-periods (i.e. $n = 10$), would your answer to (i) and (ii) change?

4.4   For the three-period, three-plant case show that total revenue is just equal to total cost. Prove that at optimum, $p_1 < p_2 < p_3$ for a three-period, three-plant problem (see (4.49)–(4.51)).

4.5   Show that when demands are *independent*, (4.2) is strictly concave.

4.6   Let $\{x_i\}_1^n$ and $\{\bar{x}_i\}_1^n$ be as in Problem **CP**. We will say that $\{\bar{x}_i\}$ is flatter than $\{x_i\}$ if $\Sigma \bar{x}_i = \Sigma x_i, \bar{x}_i \leqslant \bar{x}_j$ whenever $x_i \leqslant x_j$, and if for each i there exists an $\alpha_i \epsilon(0, 1)$ with $\bar{x}_i = \alpha_i x_i + (1 - \alpha_i)(\Sigma x_i/n)$. Show that if the supply schedule $\{x_i\}_1^n$ is flattened, the solution to Problem **CP** will involve a technology which is less diverse, in the sense that the same number, or less, of plant types will be used at optimum.

4.7   Consider a cycle of a day with periods (hours) $i = 1, 2 \ldots, 24$. Let demand curves be independent and given by $D_i(p) = 12(60 - p)$ for $i \epsilon N_o = (1, 2, \ldots, 12)$ and $D_i(p) = i(60 - p)$ for $i \epsilon N_p = (13, 14, \ldots, 24)$ (e.g. the demand curve for period 18 is $18(60 - p)$). Determine optimal prices p_o, p_p for this time-varying situation for the case of $m = 1$ where $b_1 = 1, \beta_1 = 3$.

APPENDIX

In this appendix we prove Proposition A (hereafter PA) of Section 4.2. We prove PA by induction on m. We first note that, given (4.16), whatever x and q are given, (4.29) provides an optimal vector of q_{li}s (equation (4.29) says simply that the plants should be used in the order $i = 1, \ldots, n$). Next note that for $m = 1$, PA asserts that an optimal solution is:

$$q_1 = x_n, q_{1i} = x_i, i = 1, \ldots, n. \tag{4.A1}$$

This assertion is clearly true. Suppose PA has been shown to provide the optimal solution (for arbitrary costs and demands) for $m' = 1, \ldots, m - 1$. We show it also holds then for $m' = m$. We first show that:

$$\frac{\beta_1 - \beta_2}{n - k_1 + 1} \leqslant b_2 - b_1 < \frac{\beta_1 - \beta_2}{n - k_1}, k_1 \epsilon \{0, 1, \ldots, n\} \tag{4.A2}$$

implies that $q_1 = x_{k_1} = x_{\pi(k_1)} = x_{n_1} - x_{n_0}$. (We note, by (4.21), that there exists a k_1 satisfying (4.A2).)

For $k_1 = 0$, set $k = 1$, $\hat{k} = 2$ in Lemma A above. Then $n(b_2 - b_1) < \beta_1 - \beta_2$ implies $q_1 = 0 = x_0$. Suppose therefore that $k_1 \epsilon \{1, \ldots, n\}$.

We first show that $q_1 \geqslant x_{k_1}$. Let Q be any feasible vector for Problem **CP** which satisfies (4.29) and suppose that:

$$0 \leqslant q_1 < x_{k_1} = \overline{q}_1 + \epsilon, \ \epsilon > 0. \tag{4.A3}$$

Now define a vector **Q'** as:

$$q_1' = q_1 + \epsilon \tag{4.A4}$$

$$q_2' = q_2 - \epsilon \tag{4.A5}$$

$$q_l' - q_l, l = 3, \ldots, m \tag{4.A6}$$

$$q_{li}' = q_{li}'(x, q_l') \text{ (as given in (4.29))}. \tag{4.A7}$$

By (4.A4)–(4.A7) $q_{li}' = q_{li}, l \geqslant 3, i = 1, \ldots, n$. Therefore:

$$CQ - CQ' = (\beta_2 - \beta_1)\epsilon + \sum_{l=1}^{2} b_l \sum_{i=1}^{n} (q_{li} - q_{li}'). \tag{4.A8}$$

It may be verified from (4.29) and (4.A4)–(4.A7) that:

$$q'_{1i} - q_{1i} = q_{2i} - q'_{2i} \geqslant 0, i = 1, \ldots, n, \qquad (4.A9)$$

and

$$q'_{1i} - q_{1i} = q_{2i} - q'_{2i} = \epsilon, i = k_1, \ldots, n. \qquad (4.A10)$$

therefore, (4.A8) implies:

$$\mathbf{CQ} - \mathbf{CQ'} = [(\beta_2 - \beta_1) + (b_2 - b_1)(n - k_1 + 1)] \epsilon$$

$$+ (b_2 - b_1) \sum_{i=1}^{k_1 - 1} (q'_{1i} - q_{1i}), \qquad (4.A11)$$

or using (4.A9) and $b_2 > b_1$:

$$\mathbf{CQ} - \mathbf{CQ'} \geqslant [(\beta_2 - \beta_1) + (b_2 - b_1)(n - k_1 + 1)] \epsilon. \qquad (4.A12)$$

Since $\epsilon > 0$, (4.A2) yields $\mathbf{CQ} \geqslant \mathbf{CQ'}$. Thus it can be assumed that:

$$q_1 \geqslant x_{k_1}.$$

Similarly, assume $\bar{q}_1 < x_{k_1}$ with k_1 defined by (4.A2). Then define $\mathbf{Q'}$ by

$$q'_1 = q_1 - \epsilon \qquad (4.A13)$$

$$q'_2 = q_2 + \epsilon \qquad (4.A14)$$

$$q'_l = q_l, l = 3, \ldots, m \qquad (4.A15)$$

$$q'_{li} = q'_{li}(x, q'_l) \text{ (as given in (4.29))} \qquad (4.A16)$$

Again computing the cost difference $\mathbf{CQ} - \mathbf{CQ'}$ yields, as above, $\mathbf{CQ} \geqslant \mathbf{CQ'}$ (by utilising the right inequality in (4.A2)). Thus with the above result that $q_1 \geqslant x_{k_1}$ we see that $q_1 = x_{k_1}$, as asserted in PA.

Having determined q_1 and q_{1i}, $1 \leqslant i \leqslant n$, as above, however, it is clear that $q_l, q_{li}, l > 1$, are solutions to the following problem (assuming $\pi(k_1) < n$, since otherwise all demands have already been covered in plant):

$$\text{Min} \sum_{i=n_1+1}^{n} \sum_{l=2}^{m} b_l q_{li} + \sum_{l=2}^{m} \beta_l q_l, \qquad (4.A17)$$

subject to:

$$\sum_{l=2}^{m} q_{li} = x_i, i = n_1 + 1, \ldots, n \qquad (4.A18)$$

$$0 \leqslant q_{li} \leqslant q_l, i = n_1 + 1, \ldots, n, l = 2, \ldots, m \qquad (4.A19)$$

By the induction hypothesis on m, this $(m - 1)$ plant problem has the solution as specified in PA. This completes the proof.

5 Stochastic Models of Peak-load Pricing

So far, in setting out the classic peak-load model and its extensions, we have retained the assumption of that model, i.e. that demand is deterministic. Many public utilities face demands that have not only the strong periodic element of the peak-load model, but also an important random element. Stochastic demand creates various complications which typically are not considered in the deterministic case. It is necessary to decide whether demand is to be met, and what happens, by way of rationing, when demand is not met.[1] The analysis which follows is directed at answering these questions. In Section 5.1 we describe briefly some of the main contributions to the literature on peak-load pricing under uncertainty. In Section 5.2 we provide a general framework for analysing problems of stochastic demand, comparing the results with the deterministic solutions derived in Chapters 3 and 4. Section 5.3 is concerned with examining some major issues of the stochastic problem, namely dealing with excess demand and rationing. Section 5.4 presents a brief summary and conclusions of the arguments of this chapter.

We consider the analysis of this chapter of particular importance to the issues of public-utility regulation. For this reason, and our desire to make its implications clear, we continue with its development by means of illustrative numerical results in Chapter 6. The reader may in fact just wish to skim this chapter first, and then go on to Chapter 6 for concrete illustrations of the theory presented here.

5.1 PROBLEMS OF STOCHASTIC DEMAND

The interest in stochastic demand in public utility economics is rather recent. After the contributions of French economists discussed by Drèze (1964), Brown and Johnson (1969) re-emphasised its importance. Their article initiated a controversy, confined mainly to the *American Economic Review*, as to the effects of stochastic demand on public utility pricing. Brown and Johnson (B-J) made the familiar cost assumptions of the Boiteux–Steiner–Williamson peak-load model, but they replaced the periodic demands of the peak-load model by a one-period stochastic-demand model. Like the deterministic case they assumed that the utility was welfare-maximising, or more precisely expected welfare-maximising to take into account the effect of stochastic demand. Immediately a discrepancy was apparent between their results and previous results. Their solution to the one-period stochastic model was simply $p = b$, in stark contrast to the corresponding one-period deterministic solution[2] of $p = b + \beta$. This difference was paradoxical and the more so since their solution was apparently to hold no matter how small the level of uncertainty. Thus, as the long-accepted optimal solution for deterministic demand was $p = b + \beta$, their solution of $p = b$ implied an unexplained and counter-intuitive discontinuity in the optimal stochastic solution as the degree of uncertainty approached zero.

Aside from this odd behaviour of B–J's optimal price, another unusual aspect of their development was the possibility of frequently occurring excess demand at their indicated solution. This low level of reliability at optimum was criticised by Turvey (1970) as implausible (e.g. if gas supplies are unreliable, explosions might occur as the gas comes on and off in premises temporarily unoccupied). Taking up this point, Meyer (1975) reformulated the B–J model by adding reliability constraints to it. This raised the issue of how the optimal levels of such constraints were to be determined. This issue has since been addressed by Carlton (1977) and Crew and Kleindorfer (1978), but there are still a number of problems unresolved here, as we discuss in Section 5.3 below.

Another criticism of Brown and Johnson's paper, voiced clearly by Visscher (1973), concerned their assumptions as to how demand was rationed in the event of demand exceeding capacity. B–J assumed that in this event consumers were serviced by means of a *costless rationing process* in accordance with their willingness to pay. This assumption turns out to have a crucial effect in the B–J analysis, as we will demonstrate in Section 5.3. Intuitively their assumption appears highly implausible at first sight because it implies that one of the major benefits of pricing, namely rationing according to marginal willingness to pay, is available without having to worry about the actual price charged!

To summarise, the B–J paper has been seminal in focusing recent discussion on stochastic peak-load pricing problems. In particular this discussion has underlined the importance of reliability and rationing in dealing with welfare-optimal pricing under uncertainty. Accordingly we analyse in the next section a simple model of pricing under uncertainty with special attention to these matters and to their interaction with technology choice. Thereafter, additional aspects of the recent literature on rationing are taken up.

5.2   A SIMPLE MODEL OF PRICING UNDER UNCERTAINTY[3]

In this section we extend our analysis of Chapter 4 on optimal pricing under a diverse technology to cover problems with stochastic demand. In doing so we have made a number of simplifying assumptions which must be underlined at the very beginning. First, demand uncertainty is quite simply characterised (through additive or multiplicative perturbation of a mean demand function). Second, demands are assumed independent across periods, except for possible correlations in the random components of demand. Third, we will use the expected value of the traditional welfare function, net of rationing costs, as our welfare measure.

The use of the traditional welfare function is doubtless the most serious of the simplifications undertaken here. The first implication of this is our willingness to assume risk neutrality and negligible income effects in consumer preferences. Quite aside from considerations of risk-aversion on the purely monetary side, there is a presumption in using a welfare measure that consumer preferences as regards reliability may be represented adequately through expected willingness to pay for a given (reliability-independent) demand curve. However, if reliability is viewed as an aspect of product quality, then it is clear that demand curves may shift as reliability shifts.[4] We neglect such issues here, with the partial justification that in many public utilities only a very narrow band of (high) reliability is *a priori* reasonable. In such cases demand shifts due to reliability changes in this band would also be small, so that the traditional welfare measure would continue to be reasonable for such cases.

We now spell out the assumptions of our model. When not otherwise indicated, notation and assumptions of Chapter 4 are retained.

DEMAND. Unless stated otherwise, demand in each period i is assumed independent of other period demands and is represented in additive form[5] as:

$$D_i(p_i, \tilde{u}_i) = X_i(p_i) + \tilde{u}_i, \tag{5.1}$$

where $X_i(p_i)$ represents mean demand in period i and $\tilde{u}_i$ is a disturbance term with expected value $E\{\tilde{u}_i\} = 0$. We assume X_i to be continuously differentiable and to possess an inverse denoted by P_i. X_i and P_i are assumed to satisfy the following regularity conditions:

$$-A \leqslant \frac{dP_i}{dx_i} < 0; \quad \frac{dX_i}{dp_i} < 0, \tag{5.2}$$

where $A > 0$ is some fixed constant.

Letting $\tilde{u} = (\tilde{u}_1, \ldots, \tilde{u}_n)$, we assume that $\tilde{u}$ is a continuous random variable, i.e. denoting by F and F_i the cumulative distribution functions of $\tilde{u}$ and $\tilde{u}_i$, respectively, we assume that F and F_i, $i = 1, \ldots, n$, are continuous. The random variables $\tilde{u}_i$ need not be stochastically independent.

PRODUCTION COSTS. We retain the same conventions regarding ordering, capacity costs and running costs of the n-plant model discussed in Chapter 4. In particular we exclude dominated plant types, assuming simply that:

$$0 < b_1 < b_2 \ldots < b_m, \beta_1 > \beta_2 > \ldots \beta_m > 0. \tag{5.3}$$

In Chapter 4 (see Proposition A) we noted that the optimal short-run allocation of demand to capacity is achieved by using first the plant with lowest operating costs. For emphasis we repeat the mathematical expression for the optimal amount of output of plant l in period i below:

$$q_{li}(x_i, \mathbf{q}) = \text{Min} \left[x_i - \sum_{k=1}^{l-1} q_{ki}(x_i, \mathbf{q}), q_l \right]. \tag{5.4}$$

As previously, total production costs can be derived straightforwardly using (5.4) and substituting for x_i from (5.1) as:

$$\text{Total production costs} = \sum_{l=1}^{m} \sum_{i=1}^{n} b_l q_{li}[D_i(p_i, u_i), \mathbf{q}] + \sum_{l=1}^{m} \beta_l q_l. \tag{5.5}$$

RATIONING COSTS. The presence of stochastic demand means that a situation may occur where quantity demanded exceeds capacity. Thus in terms of Figure 5.1, when price is given by p_i and demand by $D_i(p_i, u_i)$, optimal output is simply x_i. However, where demand is given by $D_i(p_i, u_i')$ output can only be z. There is an excess demand of $x_i' - z$.

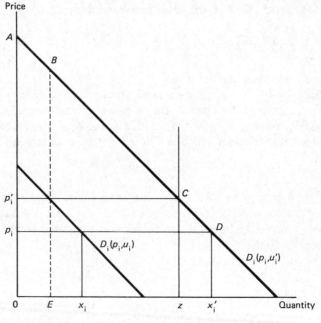

Fig. 5.1

This creates a rationing problem, which can be resolved in a number of ways. One might simply serve consumers in random order until capacity is exhausted; or when consumers must queue up for service, those with the lowest willingness to pay may be willing to stand in line the longest, leading to rationing in order of lowest willingness to pay; as a final example, the utility might determine the marginal valuations of individual consumers and then ration according to these, i.e. in order of marginal willingness to pay.

It should be clear that different rationing schemes may yield different consumers' surplus in the event of excess demand. Considering Figure 5.1, for example, and assuming the demand curve $D_i(p_i, u_i')$

obtains, rationing in order of willingness to pay leads to gross surplus $0ACz$, whereas rationing in order of lowest willingness to pay yields a surplus of $EBDx_i'$, where $E = x_i' - z$ is the excess demand for p_i, z, u_i' as shown. Of course, rationing according to (highest) willingness to pay will always lead to higher gross surplus than other rationing schemes, and in this case, indeed, $0ACz > EBDx_i'$.

Besides the differential effects of rationing on consumers' surplus, different rationing schemes may also have different costs of administering them. In representing the total welfare impact, we need to consider both surplus losses and administrative costs. Our approach will be to take as a base case the (perfect) rationing scheme proposed originally by Brown and Johnson (1969) which assumes costless rationing according to willingness to pay. For a specific rationing scheme r, we then define (incremental) rationing costs R_r (or just R when r is clear) to be any surplus losses and administrative costs over and above those incurred under the B-J scheme. Alternatively, the reader may think of r as rationing according to willingness to pay and of R_r as the costs of implementing this scheme.

In general one may expect R_r to depend on price, output and capacity in complex ways. We restrict attention in this section, however, to rationing costs which depend only on the level of excess demand. Specifically, we assume that R_r is of the form:

$$\text{Total rationing costs} = R = \sum_{i=1}^{n} r_i(D_i(p_i, \tilde{u}_i) - z), \qquad (5.6)$$

where $z = q_1 + q_2 + \ldots + q_m$ is total capacity, and where rationing costs in period i are just $r_i(D_i - z)$, where r_i is assumed non-negative, convex and continuously differentiable and such that $dr_i(y)/dy = 0$ when $y \leqslant 0$.

THE SOCIAL-WELFARE FUNCTION. As announced earlier, we will use the expected value of the traditional welfare function as our measure of net benefit. To obtain a formal expression for this requires some care, however.

Let us first consider the problem of measuring gross benefits using Figure 5.1. In case of $D_i(p_i, u_i)$ total revenue plus consumers' surplus is given in exactly the same way as in the deterministic case by the area under the curve to z, provided we make our base-case assumption that rationing takes place according to marginal willingness to pay. In this case, therefore, gross surplus is the integral under the (inverse) demand curve up to the actual amount supplied. We can incorporate these considerations mathematically as follows. For any given value of the disturbance term, $\mathbf{u} = (u_1, \ldots, u_n)$, and for given price and capacity vectors $\mathbf{p}$ and $\mathbf{q}$, the actual output in any period is:

$$S_i(p_i, u_i, z) = \text{Min}\{D_i(p_i, u_i), z\}. \tag{5.7}$$

Using (5.7) we see that, for given $\mathbf{u}$, $\mathbf{p}$ and $\mathbf{q}$, consumers' surplus under rationing according to willingness to pay is therefore (note: $z = q_1 + q_2 + \ldots + q_m$);

$$CS(\mathbf{u}, \mathbf{p}, \mathbf{q}) = \sum_{i=1}^{n} \int_0^{S_i(p_i, u_i, z)} P_i(x_i - u_i) dx_i, \tag{5.8}$$

since, from (5.1), the inverse demand curve for given u_i is $X_i^{-1}(x_i - u_i) = P_i(x_i - u_i)$.

Now using (5.8) and recalling our definition of rationing costs as being relative to B-J rationing, we obtain the following measure of welfare returns $W_r(\mathbf{u}, \mathbf{p}, \mathbf{q})$ for any given rationing scheme r and fixed $\mathbf{u}, \mathbf{p}, \mathbf{q}$:

$$W(\mathbf{u}, \mathbf{p}, \mathbf{q}) = \sum_{i=1}^{n} \int_0^{S_i(p_i, u_i, z)} P_i(x_i - u_i) dx_i$$

$$- \sum_{i=1}^{n} \sum_{l=1}^{m} b_l q_{li}(D_i(p_i, u_i), \mathbf{q}) - \sum_{l=1}^{m} \beta_l q_l - \sum_{i=1}^{n} r_i(D_i(p_i, u_i) - z). \tag{5.9}$$

Taking expected values, the desired welfare function may now be expressed as:

$$\overline{W}_r(\mathbf{p}, \mathbf{q}) = E_{\widetilde{u}}\{W_r(\mathbf{u}, p, \mathbf{q})\}. \tag{5.10}$$

The problem of interest is to maximise $\overline{W}$ over the set of feasible rationing schemes and non-negative price and capacity vectors. In this section we will assume a fixed rationing scheme r, and we write simply $\overline{W}(\mathbf{p}, \mathbf{q})$ for welfare returns. We return to comparative rationing results in the next section. We also assume that the random variable $\widetilde{\mathbf{u}}$ is such that $\overline{W}(\mathbf{p}, \mathbf{q})$ exists for all feasible price and capacity vectors.[6]

OPTIMALITY CONDITIONS.[7] As the derivation of the optimality conditions is rather technical, we have placed it in the appendix to this chapter. After giving below the optimality conditions, we proceed to derive first some results concerning optimal capacity and efficient technology, and second some implications for price:[8]

$$\frac{\partial W}{\partial p_i} = p_i X_i'(p_i) F_i(z - X_i(p_i))$$

$$- \sum_{l=1}^{m} b_l X_i'(p_i) \left[F_i(Q_l - X_i(p_i)) - F_i(Q_{l-1} - X_i(p_i)) \right]$$

$$- X_i'(p_i) E_{\widetilde{u}_i} \{ r_i'(X_i(p_i) + \widetilde{u}_i - z) \}, i = 1, \ldots, n. \tag{5.11}$$

$$\frac{\partial \overline{W}}{\partial q_k} = \sum_{i=1}^{n} \{ \int_{z - X_i(p_i)}^{\infty} P_i(z - u_i) dF_i(u_i)$$

$$- b_k [1 - F_i(Q_k - X_i(p_i))] \} + \sum_{l=k+1}^{m} b_l \ [F_i(Q_l - X_i(p_i))$$

$$- F_i(Q_{l-1} - X_i(p_i))] + E_{\widetilde{u}_i} \{ r_i'(X_i(p_i) + \widetilde{u}_i - z) \} - \beta_k,$$

$$k = 1, \ldots, m. \tag{5.12}$$

In the above expressions prime denotes derivative and capacity through plant l is denoted by Q_l, so that:

$$Q_l = \sum_{k=1}^{l} q_k, \, l = 1, \ldots, m, \tag{5.13}$$

where we continue to use z for total capacity so that $z = Q_m$. Also, since F_i is the cumulative distribution function (CDF) of $\widetilde{u}_i$, note that $F_i(Q_l - X_i(p_i))$ is just the probability $Pr\{\widetilde{u}_i \leqslant Q_l - X_i(p_i)\} = Pr\{X_i(p_i) + \widetilde{u}_i \leqslant Q_l\}$, i.e. the probability that demand does not exceed capacity (Q_l) of the first l types.

The above expressions were obtained essentially by a marginal argument and can be best understood intuitively in this light. Regarding (5.11), for example, if we use the just-stated meaning of $F_i(Q_l - X_i(p_i))$ and set $\partial W/\partial p_i = 0$, we obtain the following condition which the optimal prices must satisfy:

$$p_i X_i'(p_i) Pr\{ D_i(p_i, \widetilde{u}_i) \leqslant z \} =$$

$$\sum_{l=1}^{m} b_l X_i'(p_i) Pr\{ Q_{l-1} \leqslant D_i(p_i, \widetilde{u}_i) \leqslant Q_l \}$$

$$+ X_i'(p_i) E_{\widetilde{u}_i} \{ r_i'(D_i(P_i, \widetilde{u}_i) - z) \}. \tag{5.14}$$

Now when demand is greater than capacity z, increasing the price slightly will leave the sum of revenue and consumers' surplus unchanged. On the other hand, if demand is less than z, a slight increase in price will clearly decrease consumers' surplus plus revenue by an amount equal to the prevailing price times the resulting decrease in demand. Thus the left-hand side of (5.14) represents the expected marginal benefits in the form of revenue and consumers' surplus at price p_i. Similarly, the right-hand side is seen to be the sum of expected marginal operating and rationing costs. To see that the first term represents expected marginal operating costs, simply note that plants are operated in the order 1 through m; so if demand falls between Q_{l-1} and Q_l, then plant l is the last plant in use and small changes in price therefore yield marginal operating-cost changes equal to $b_l X_i'(p_i)$.

A similar argument to the above leads to an understanding of (5.12) in terms of expected marginal costs and benefits of capacity increases. We delay this discussion until we have recast the conditions (5.12) in a more convenient form, but the interested reader may refer to Brown and Johnson (1969) for a discussion of the single-plant, single-period case. Note, in particular, that (5.11) and (5.12) reduce to their first-order conditions when $m = n = 1$ and when rationing costs are zero.

Before proceeding some notational conventions will be useful. Since F_i is the CDF of $\tilde{u}_i$ it follows that $F_i(u_i) = Pr\{\tilde{u}_i \leqslant u_i\}$ for any $u_i \epsilon R$. Using this fact we define the quantities:

$$F_i^l = F_i(Q_l - X_i(p_i)) = Pr\{D_i(p_i, \tilde{u}_i) \leqslant Q_l\}, \text{ for all } i, l.$$

$$(5.15)$$

Note that since $z = Q_m$, $F_i^m = F_i(z - X_i(p_i))$. Now, using the property of any cumulative distribution function that $x \leqslant y$ implies $0 \leqslant F_i(x) \leqslant F_i(y) \leqslant 1$, we have:

$$0 = F_i^0 \leqslant F_i^1 \leqslant \ldots \leqslant F_i^m \leqslant 1, \ i = 1, \ldots, n, \qquad (5.16)$$

where we set $F_i^0 = 0$ for convenience.

We can now restate the first-order conditions (5.11) (or (5.14)) for price by cancelling $X_i'(p_i)$ from all terms and dividing by F_i^m (assuming, of course, that $F_i^m > 0$, so that demand in period i does not always exceed capacity):[9]

$$p_i = \sum_{l=1}^{m} \gamma_{li} b_l + E\{r_i'(X_i(p_i) + \tilde{u}_i - z)\}/F_i^m, \ i = 1, \ldots, m,$$

$$(5.17)$$

where $0 \leqslant \gamma_{li} \leqslant 1$ is given by:

$$\gamma_{li} = (F_i^l - F_i^{l-1})/F_i^m$$

$$= Pr\{Q_{l-1} \leqslant D_i(p_i, \widetilde{u}_i) \leqslant Q_l | D_i(p_i, \widetilde{u}_i) \leqslant z\}, \quad (5.18)$$

so that, for all i, $\gamma_{1i} + \ldots + \gamma_{mi} = 1$.

We note that (5.17) and (5.18) imply that p_i is between b_1 and b_m in the absence of rationing costs, and increased by an appropriate amount when rationing costs are present. From (5.18) we can see that γ_{li} is the probability that plant l will be the last plant to be used, conditional on the event that there is sufficient capacity to meet demand. Thus price in each period must equal the conditional expected marginal operating plus rationing costs.

OPTIMAL CAPACITY AND EFFICIENT TECHNOLOGY. The conditions characterising optimal technology and order of operation are similar for the stochastic case to those derived in Chapter 4 for the deterministic case. We therefore only summarise these results and give intuitive demonstrations here. The reader wishing to see full-blown proofs of these results should consult Crew and Kleindorfer (1976).

Result 1: For each $k \in \{1, \ldots, m\}$, the following must hold if plant k is to be used in any optimal solution:

$$n(b_{\hat{k}} - b_k) > \beta_k - \beta_{\hat{k}}, \text{ for all } \hat{k} > k. \quad (5.19)$$

Notice that Result 1 is just the left half of Lemma A of Chapter 4. The right half of Lemma A need not hold in the stochastic case.

Result 2: Assuming (5.19) holds for $k = 1$, plant type 1 will always be used (unless no capacity whatsoever is installed).

As noted in Chapter 4, this result applies in the deterministic case. It applies for stochastic demand for similar reasons. Since plant type 1 is the one with minimum operating costs and maximum capacity costs, Result 2 simply states that this should be the base-load plant type. The only requirement is, of course, that (5.19) hold, so that, for all other plant types k, $nb_1 + \beta_1 < nb_k + \beta_k$, i.e. the marginal cost of installing and operating the base-load plant over the entire cycle should be less than that of any other available plant type.

Result 3: The efficient technological frontier in the (b, β) plane is downward-sloping and convex. In particular, together with (5.4) and

(5.19), the relations:

$$\frac{\beta_l - \beta_{l+1}}{b_{l+1} - b_l} < \frac{\beta_{l-1} - \beta_l}{b_l - b_{l-1}} < n, \text{ for } l = 2, \ldots, m - 1 \qquad (5.20)$$

must hold if the plant mix$\{1, \ldots, m\}$ is to be used.

The rationale behind Result 3 is as follows. Suppose two plants with cost characteristics (b_1, β_1) and (b_2, β_2) were available. Then every convex combination of these cost characteristics is also available as a plant type by simply operating plants 1 and 2 the appropriate proportions of time. Given the above it is clear that any plant lying above the line segment joining any two plants in the (b, β) plane cannot be efficient since an appropriate fictitious plant can be achieved on this line segment which would have both a lower b and a lower β.

Result 4: Assuming (5.20), if $q_k > 0$ for some $k \epsilon \{2, \ldots, m\}$, then in any optimal solution $q_l > 0$ for every $l \epsilon \{1, \ldots, k - 1\}$. Thus every optimal plant mix consists of contiguous plant types arranged in order of increasing operating costs.

Result 4 can be understood by reversing the above argument for Result 3. If a plant type on the technological frontier is skipped, then some fraction of the two plants adjacent to the skipped plant could be thought of as equivalent to a fictitious plant which would be dominated by the skipped plant. This result contrasts somewhat with the deterministic case where the optimal plant mix may consist of non-contiguous plant types.[10] The deterministic case is explicitly ruled out here by our assumptions, which preclude non-continuous random variables which, for example, arise from deterministic demand where $Pr\{\widetilde{u} = 0\} = 1$.

Let us now summarise succinctly the above results. We first note that $\partial \overline{W}/\partial q_k$ in (5.12) contains the following common term M for each $k = 1, 2, \ldots, m$:

$$M = \sum_{i=1}^{n} \int_{z-X_i(p_i)}^{\infty} P_i(z - u_i)dF_i(u_i) + E\{r_i'(X_i(p_i) + \widetilde{u}_i - z)\}.$$

$$(5.21)$$

In view of the above results the optimal plant mix is of the form $\{1, \ldots, \hat{m}$, where $\hat{m} \epsilon 1, \ldots, m\}$ is the number of the last plant used in the optimal solution. Now using $\partial \overline{W}/\partial q_l = 0$ if $q_l > 0$, and successively eliminating M from $\partial \overline{W}/\partial q_{l+1} - \partial \overline{W}/\partial q_l = 0$ for $l = 1, \ldots,$ $\hat{m} - 1$, yields from (5.11) and (5.12) the following $\hat{m} + n$ necessary conditions for the $\hat{m} + n$ variables $(p_1, \ldots, p_n), (q_1, \ldots, q_{\hat{m}})$:

$$p_i F_i^{\hat{m}} = \sum_{l=1}^{\hat{m}} b_l (F_i^l - F_i^{l-1}) + E\{r_i'(X_i(p_i) + \tilde{u}_i - z)\},$$
$$i = 1, \ldots, n \qquad (5.22)$$

$$n - \frac{\beta_l - \beta_{l+1}}{b_{l+1} - b_l} = \sum_{i=1}^{n} F_i^l, l = 1, \ldots, \hat{m} - 1 \qquad (5.23)$$

$$\sum_{i=1}^{n} \int_{z - X_i(p_i)}^{\infty} [P_i(z - u_i) - b_{\hat{m}}$$
$$+ r_i'(X_i(p_i) + u_i - z)] dF_i(u_i) = \beta_{\hat{m}}. \qquad (5.24)$$

We may rewrite (5.23) as:

$$\beta_l - \beta_{l-1} = (b_{l+1} - b_l) \sum_{i=1}^{n} (1 - F_i^l)$$
$$= \sum_{i=1}^{n} (b_{l+1} - b_l) Pr\{ D_i(p_i, \tilde{u}_i) \geqslant Q_l \}, \qquad (5.25)$$

which implies that the marginal capacity cost of using additional units of plant l to replace units of $l + 1$ should equal the expected marginal operating cost savings of making the incremental change to plant l. Notice that (5.24) is precisely the condition that would be obtained if only one plant type, namely $\hat{m}$, were available.

EFFICIENT PRICES. Our main results concern bounds on the optimal prices and a demonstration that peak-load pricing is efficient. Again, the detailed proofs of these results are left to the appendix.

Result 5: The following bounds obtain for the optimal prices p_i:

$$b_1 \leqslant b_1 + R_i \leqslant p_i \leqslant b_m + R_i, \text{ for all } i,$$

and

$$nb_1 \leqslant \sum_{i=1}^{n} p_i \leqslant nb_1 + \beta_1, \qquad (5.27)$$

where $R_i (= E\{ r_i'/F_i^m \})$ represents expected marginal rationing costs in period i.

The bounds in (5.26) have already been indicated in connection with (5.17) and follow simply from observation that p_i is to be set equal to the sum of conditional expected marginal running and rationing costs.

Given this, the left-hand inequality in (5.27) follows immediately, since marginal running costs are always at least b_1. As for the right-hand inequality in (5.27), suppose for the moment that the sum of all prices exceeded $nb_1 \cdot + \beta_1$. We would then simultaneously increase capacity of type 1 by, say, ϵ units and decrease each price slightly, still maintaining their sum greater than $nb_1 + \beta_1$ so as to generate ϵ units of expected additional demand. Rationing costs will not have changed, but these changes would lead to an increment of more than $(nb_1 + \beta_1)\epsilon$ in expected revenue alone (i.e. neglecting the additional consumers' surplus). Moreover, the increase in expected costs from these changes is only $(nb_1 + \beta_1)\epsilon$, the cost of installing and operating the additional units of type 1 capacity over the entire cycle. Thus the original situation could not have been optimal.

Note that (5.26)–(5.27) imply that p_i actually lies between b_1 and $b_1 + \beta_1$, as in the deterministic case.[11] Also, the right-hand inequality in (5.27) holds as an equality in the deterministic case, whether the technology is diverse or not. This is not so in the stochastic case, as we show by example below.

We now examine the pricing implications of peak-load effects. As a simple example, we may rewrite (5.14) when $m = 1$ as follows:

$$p_i = b_1 + E\{r_i'(X_i(p_i) + \tilde{u}_i - z)\} / F_m^1. \tag{5.28}$$

Now, if $r_i \equiv r_j$, $X_i(p) > X_j(p)$, for all p, and if $\tilde{u}_i, \tilde{u}_j$ are identically distributed, then it is readily seen from (5.28) that $p_i \geqslant p_j \geqslant b_1$, this result following directly from the increasing nature of marginal rationing costs. Accordingly, when rationing costs and peak loads are present, it follows that a peak-load pricing policy is optimal.[12]

It is interesting to illustrate the effects of rationing costs by specialising (5.28) to the case where r_i is of the linear form $r_i(y) = cy$ $(y \geqslant 0)$ and $r_i(y) = 0$, $y \leqslant 0$, where $c > 0$ is the unit cost of excess demand (above costless rationing, according to willingness to pay). In this case (5.28) becomes:

$$p_i = b_1 + (1 - F_i^1) c/F_i^1. \tag{5.29}$$

Concentrating on the two-period case, and assuming $F_i^1 = 1$, perfect reliability in the off-peak period, (5.29) yields the following optimal prices:

$$p_1 = b_1, \quad p_2 = b_1 + (1 - F_2^1) c/F_2^1. \tag{5.30}$$

Thus peak-load pricing is optimal here as long as $c > 0$. The reader should also note that Result 5 implies that z will be adjusted so that always $p_2 \leqslant b_1 + \beta_1$. In particular non-positive profits always obtain in this case.

Even in the absence of rationing costs peak-load pricing can be shown to be efficient. The essential rationale for this is that prices are to be set equal to conditional expected marginal operating costs. These costs, in turn, are monotonically increasing with output, which thus implies a peak-load pricing policy. We summarise these remarks informally in Result 6.

Result 6: If rationing costs in periods i and j are functionally identical $(r_i \equiv r_j)$ and if mean demand is higher in period i than in j $(X_i(p) > X_j(p)$ for all $p)$, then, under mild regularity assumptions, price in period i should be higher than in period j $(p_i > p_j \geqslant b_1)$.

· The 'mild regularity conditions' referred to above amount to conditions which ensure that, for any fixed price $p_i = p_j = p$, the *conditional* (on demand not exceeding capacity) distribution of demand in period i is to the right of the corresponding distribution for period j. When this is so, then charging the same or higher price in period j as in period i would lead to a (stochastically) larger conditional demand in period i than in period j. Since marginal operating and rationing costs are increasing, their conditional expected value would then be higher in period i than in period j. As noted, however, price is to be set equal to this expected value so it must be that $p_i > p_j \geqslant b_1$.

An example of when the regularity condition in question holds is the case where period i is a strong peak relative to period j, in the sense that $Pr\{ D_i (p, \tilde{u}_i) \geqslant D_j (p, \tilde{u}_j) \} = 1$ for any (reasonable) price p (i.e. for $b_1 \leqslant p \leqslant b_1 + \beta_1$). Another example is when $\tilde{u}_i$ and $\tilde{u}_j$ are identically distributed according to a normal, exponential, or uniform distribution. The interested reader should consult the appendix for technical details on these matters.

Summarising the above discussion and results, an upward-sloping system-wide marginal operating-cost curve (which is a natural consequence of a diverse technology), when coupled with marginal-cost pricing, implies the efficiency of peak-load pricing under uncertainty. Departures from perfect, costless rationing also contribute to the optimality of peak-load pricing. In fact the more inefficient the rationing scheme is, the more pronounced will be the price differential between peak and off-peak prices.

Before continuing it is interesting to note a few straightforward extensions of the above analysis to cover multiplicative demand uncertainty and other specifications of technology. The case of multiplicative uncertainty is obtained by replacing (5.1) with the following specification:

$$D_i (p_i, \tilde{v}_i) = \tilde{v}_i X_i (p_i), \qquad (5.31)$$

where $\tilde{v}_i$ is a non-negative random variable with expected value $E\{\tilde{v}_i\}$ = 1. Leaving all else as above, one easily derives optimality conditions for this case which are exactly analogous to (5.11)–(5.12) (see Exercise 5.2 in this regard). From this all the above results carry over to the demand specification (5.31).

A second extension of the above analysis concerns replacing the technology specification embodied in (5.5) by a more aggregate specification (see also Section 4.3 for similar results for the deterministic case) as follows:

$$\text{Total production costs} = \sum_{i=1}^{n} C_0 (S_i, z) + C_1 (z), \qquad (5.32)$$

where $S_i = S_i(p_i, u_i, z)$ is output in period i as given in (5.7). As we ask the reader to verify in Exercise 5.3, the technology specification (5.32) leads to the same pricing and total capacity rules as did the earlier diverse technology specification. In particular price is to be set to the sum of conditional expected marginal operating and rationing costs.

From the above extensions we see that the results derived thus far are fairly robust to changing assumptions on demand and technology specification. We next investigate the effects of alternative rationing policies in more detail.

5.3 RATIONING, RELIABILITY AND PROFITS

In the previous section we studied the problem of maximising a welfare function of the form:

$$W_r(\mathbf{p}, \mathbf{q}) = E\{W_{BJ}(\mathbf{u}, \mathbf{p}, \mathbf{q}) + \Sigma r_i(D_i(p_i, \tilde{u}_i), z)\}, \qquad (5.33)$$

where W_{BJ} represents welfare returns under B–J perfect rationing (costless rationing according to willingness to pay) and where Σr_i represents additional surplus losses and administrative costs associated with the rationing scheme in actual use. We have thus far only concerned ourselves with a given, fixed rationing scheme, and then only under the assumption that r_i in (5.33) is of the form $r_i(D_i - z)$, depending only on excess demand. In this section we relax these assumptions and study the effect of alternative rationing schemes on optimal reliability and profitability of the welfare-maximising monopoly. We restrict attention throughout to the case $m = n = 1$, where plant type 1 has cost parameters b and β.[13] We first reconsider our results of the previous section and then turn our attention to other rationing schemes (whose costs Σr_i in (5.33) need not be expressed in terms of excess demand as we have assumed to this point).

RATIONING WITH COSTS PROPORTIONAL TO EXCESS DEMAND. Let us reconsider the results of the previous section (for additively perturbed demand (5.1)) when $m = n = 1$ and $r_i(y) = c$ Max (y, o), i.e. costs beyond perfect rationing are proportional to excess demand. The welfare function (5.9)-(5.10) then becomes (suppressing the subscript $i = 1$):

$$\overline{W}(p, z) = E\{\int_0^{S(p, \tilde{u}, z)}[P(x - \tilde{u}) - b]\, dx - \beta z$$
$$- c \operatorname{Max}[D(p, \tilde{u}) - z, 0]\} \tag{5.34}$$

The first-order conditions for optimal price and capacity are (5.22) and (5.24), which we may rewrite as follows when $m = 1$:

$$(p - b)F(z - X(p)) = c(1 - F(z - X(p))) \tag{5.35}$$

$$\int_{z-X(p)}^{\infty}(P(z - u) - b + c)dF(u)) = \beta, \tag{5.36}$$

where $F(u) = Pr\{\tilde{u} \leq u\}$ is the *CDF* of the disturbance term in (5.1). We deal with two cases below, $c = 0$ and $c > 0$.

The B-J case (c = 0): We first recall the B-J results, which B-J obtained for the case $c = 0$. For this case B-J cancelled the term $F(z - X(p))$ in (5.35) to obtain $p = b$. This clearly assumes that $F(z - X(p)) = Pr\{X(p) + \tilde{u} \leq z\} =$ reliability is non-zero at optimum, an assumption which we now show need not hold.

To see when zero reliability is optimal, note that if $Pr\{X(p) + \tilde{u} \leq z\} = 0$, then the lower limit of integration in (5.36) becomes effectively $-\infty$ and (5.36) then reduces to:

$$E\{P(z - \tilde{u})\} = b + \beta, \tag{5.37}$$

a condition on z alone. Thus any price yielding $F(z - X(p)) = 0$, with z as in (5.37), is optimal.[14] Clearly if p is such a price, then so is any price $p' \leqslant p$ (although we will typically only consider prices which at least recover operating expenses). Also, satisfying (5.37) and $F(z - X(p)) = 0$ is easiest when the range of the disturbance term $\widetilde{u}$ is small. Indeed, as the range of the disturbance term $\widetilde{u}$ goes to zero, (5.37) converges[15] to $P(z) = b + \beta$, i.e. optimal capacity converges the deterministic optimal capacity $z_d = X(b + \beta)$. As the range of $\widetilde{u}$ increases, one may expect the range of prices satisfying $F(z - X(p)) = 0$ to behave as illustrated in Figure 5.2.[16] There we plot optimal prices versus the variance of u. Up until $\hat{v}$ it is seen that a (decreasing) range of optimal prices obtains. Thereafter, only the B-J solution is optimal.

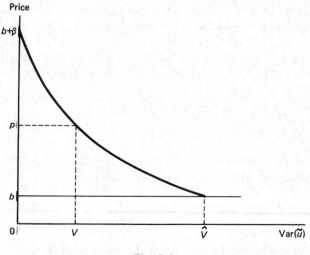

Fig. 5.2

When there are multiple optima, each such optimal solution yields the same expected welfare, but with different revenue effects. Considering the point v in Figure 5.2, for example, revenue and profits increase in going from the B-J solution to the maximal optimal solution p, while expected surplus decreases correspondingly. Note that since output can never exceed z and since price always satisfies $p < b + \beta$ (see also Result 5), welfare-optimal solutions to the B-J problem all entail strictly negative profits, except in the deterministic case.

Considering the deterministic case in Figure 5.2, it is interesting to note that $p = b$ is indicated to be optimal. The fact that this solution has not generally been recognised as optimal stems from the fact that previous derivations for the deterministic case have only considered solutions satisfying the constraint that sufficient capacity be installed to meet peak demand. In the absence of such a (reliability) constraint, it may easily be verified that the B–J solution is indeed 'optimal' for the familiar welfare criterion which does not discriminate between producers' and consumers' surplus. It is in fact the optimal solution which provides minimum profit, minimum revenue and maximum consumers' surplus and excess demand.

As a final point on the B–J case the reader should note that when demands are linear the left-hand side of (5.36) is exactly $P(z)$, since $E\{\widetilde{u}\} = 0$. Thus, when demands are linear, there is a range of levels of sufficiently low uncertainty over which the optimal capacity decision is precisely z_d. Corresponding optimal prices are simply those satisfying $F(z_d - X(p)) = 0$. When demands are not linear, optimal capacity may be greater than, or less than, deterministic optimal capacity when uncertainty is small, depending on the concavity or convexity of the demand curve. That is, $E\{P(z - \widetilde{u})\}$ may be less than, or greater than, $P(z - E\{\widetilde{u}\} = P(z_d)$.

The Case $c > 0$: We now return to the case $c > 0$ in (5.35)–(5.36). It is clear in this case that $F(z - X(p)) > 0$, i.e. reliability will be positive at optimum. From this and the fact that $P(z - u) < P(X(p)) = p$ for almost all u in the integral in (5.36), we have from (5.36):

$$\int_{z-X(p)}^{\infty} (p - b + c)dF(u) < \beta. \tag{5.38}$$

Rewriting the integral in (5.38) as $(p - b + c)(1 - F(z - X(p))$, we see from (5.35) that this implies $p < b + \beta$. In particular profits are strictly negative at the welfare-optimal solution.

Comparative statics easily establishes under mild regularity conditions that as c increases, i.e. as rationing gets more inefficient, capacity, price and reliability all increase.[17] From this it also follows that profits, gross of rationing costs, also increase as c increases. The rationale for this behaviour is clear. As non-price rationing (in the event of excess demand) becomes more inefficient, more reliance must be placed on price rationing and increased capacity to decrease excess demand.

An interesting footnote to this analysis is the behaviour of the optimal solution as c approaches infinity. In this case, as the reader may verify from (5.35)–(5.36), price approaches $b + \beta$ and reliability approaches unity, i.e. capacity approaches $X(b + \beta) + u^*$, where $Pr\{\widetilde{u} > u^*\} = 0$. Thus, for rationing schemes whose costs above perfect rationing depend only on excess demand, reasonably high rationing costs lead to the deterministic price as the welfare-optimal solution. This, and the fact that $p \leqslant b + \beta$ no matter what c is, stem from the symmetrical way in which z and $X(p)$ enter rationing costs here. The flavour of these results changes when other forms of rationing-cost functions are assumed in (5.33), as we now demonstrate.

RANDOM AND OTHER RATIONING SCHEMES. Visscher (1973) and Carlton (1977) have studied other forms of rationing than those we have been concerned with thus far. We first summarise their results, discuss them briefly in relation to the above analysis, and then examine one case, random rationing, in somewhat more detail.

Table 5.1 summarises the Visscher–Carlton results. The rationing schemes listed are as follows:

B–J = Costless rationing according to willingness to pay.

CED = Rationing whose costs above B–J rationing depend only on excess demand (as we have dealt with to this point).

RAN = Random rationing: consumers are served randomly in the event of excess demand, until capacity is exhausted.

LWP = Rationing in order of lowest willingness to pay until capacity is exhausted.

Gross profit refers to expected revenues minus expected operating and capacity costs and excludes any rationing costs or surplus losses.[18] The additive and multiplicative disturbance specifications are those given by (5.1) and (5.31) respectively.

The results on RAN and LWP are due to Visscher (additive disturbance) and Carlton (multiplicative disturbance). The results on B–J and CED rationing are derived in the text above (see also Exercise 5.2). A detailed discussion of the additive case is also contained in Sherman and Visscher (1978).

If we think of rationing inefficiency as increasing in the order B–J, RAN, LWP, then we see reflected in Table 5.1 the following conclusion which we derived earlier for the class of CED rationing schemes. As rationing becomes less efficient, the welfare-optimal solution entails increased prices, capacity, reliability, (gross) profit, and, of course, decreasing welfare.

Table 5.1 Comparing various rationing schemes

Rationing scheme	Additive disturbance		Multiplicative disturbance	
	Price	Gross profit	Price	Gross profit
B-J	$b \leqslant p < b+\beta$	Negative	$b \leqslant p < b+\beta$	Negative
CED ($c > 0$)	$b < p < b+\beta$	Negative ($>$ B-J)	$b < p < b+\beta$	Negative ($>$ B-J)
RAN	$b < p < b+\beta$	Negative	$p > b+\beta$	Zero
LWP	$b+\beta$	Negative	$p > b+\beta$	Positive
Deterministic	$b+\beta$	Zero	$b+\beta$	Zero

In order to give some further substance to the principles just noted, let us consider the case of random rationing with multiplicative demand in more detail. We follow the development of Carlton (1977).

Suppose demand is given by $D(p, \tilde{v}) = \tilde{v}X(p)$. Then, if in the event of excess demand, a service is distributed randomly among those willing to pay the quoted price, welfare returns are given for any fixed v by:

$$W_R(v, p, z) = \begin{cases} \int_0^{vX(p)}(P(x/v) - b)dx - \beta z, & \text{if } vX(p) \leqslant z \\[2ex] \dfrac{z}{vX(p)} \int_0^{vX(p)}(P(x/v) - b)dx - \beta z, & \text{else.} \end{cases}$$

(5.39)

Taking expected values in (5.39) over $\tilde{v}$, we obtain the following expected welfare returns under random rationing:

$$\overline{W}_R(p, z) = \int_0^{z/X(p)}\int_0^{vX(p)}(P(x/v) - b)dx \, dF(v)$$

$$+ \int_{z/X(p)}^{\infty} \frac{z}{X(p)} \int_0^{vX(p)}(P(x/v) - b)dx \, dF(v) - \beta z.$$

(5.40)

We will in fact generalise (5.40) to the form:

$$\overline{W}_R(p, z) = \int_0^{z/X(p)}\int_0^{vX(p)}(P(x/v) - b)dx \, dF(v)$$

$$+ \int_{z/X(p)}^{\infty} \frac{ez}{X(p)} \int_0^{vX(p)}(P(x/v) - b)dx \, dF(v) - \beta z,$$

(5.41)

where $e > 0$ will be varied to allow a comparison across a class of rationing schemes 'centred' on random rationing (where $e = 1$). Clearly, the greater is e, the more efficient is the rationing process.

Now define $s = z/X(p)$ and change variables in the inner integrals in (5.41) to obtain $\overline{W}$ in terms of the decision variables p, s as follows:

$$W(p, s) = \int_0^s v \int_0^{X(p)}(P(x) - b)dx \, dF(v)$$

$$+ \int_0^{\infty} es \int_0^{X(p)}(P(x) - b)dx \, dF(v) - \beta sX(p). \quad (5.42)$$

Setting $\partial \overline{W}/\partial p = \partial \overline{W}/\partial s = 0$, we obtain the following first-order conditions for maximising $\overline{W}$:

$$(p - b)\left[\int_0^s vdF(v) + e\int_s^{\infty} sdf(v)\right] - \beta s = 0 \quad (5.43)$$

$$[\int_0^{X(p)}(P(x) - b)dx] [(1 - e)sf(s) + e(1 - F(s))]$$
$$- \beta X(p) = 0 \qquad (5.44)$$

Denote by $I(e, s)$ the quantity:

$$I(e, s) = \frac{1}{s} [\int_0^s vdF(v) + es\int_s^\infty dF(v)]$$

$$= \frac{1}{s} [\int_0^s (v - es)dF(v) + es] < e. \qquad (5.45)$$

Then, from (5.43), optimal price is:

$$p = b + \frac{\beta}{I(e, s)}, \qquad (5.46)$$

so that for sufficiently inefficient rationing (e.g. for any $e \leqslant 1$), price exceeds $b + \beta$).

Expected profits (excluding any rationing costs) are:

$$\overline{\Pi} = (p - b)X(p)\int_0^s vdF(v) + (p - b)sX(p)\int_s^\infty dF(v)$$

$$- \beta sX(p). \qquad (5.47)$$

Multiplying (5.43) by $X(p)$ and comparing with (5.47) yields:

$$\Pi = (p - b)sX(p) (1 - e) (1 - F(s)). \qquad (5.48)$$

From this and (5.46) we see that profits are negative, zero, or positive as e is > 1, $= 1$, or < 1, respectively.

The above provides further confirmation of the general principle enunciated earlier that the more inefficient the rationing scheme, the more reliance will have to be placed on normal price rationing to clear the market, i.e. the higher will be the welfare-optimal price and profits. In addition it is interesting to note that welfare-optimal prices (and profits) are higher under multiplicative demand uncertainty than under additive uncertainty. This is doubtless because under multiplicative uncertainty, price and uncertainty interact, with the consequence that random outcomes on the high side are magnified by price effects, lending even greater importance to the rationing effects of price in avoiding excess demand.

The rather different consequences of the above alternative demand uncertainty specifications will hardly be greeted with pleasure outside of econometric circles. None the less they indicate the strong inter-action of price, uncertainty and rationing methods and the need to deal with these issues within a unified framework.

SECOND-BEST PRICING. Let us now briefly consider how the above results might change if a minimum profit constraint were imposed.[19] To analyse this we return to our assumption that demand is of the form (5.1) and rationing costs are proportional to excess demand. We con-sider the following problem:

$$\text{Max } W(p,z) = \int_0^{z-X(p)}\int_0^{X(p)+u}(P(z-u)-b)dx\,dF(u)$$

$$+ \int_{z-X(p)}^{\infty}\int_0^{z}(P(z-u)-b)dx\,dF(u)$$

$$- \int_{z-X(p)}^{\infty}c(X(p)+u-z)dF(u) - \beta z, \quad (5.49)$$

subject to:

$$\overline{\Pi}(p,z) = \int_0^{z-X(p)}(p-b)(X(p)+u)dF(u)$$

$$+ \int_{z-X(p)}^{\infty}(p-b)zdF(u) - \beta z \geqslant \Pi_0. \quad (5.50)$$

Note that the objective function in (5.49) is just (5.34) and the con-straint (5.50) is a minimum expected profit constraint.

Forming the Lagrangian for (5.49)–(5.50) we have:

$$L = W(p,z) + \theta(\Pi(p,z) - \Pi_0). \quad (5.51)$$

The first-order conditions for solving (5.49)–(5.50) are $\partial L/\partial p = \partial L/\partial z = 0$ and $\theta \geqslant 0$. After simplification these yield the following:

$$(p-b)X'(p)F(z-X(p))(1+\theta) - cX'(p)(1-F(z-X(p)))$$

$$+ \theta[X(p) - \int_{z-X(p)}^{\infty}(X(p)+u-z)dF(u)] = 0 \quad (5.52)$$

$$\int_{z-X(p)}^{\infty}[P(z-u)-b+c+\theta(p-b)]dF(u) - (1+\theta)\beta = 0 \quad (5.53)$$

From (5.52) we have:

$$\frac{p-b}{p} = \frac{\theta}{1+\theta}\frac{E\{S(p,z,\tilde{u})\}}{pX'(p)F(z-X(p))} + \frac{1}{1+\theta}\frac{c(1-F(z-X(p)))}{pF(z-X(p))}, \quad (5.54)$$

where $S(p,z,\tilde{u})$ is output as in (5.7). We may rewrite (5.54), as in

Sherman and Visscher (1978):

$$\frac{p - b}{p} = \frac{\theta}{1 + \theta} \frac{1}{\eta F(z - X(p))} \left[1 - \frac{E\{\widetilde{ed}\}}{X(p)} \right]$$

$$+ \frac{1}{1 + \theta} \frac{c(1 - F(z - X(p))}{pF(z - X(p))}, \quad (5.55)$$

where η is (mean) demand elasticity and $E\{\widetilde{ed}\}$ is expected excess demand.

To understand (5.54)–(5.55) better, let us note, taking derivatives in (5.50), that the profit margin for the expected profit-maximiser is given by:

$$\frac{p - b}{p} = \frac{1}{\eta F(z - X(p)} \left[1 - \frac{E\{\widetilde{ed}\}}{X(p)} \right]. \quad (5.56)$$

When $c = 0$ we see that (5.55) and (5.56) produce a result analogous to the deterministic case (see Section 4.3) whereby the rules for setting profit margins for the welfare-maximiser and the profit-maximiser differ only by a constant ($\theta/1 + \theta$ above). As Sherman and Visscher have noted, this similarity is not surprising when perfect rationing obtains, since then both the profit- and the welfare-maximiser can ignore rationing in their pricing policies and concentrate on raising revenue.

Returning to the general case $c \geqslant 0$, we see that welfare-optimal profit margins are increased when rationing is inefficient. As c approaches infinity, it may be verified from (5.52)–(5.53) that $F(z - X(p))$ tends to unity, and that $c(1 - F(z - X(p))$ tends to $(1 + \theta)\beta$, so that the pricing rule (5.54) reduces to:

$$\frac{p - b}{p} = \frac{\theta}{1 + \theta} \frac{1}{\eta} + \frac{\beta}{p}, \quad (5.57)$$

which, as the reader may verify from Chapter 4, is the deterministic second-best optimal profit margin (when θ is determined so as to satisfy (5.50)).

Note that as the constraint (5.50) becomes more stringent, θ increases, and the pricing rule (5.55) becomes more like the profit-maximising rule (5.56). This last statement depends, of course, on our definition of profit as excluding any rationing costs. If some portion of these costs were included in the monopolist profit function,[20] then less divergence would emerge between the profit- and welfare-maximising solutions.

As regards optimal capacity, we may rewrite (5.57) as:

$$\frac{1}{1 + \theta} \; [\int_{z-X(p)}^{\infty} (P(z - u) - b + c)dF(u) - \beta] + \frac{\theta}{1 + \theta}$$

$$[\int_{z-X(p)}^{\infty} (p - b)dF(u) - \beta] = 0. \tag{5.58}$$

The first term in (5.58) (set to zero) is the first-order condition an expected welfare-maximiser must satisfy and the second is the corresponding condition for an expected profit-maximiser. Again, the multiplier θ measures the tautness of the constraint (5.50). As θ increases, (5.58) becomes more like the profit-maximising condition. As the constraint (5.50) becomes more stringent, capacity would therefore tend to decrease to the expected profit-maximising level, while price and profits would tend to increase.

Concluding this brief discussion of second best, it can be seen that something like an inverse elasticity rule continues to obtain for the optimal price, though now excess demand and rationing compound the problem of raising revenues in the least distorting way. We noted though that there again pricing rules approaching the deterministic case emerge when reliability is high at optimum. We consider the intuitive rationale for this immediately below.

RATIONING COSTS AND RELIABILITY CONSTRAINT. We continue to assume that rationing costs depend only on excess demand. We are interested in comparing the welfare-optimal procedures described above with the approach suggested by Meyer (1975) of adding explicit reliability constraints to the B-J problem formulation. To do so we reconsider our original problem of maximising (5.10), now omitting rationing costs and instead constraining reliability. Thus we are interested in the following problem:

$$\text{Max } \overline{W}'(p, q) = E\{W'(p, q, \tilde{u})\} , \tag{5.59}$$

subject to:

$$F_i[z - X_i(p_l)] \geqslant \epsilon_i, i = 1, 2, \tag{5.60}$$

where $\epsilon_i(0 \leqslant \epsilon_i \leqslant 1)$ is a specified reliability level for period i and where the welfare function $\overline{W}'$ in (5.59) is defined through (5.9) by assuming

$r_i \equiv 0$, $i = 1, \ldots, n$, i.e. by omitting rationing costs from the welfare function.

Now suppose the reliability levels ϵ_i in (5.60) are set to $\epsilon_i = \hat{\epsilon}_i = F_i[\hat{z} - D_i(\hat{p}_i)]$, with $(\hat{p}, \hat{q})$ an optimal solution to our original problem of maximising the expected value $\overline{W} = \overline{W}' - \Sigma E\{r_i\}$ in (5.10). Since rationing costs are increasing monotonically and are convex in excess demand, it is clear that the higher the required reliability levels ϵ_i in (5.60), the lower will be the expected rationing costs at optimum. Therefore, (5.60) may be regarded as a constraint on expected rationing costs, and if the reliability levels ϵ_i are (optimally) specified as $\epsilon_i = \hat{\epsilon}_i$, then the solution $(\hat{p}, \hat{q})$ to maximising $\overline{W}$ also solves the reliability-constrained problem (5.59)–(5.60).

Thus reliability constraints may be thought of as a surrogate for rationing costs, provided of course that they are specified optimally. We will return to this point in Chapter 9 in discussing regulation. For the moment, though, we may note that this equivalence between rationing costs and reliability constraints (when rationing costs are of the form (5.6)) explains why essentially deterministic pricing behaviour occurs when rationing becomes inefficient (as we have noted on several occasions). This is so because highly inefficient rationing requires very high reliability at optimum and the original problem then reduces to an equivalent deterministic problem with demands specified by taking the appropriate (very high) fractile of the original, given, stochastic demand distribution.

5.4 CONCLUSIONS

We will now briefly recount the main arguments of this chapter. In Section 5.2 we developed a framework which showed some of the main effects of stochastic demand on peak-load pricing. We dealt with the crucial question of how capacity is rationed when demand exceeds capacity by introducing the notion of rationing costs. Within this framework the earlier results for deterministic peak loads were modified to give the appropriate peak-load prices and diverse technological solutions. In Section 5.3 we extended this approach to provide a discussion of rationing and reliability.

The results of this chapter might be summarised briefly by saying that welfare-optimal pricing under uncertainty entails marginal-cost pricing rules similar to those obtaining under certainty. However, determining and quantifying the appropriate marginal costs here requires that rationing and excess-demand conditions be considered explicitly. We may summarise the essence of the various welfare-optimal policies derived as follows. Optimal capacity should be set so that losses in consumers' surplus net of operating costs (as determined by the rationing scheme in use) are just equal to the *LRMC* of increasing capacity, all of this to take place at optimal prices. The optimal prices are complicated (although typically they may be expected to be close to deterministic optimal prices when reliability is high); but essentially they are obtained by equating expected benefits from the *actual* marginal unit of demand met to the expected *SRMC*. Given the above capacity rule, this amounts to determining price by maximising expected consumers' surplus (given the rationing scheme or load-shedding procedure used) subject to optimal reliability levels.

An issue which we have not addressed, but which is clear in principle, is the selection of an optimal rationing scheme. This would simply proceed by comparing the optimal welfare returns and costs of implementation associated with each such scheme. A further issue which we have dodged is that of redistributing the social costs of excess demand. It should at least be clear, however, that an unregulated monopolist will take a fairly callous view of these costs unless he has to bear a portion of them.

We may expect some additional complications on the reliability problem in dealing with the regulated firm. These are dealt with in Part Three. As a prelude to the major policy issues involved there we first attempt in the next chapter to strengthen the reader's intuitive grasp of welfare-optimal pricing policies under uncertainty through some illustrative numerical examples.

EXERCISES

5.1   For the case $m = 1$ show that the first-order conditions (5.11)–(5.12) are also sufficient. Do this by converting the welfare-maximisation problem in (p, q) space into an equivalent problem (with equivalent first-order conditions) in (x, q) space, i.e. by solving:

$$\text{Max}_{x, q} \overline{w}(x, q),$$

where $\overline{w}(x, q) = \overline{W}(P(x), q)$, instead of Max $\overline{W}(p, q)$. The function

$\overline{w}(x, q)$ can then be shown to be concave, which implies the desired result.

5.2 Imitate the derivation in the appendix to this chapter for the demands (5.31). Show that the only change in the corresponding first-order conditions (5.11)–(5.12) is that $z - X_i(p_i)$ (respectively, $Q_l - X_i(p_i)$, or $Q_k - X_i(p_i)$) is replaced wherever it occurs by $z/X_i(p_i)$ (respectively, $Q_l/X_i(p_i)$, or $Q_k/X_i(p_i)$) and $z - u_i$ is replaced by z/v_i. Verify, in particular, that (5.17) holds with the substitution of $\widetilde{v}_i X_i(p_i)$ for $X_i(p_i) + \widetilde{u}_i$.

5.3 Imitate the derivation in the appendix to this chapter for the production costs (5.32). Show that the same qualitative results obtain for optimal price and capacity for these costs as for the proportional-cost technology specified in the text.

5.4 Assume that $\widetilde{u}$ is such that $f'(u) \leqslant 0$, where $u \geqslant 0$. Assume as well that $z \geqslant X(p)$ at optimum. Now show that optimal price and capacity, and therefore also reliability, increases as c increases in (5.35)–(5.36).

APPENDIX

In this appendix we are concerned with derivations and proofs of various results given in the text.

DERIVATION OF FIRST-ORDER CONDITIONS

We derive the first derivatives of the expected welfare function $\overline{W}$, equation (5.10) of Section 5.2. We shall assume that $\overline{W}$ is sufficiently regular to allow interchanging the expectation and differentiation operators. This being so, we have from (5.1) and the chain rule:

$$\frac{\partial}{\partial p_i} \left(\sum_{i=1}^{n} \int_0^{S_i(p_i, u_i, z)} P_i(x_i - u_i) dx_i \right)$$

$$= P_i(S_i(p_i, u_i, z) - u_i) \frac{\partial}{\partial p_i} S_i(p_i, u_i, z)$$

$$= \begin{cases} p_i X_i'(p) & \text{if } u_i < z - X_i(p_i) \\ 0 & \text{if } u_i > z - X_i(p_i), \end{cases} \tag{5.A1}$$

where $'$ denotes differentiation and S_i is as defined in (5.8), and $P_i = X_i^{-1}$, so that $P_i(X_i(p_i)) = p_i$. Thus, after interchanging expectation and differentiation, (5.A1) yields:

$$\frac{\partial}{\partial p_i} \left(E\left\{ \sum_{i=1}^{n} \int_0^{S_i(p_i, \tilde{u}_i, z)} P_i(x_i - \tilde{u}_i) dx_i \right\} \right)$$

$$= \sum_{i=1}^{n} p_i X_i'(p_i) F_i(z - X_i(p_i)). \tag{5.A2}$$

From (5.5) and (5.3) plant l will be used in period i precisely when $Q_{l-1} - X_i(p_i) \leqslant \tilde{u}_i \leqslant Q_l - X_i(p_i)$, so that:

$$E\{b_l q_{li}(D_i(p_i, u_i), \mathbf{q})\} = b_l \int_{Q_{l-1} - X_i(p_i)}^{Q_l - X_i(p_i)}$$

$$(D_i(p_i, \tilde{u}_i) - Q_{l-1}) dF_i(u_i). \tag{5.A3}$$

From (5.42) an interchange of expectation and differentiation yields:

$$\frac{\partial}{\partial p_i} E\{b_l q_{li}(D_i(p_i, \tilde{u}_i), \mathbf{q})\}$$

$$= b_l \int_{Q_{l-1} - X_i(p_i)}^{Q_l - X_i(p_i)} \frac{\partial}{\partial p_i} (D_i(p_i, u_i) - Q_{l-1}) dF_i(u_i)$$

$$= b_l X_i'(p_i)[F_i(Q_l - X_i(p_i)) - F_i(Q_{l-1} - X_i(p_i))]. $$

$$\tag{5.A4}$$

Similarly:

$$\frac{\partial}{\partial p_i} E\{r_i(X_i(p_i) + \tilde{u}_i - z)\} = X_i'(p_i) E\{r_i'(X_i(p_i) + \tilde{u}_i - z)\}. $$

$$\tag{5.A5}$$

Combining (5.A2), (5.A4) and (5.A5) with (5.10), we obtain (5.11).

Proceeding to the derivation of $\partial W/\partial q_k$, we recall that $z = q_1 + \ldots + q_m$ so that:

$$\frac{\partial}{\partial q_k} \left(\sum_{i=1}^{n} \int_0^{S_i(p_i, \tilde{u}_i, z)} P_i(x_i - \tilde{u}_i) dx_i \right)$$

$$= \begin{cases} 0 & \text{if } u_i < z - X_i(p_i) \\ P_i(z - u_i) & \text{if } u_i > z - X_i(p_i) \end{cases} \tag{5.A6}$$

so that, interchanging expectation and differentiation:

$$\frac{\partial}{\partial q_k}\left(E\left\{\sum_{i=1}^{n} \int^{S_i(p_i,\, u_i,\, z)} P_i(x_i - u_i)dx_i\right\}\right)$$

$$= \sum_{i=1}^{n} \int_{z-X_i(p_i)}^{\infty} P_i(z - u_i)dF_i(u_i). \tag{5.A7}$$

Also, (5.A3) implies:

$$\frac{\partial}{\partial q_k}\left(E\left\{\sum_{i=1}^{n} \sum_{l=1}^{m} b_l q_{li}(D_i(p_i, \widetilde{u}_i)\mathbf{q})\right\}\right) =$$

$$-b_k[1 - F_i(Q_k - X_i(p_i))] + \sum_{l=k+1}^{m} b_l[F_i(Q_l - X_i(p_i))$$

$$- F_i(Q_{l-1} - X_i(p_i))]. \tag{5.A8}$$

Finally, interchanging expectation and differentiation:

$$\frac{\partial}{\partial q_k} E\{r_i(X_i(p_i) + \widetilde{u}_i - z)\} = E\{r_i'(X_i(p_i) + \widetilde{u}_i - z)\}, \tag{5.A9}$$

so that (5.10) and (5.A7)–(5.A9) yield (5.12), as desired.

PROOF OF RESULT 5

Note first that the monotonicity of the inverse demand function P_i implies that:

$$\int_{z-X_i(p_i)}^{\infty} P_i(z - u_i)dF_i(u_i) \geqslant P_i(z - X_i(p_i))\int_{z-X_i(p_i)}^{\infty} dF_i(u_i)$$

$$= p_i(1 - F_i(z - X_i(p_i))) = p_i(1 - F_i^m). \tag{5.A10}$$

Thus, from (5.12), if $q_k > 0$ in an optimal solution:

$$0 = \frac{\partial \overline{W}}{\partial q_k} \geqslant \sum_{i=1}^{n} (p_i(1 - F_i^m) - b_k(1 - F_i^k(1 - F_i^k)$$

$$+ \sum_{l=k+1}^{n} b(F_i^l - F_i^{l-1}) + E_{\widetilde{u}_i}\{r_i'\}) - \beta_k. \tag{5.A11}$$

Since, by Result 2, plant 1 will always be used in an optimal solution,

(5.A11) implies for $k = 1$:

$$0 \geqslant \sum_{i=1}^{n} p_i - \left[\sum_{i=1}^{n} (p_i F_i^m - \sum_{l=1}^{m} b_l (F_i^l - F_i^{l-1}) - E_{\widetilde{u}_i}\{r_i'\}) \right]$$

$$- nb_1 - \beta_1.$$
(5.A12)

But using (5.15) to rewrite (5.11) implies for all i:

$$p_i F_i^m = \sum_{l=1}^{m} b_l (F_i^l - F_i^{l-1}) + E_{\widetilde{u}_i}\{r_i'\},$$
(5.A13)

so that the term in brackets in (5.A12) is zero. Thus (5.A12)–(5.A13) and (5.17) imply the asserted bounds in (5.26)–(5.27).

PROOF OF RESULT 6

Suppose $X_i(p) > X_j(p)$ for any price p and that $r_i(y) = r_j(y)$ for all y. Let the marginal operating-cost function be denoted by $g(y)$ so that:

$$g(y) = \begin{cases} 0 \text{ if } y \leqslant 0 \\ b_l \text{ if } Q_{l-1} < y \leqslant Q_l, l = 1, \ldots, m \\ 0 \text{ if } y > Q_m = z. \end{cases}$$
(5.A14)

Then, we may rewrite (5.17) as:

$$p_i = E_{\widetilde{u}_i}\{g(X_i(p_i) + \widetilde{u}_i) | X_i(p_i) + u_i \leqslant z\}$$
$$+ E_{\widetilde{u}_i}\{r_i'(X_i(p_i) + \widetilde{u}_i - z)\}/F_i^m.$$
(5.A15)

We wish to show that $p_i < p_j$. Suppose the contrary: $p_i > p_j$. Then the convexity of r_i and $X_i'(p_i) < 0$ imply that:

$$r_i'(X_i(p_i) + u - z) \geqslant r_j'(X_i(p_j) + u - z), \text{ for all } u \in R.$$
(5.A16)

We now assume that $F_i(z - X_i(p_i)) \leqslant F_j(z - X_j(p_j))$. Since $X_i(p_i) > X_j(p_j)$, this would be the case if either $\widetilde{u}_i$ and $\widetilde{u}_j$ were identically distributed or if period i were a strong peak relative to period j, in the sense that $Pr\{D_i(\mathbf{p}, \widetilde{u}_i) \geqslant D_j(\mathbf{p}, \widetilde{u}_j)\} = 1$ for all reasonable prices p (i.e. $b_1 \leqslant p \leqslant b_1 + \beta_1$). Using this regularity assumption, it follows that

$p_i < p_j$ implies:

$$E_{\widetilde{u}_i}\{r_i'\}/F_i^m \geqslant E_{\widetilde{u}_i}\{r_j'\}/F_j^m \tag{5.A17}$$

Thus $p_i < p_j$ would imply from (5.A16) and (5.A17) that

$$E_{\widetilde{u}_i}\{g(X_i(p_i) + \widetilde{u}_i)|X_i(p_i) + u_i \leqslant z\} \leqslant$$
$$E_{\widetilde{u}_i}\{g(X_j(p_j) + \widetilde{u}_j)|X_i(p_i) + \widetilde{u}_i \leqslant z\}. \tag{5.A18}$$

We show below, under a mild regularity condition on $\widetilde{u}_i$, that (5.A18) cannot hold, i.e. conditional expected marginal operating costs are increasing monotonically in output. To show this we note the following lemma (see Lehmann, 1959, p. 112).

LEMMA. If F_0, F_1 are two cumulative distribution functions on the real line such that $F_1(x) \leqslant F_0(x)$ for all x, then $E_0 \Psi(\widetilde{X}_0) \leqslant E_1 \Psi(\widetilde{X}_1)$ for all non-decreasing functions Ψ, where $\widetilde{X}_0$, $\widetilde{X}_1$ are the random variables corresponding to F_0, F_1, respectively.

Now let F_0 (respectively, F_1) of the above lemma be the conditional distribution of $X_j(p_j) + \widetilde{u}_j$ (respectively, $X_i(p_i) + \widetilde{u}_i$), given $X_j(p_j) + \widetilde{u}_j \leqslant z$ (respectively, given $X_i(p_i) + \widetilde{u}_i \leqslant z$). Using this notation (5.A18) becomes $E_1\{g(\widetilde{X}_1)\} \leqslant E_0\{g(\widetilde{X}_0)\}$. Since g is increasing monotonically, this would be a contradiction if we can show that $F_1(x) \leqslant F_0(x)$ for all x. With the above definitions of F_0 and F_1 this means that we wish to provide conditions under which, for $p_i \leqslant p_j$:

$$F_1(u) = \frac{F_i(u - X_i(p_i))}{F_i(z - X_i(p_i))} \leqslant \frac{F_j(u - X_j(p_j))}{F_j(z - X_j(p_j))} = F_0(u), \tag{5.A19}$$

where $-X_j(p_j) \leqslant u \leqslant z$, and $0 < F_i(z - X_i(p_i)) \leqslant F_j(z - X_j(p_j))$. In particular (5.A19) would be fulfilled if period i is a strong peak relative to period j in the sense stated above, or if $\widetilde{u}_i, \widetilde{u}_j$ were identically distributed with common distribution function $F_i = F_j = F$ satisfying:

$$F(y) > 0 \Rightarrow \frac{F(x)}{F(y)} \leqslant \frac{F(x + a)}{F(y + a)}, \text{ for all } x \leqslant y \text{ and } a \geqslant 0. \tag{5.A20}$$

The regularity condition (5.A20) may be shown to hold for a wide class of random variables including uniform, exponential and normal random variables. Clearly much weaker conditions would also ensure the validity of (5.A19). With (5.A19), however, we have the desired result that conditional expected marginal operating costs rise as output rises. This, then, contradicts (5.A18) and asserts the efficiency of peak-load pricing.

6 Some Numerical Illustrations

The purpose of this chapter is to illustrate by means of numerical examples the theory set out in earlier chapters. This should help to clarify some of our earlier analysis, as well as illustrate a number of extensions not otherwise obvious.[1] We restrict attention to a simple example with linear demands and additive random disturbances. Given these assumptions a number of interesting insights emerge to support our theoretical discussion of the preceding chapter. We illustrate, in particular, that deterministic solutions are good approximations of stochastic optimal solutions when the optimal reliability level is required to be high.

6.1 BASIC DATA AND DETERMINISTIC SOLUTIONS

We are concerned with a case where there are two periods ($n = 2$) with linear demands given by $D_i(p_i, \widetilde{u}_i) = X_i(p_i) + \widetilde{u}_i$, where:

$$X_1(p_1) = 40 - \tfrac{1}{7}p_1 \tag{6.1}$$

$$X_2(p_2) = 80 - \tfrac{5}{7}p_2. \tag{6.2}$$

We assume that the disturbance terms $\widetilde{u}_i$ are uniformly distributed on $[-\gamma, \gamma]$, where γ is a positive constant.

We continue to assume that surplus losses and administrative costs of rationing, beyond those incurred under costless rationing according to marginal willingness to pay, depend only on the level of excess demand. Accordingly, we define rationing costs as:

$$r_i(y) = \begin{cases} 0 \text{ if } y \leqslant 0 \\ \alpha y^2 \text{ if } y > 0, \end{cases} \tag{6.3}$$

where $\alpha > 0$, and y is of course the excess of demand over capacity as defined in equation (5.7).

For purposes of our examples we have three plant types whose cost characteristics are given in Table 6.1. Let us consider the following

Table 6.1

	b	β
Plant 1	1	15
Plant 2	3	12
Plant 3	5	10

combinations of the above:

$$\text{Mix } A = \{1\}; \text{Mix } B = \{1, 2\}; \text{Mix } C = \{1, 2, 3\}; \text{Mix } D = \{3\}.$$
(6.4)

Let us begin our comparison by noting some results for the deterministic case. These are given in Table 6.2. Note, in particular, that Proposition A of Chapter 4 implies that only plants 1, 2 are used in Mix C.

Table 6.2

Mix	Period 1 Price (p_1)	Period 2 Price (p_2)	Total capacity (z)
A	$p_1 = b_1 = 1$	$p_2 = b_1 + \beta_1 = 16$	68.57
B	$p_1 = 2b_1 + \beta_1 - (b_2 + \beta_2) = 2$	$p_2 = b_2 + \beta_2 = 15$	69.29
C	$p_1 = 2b_1 + \beta_1 - (b_2 + \beta_2) = 2$	$p_2 = b_2 + \beta_2 = 15$	69.29
D	$p_1 = b_3 = 5$	$p_2 = b_3 + \beta_3 = 15$	69.29

6.2   SOLUTIONS FOR THE STOCHASTIC CASE

We first examine the case of stochastic demand and finite rationing costs. The effect of rationing costs are in line with intuition. In Figure 6.2 we consider the case where $\gamma = 10$ and Mix B is used. As a result of the stochastic demand, we have a rationing problem. By varying rationing costs $0 \leqslant \alpha < \infty$ we alter the magnitude of the rationing problem. We see clearly the effect of changing rationing costs in Figure 6.1. When rationing costs are zero irrespective of the level of excess demand, we have a Brown–Johnson-type solution of $p_1 = 2$ and $p_2 = 3$. (The reader should check his intuition on this through Exercise 6.3.) However, as

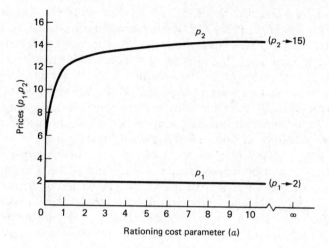

Fig. 6.1

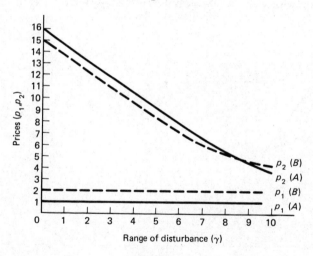

Fig. 6.2

rationing becomes more expensive, pricing becomes more attractive, and price increases, eventually converging to the deterministic optimum. Similarly, Figure 6.2 illustrates, for the case $\alpha = 0.01$ and Mixes A and B, that the optimal solution converges to the deterministic solution as the range of the disturbance term decreases.

The effects described above are very much along the lines of intuition. As α gets large, a very high level of reliability is optimal, so that the public utility is faced with the essentially deterministic problem of planning to meet a very high fractile of the demand distribution. This leads to the optimality of the deterministic prices. Of course, as γ gets small, a nearly deterministic problem also results. Although not shown, the reader will also find it intuitively obvious that total capacity installed at optimum approaches the upper fractile of the peak-period demand distribution as either α gets large or γ gets small.

Some light is thrown on the B–J solution as well as the problem of stochastic demand by means of an example where rationing costs are zero ($\alpha = 0$) and where the strength of the randomness in demand is allowed to vary. Figure 6.3 illustrates the case for Mix D, with optimal prices for any value of the random disturbance. At $\gamma = 0$ (the deterministic case) any price between 5 and 15 is optimal.[2] As γ increases, the range of optimal prices decreases until at a little over $\gamma = 7$ it converges to zero, with the B–J solution of $p_1 = p_2 = b_3 = 5$ as the unique

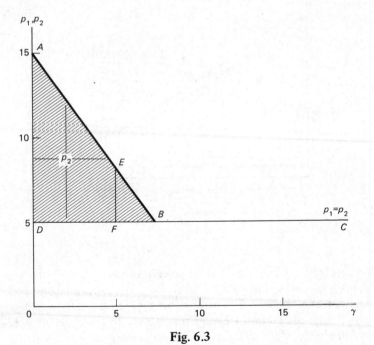

Fig. 6.3

optimal solution. As we discussed in Chapter 5, the existence of multiple optima when γ is small arises from the fact that the traditional welfare function, as interpreted by B–J, does not distinguish between consumers' and producers' surplus. Thus the effect of the assumption of costless rationing according to willingness to pay ($\alpha = 0$) is for the deterministic price to be just one of an infinity of prices within the range described above for the case of deterministic demand, this range shrinking as demand becomes 'more random'. Intuitively, in Figure 6.3 the curve AB is the locus of points for which peak-period reliability is just equal to zero. Thus as γ approaches zero the range of peak-period excess demand along AB (i.e. $\alpha\gamma$) shrinks to zero and deterministic pricing emerges.

In Figure 6.4 we explore these relations between optimal prices and reliability in more detail for Mix D and two values of the random disturbance term $\gamma = 5$ and $\gamma = 15$. In this case, however, we impose an

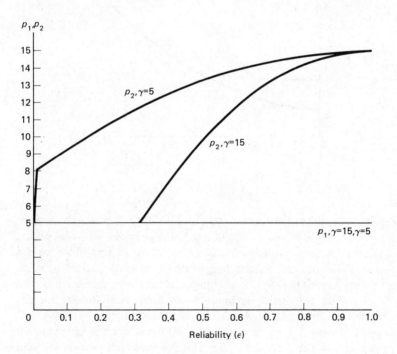

Fig. 6.4

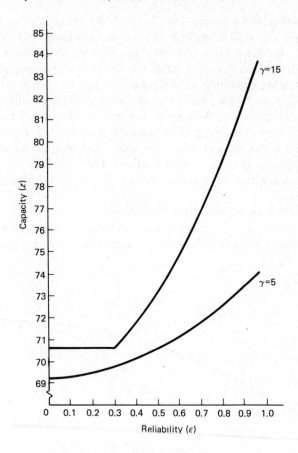

Fig. 6.5

explicit reliability constraint $Pr\{D_i(p_i, \tilde{u}) \leqslant z\} > \epsilon$, $i = 1, 2$, in place of the rationing costs (6.3). As expected, similar behaviour is observed at optimum for these explicit reliability constraints to that which we just discussed for the case of rationing costs. In particular prices converge to the deterministic optima as required reliability is increased to one. These results are further summarised in Table 6.3. Results for the expected profit-maximising case are also shown for comparative purposes. In Figure 6.5 we show (for Mix D) the interaction between reliability and optimal capacity. Here it is assumed that price is adjusted optimally (according to Figure 6.4) to maintain the desired reliability

Table 6.3 Optimal solutions for the example

		Range of disturbance term (γ)					
		Welfare-maximising case			Profit-maximising case		
		$\gamma = 0^*$	$\gamma = 5$	$\gamma = 15$	$\gamma = 0^*$	$\gamma = 5$	$\gamma = 15$
$\epsilon = 0$†	p_1	5.00	5.00	5.00	142.50	142.50	142.50
	p_2	5.00–15.0	5.00–8.0	5.00	63.50	63.39	63.19
	Q	69.29	69.29	70.73	34.65	38.00	44.71
$\epsilon = 0.5$	p_1	5.00	5.00	5.00	142.50	142.50	142.50
	p_2	15.00	13.24	9.74	63.50	63.39	63.19
	Q	69.29	70.54	73.04	34.65	38.00	44.71
$\epsilon = 0.9$	p_1	5.00	5.00	5.00	142.50	142.50	142.50
	p_1	15.00	14.92	14.77	63.50	63.45	63.40
	Q	69.29	73.34	81.44	34.65	38.67	46.76
$\epsilon = 0.98$	p_1	5.00	5.00	5.00	142.50	142.50	142.50
	p_2	15.00	14.99	14.98	63.50	63.49	63.49
	Q	69.29	74.09	83.70	34.65	39.45	49.05
$\epsilon = 1.0$	p_1	5.00	5.00	5.00	142.50	142.50	142.50
	p_2	15.00	15.00	15.00	63.50	63.50	63.50
	Q	69.29	74.29	84.29	34.65	39.65	49.65

Reliability Level Required (row label along left margin)

*The deterministic case.
†The B–J case.

level. As more reliability is required, more capacity is also required. The trade-off is simple. If more reliability is desired, it can be achieved by either increasing price or capacity, and optimality in the sense of maximising expected welfare can be achieved by some (optimal) combination of both of these.

We also examined some effects of technology through cost changes on optimality in the stochastic case. We show (for Mix B) in Figure 6.6 the effects of a change in the value of b_2 on optimal prices for $\gamma = 10$ and $\alpha = 0$. As b_2 rises, p_2 rises with a kink at A, where $p_2 = 4.05$ and p_2 drops sharply. Similarly, p_1 increases until B and then decreases sharply. The kinks at B and A arise from the fact that along CB only plant 2 is used; along BA both plants 1 and 2 are used; and along ADE only plant 1 is used. For Mix B we show in Figure 6.7 the correspond-

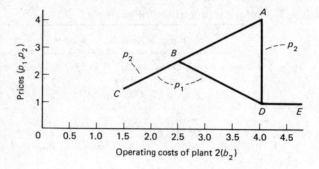

Fig. 6.6

ing effects of changes in b_2 upon capacity. As b_2 rises, total capacity decreases until at a price of 4.05 plant 2 ceases to be used and therefore total capacity ($z = q_1 = 68.56$) is no longer affected in any way by further increases in b_2.

Use of numerical examples has served to illustrate a number of important points about the relationship between deterministic and stochastic demand, in particular the extent to which the deterministic solution approximates the stochastic solution when randomness is small or optimal reliability is high. We also illustrated the fact that rationing costs and explicit reliability constraints are symmetrical in their effects on optimal pricing and capacity. Finally, we examined the impact of alternative technologies and illustrated the sensitivity of optimal prices to available technology.

EXERCISES

6.1   Refer to Table 6.1 and decide whether any of the three plant types would be excluded in the deterministic case.

6.2   Verify that necessary conditions (5.22)–(5.24) are satisfied for Mix B with $\gamma = 10$ and no rationing costs ($\alpha = 0$) at $p_1 = 2, p_2 = 3$, $q_1 = X_1(2) = 39\frac{5}{7}$, and $z = 69.34$.

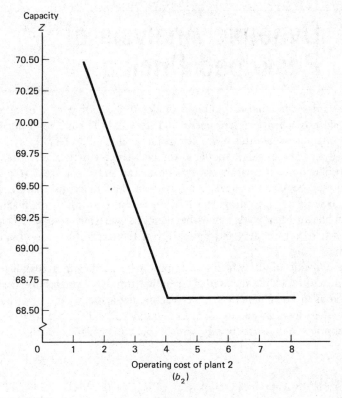

Fig. 6.7

6.3   When we have $\gamma = 15$, and optimal capacity for Mixes A, B, C given respectively by 68.93, 70.18 and 70.73, find reliability levels implied for $\alpha = 0$. Denote reliability levels in period 2 for Mixes $A, B,$ C respectively as $F_{2A}^m, F_{2B}^m, F_{2C}^m$. (*Hint*: first derive optimal prices.)

7 Dynamic Analysis of Peak-load Pricing

In the earlier chapters we explored in detail the nature of the static peak-load problem for deterministic and stochastic demand conditions. In this chapter we address ourselves to the peak-load problem in dynamic analysis. The dynamic model developed here is simple and is intended to illustrate comparatively dynamic and static analyses. Where steady-state conditions prevail it has been customary to transform dynamic problems into static ones. To the extent that this is reasonable with public utilities gives our earlier analysis widespread appeal. Our concern here is to understand the nature of the trade-offs involved in a dynamic setting.

The dynamic model which we employ here deals with a peak-load problem with available technology specified through a production cost function as in Pressman (1970). We describe the assumptions and structure of the model in Section 7.1. In Section 7.2 and 7.3 we solve for optimal prices and discuss briefly some implications of the model.

7.1 A DYNAMIC MODEL OF PRICING AND INVESTMENT

We will use the following notation in the rest of this chapter:

$K(t)$ = installed capacity or capital stock at time t.

$x(t)$ = production rate or output at time t, constrained by the capital stock. We assume that the production rate is equal to the demand rate and we will use 'production' or 'demand' interchangeably.

$P(x(t), t)$ = inverse demand function at time t. It is assumed continuous such that $\partial P/\partial x < 0$.

$I(t)$ = investment rate at time t which is required for maintaining or increasing existing capital stock.

$C(x(t), K(t), t)$ = operating-cost function at time t. We assume that C is twice continuously differentiable and that $\partial C/\partial x > 0$, $\partial^2 C/\partial x^2 \geqslant 0$, $\partial C/\partial K \geqslant 0$ and $\partial^2 C/\partial x\partial K \leqslant 0$. Also $\partial C/\partial x > 0$ and $\partial^2 C/\partial x^2 \geqslant 0$ is reasonable for most public utilities. $\partial C/\partial K \geqslant 0$ and $\partial^2 C/\partial x\partial K \leqslant 0$

108

imply the existence of scale economies.[1]

$\phi(I(t), t)$ = investment cost function, assumed continuously differerentiable and such that, for all t, $\phi(0, t) = 0$ and $\phi'(I, t) > 0$.

δ = rate of depreciation of capital stock.

T = planning horizon.

r = discount rate.

$M(t)$ = upper bound on investment at time t.

Now, a dynamic formulation of the peak-load pricing problem using control theory[2] can be given.

DYNAMIC PRICING PROBLEM (DPP)

$$\text{Max } \int_0^T e^{-rt}\left\{\int_0^X P(y(t),t)dy(t) - C(K(t),x(t),t)\right.$$

$$\left. - \phi(I(t), t)\right\}dt, \tag{7.1}$$

subject to:

$$\dot{K}(t) = -\delta K(t) + I(t) \qquad [\lambda_0(t)] \tag{7.2}$$

$$0 \leqslant x(t) \qquad\qquad [\lambda_1(t)] \tag{7.3}$$

$$x(t) \leqslant K(t) \qquad\qquad [\lambda_2(t)] \tag{7.4}$$

$$0 \leqslant I(t) \qquad\qquad [\lambda_3(t)] \tag{7.5}$$

$$I(t) \leqslant M(t) \qquad\qquad [\lambda_4(t)] \tag{7.6}$$

$$K(0) = K_0, K(T) \geqslant K_T, K_0 \text{ and } K_T \text{ given constants}, \tag{7.7}$$

where $K(t)$ is the 'state variable', $x(t)$ and $I(t)$ are 'control variables', $\lambda_0(t)$ is the adjoint variable, and $\lambda_1(t), \lambda_2(t), \lambda_3(t), \lambda_4(t)$ are Lagrange multipliers.

It should be noted as an essential feature of the above problem that prices can be varied instantaneously. A more general model might include a transactions cost for price changes. In fact, however, our concern here is to understand the long-run ideal path of price adjustment, making the assumption of free price adjustment seem appropriate for our purposes. In a short-run analysis, (for example, Dansby, 1976), greater consideration would be given to the issue of intra-period price stability.

A major question for a control formulation of a problem in general and for DPP in particular concerns the existence of a unique bounded measurable solution to the model. Existence and uniqueness issues present some difficulties mathematically. Readers interested in these aspects of DPP may consult Chang (1978), which proves existence of solutions to DPP for a wide class of problems. In this chapter we will in fact assume a piecewise continuous solution exists to Problem DPP.

7.2   OPTIMAL SOLUTIONS IN A DYNAMIC SETTING

In this section we will apply the necessary conditions of optimal control theory reported by Arrow (1968) and others.[3] We first derive our most important results and then discuss these in relation to the static case in Section 7.3. Let the Hamiltonian and Lagrangian functions of DPP be as follows:

$$H(K, x, I, \lambda_0, t) = \int_0^x P(y, t)dy - C(K, x, t) - \phi(I, t)$$
$$+ \lambda_0(-\delta K + I) \tag{7.8}$$

$$L(K, x, I, \lambda_0, \lambda_1, \lambda_2, \lambda_3, \lambda_4, t) = H(K, x, I, \lambda_0, t)$$
$$+ \lambda_1 x + \lambda_2(K - x) + \lambda_3 I + \lambda_4(M - I). \tag{7.9}$$

The Maximum Principle of Pontryagin yields directly the following result:

RESULT 7.1. Assume that a piecewise continuous solution to Problem DPP exists. Denote this solution $\hat{K}(t)$, $\hat{x}(t)$ and $\hat{I}(t)$. Then there exists an adjoint trajectory $\lambda_0(t)$ and Lagrange multipliers, $\lambda_1(t)$, $\lambda_2(t)$, $\lambda_3(t)$, $\lambda_4(t)$ such that:

$$\dot{\lambda}_0 = r\lambda_0 - \frac{\partial L}{\partial K} = (r + \delta)\lambda_0 + \frac{\partial C(\hat{K}, \hat{x}, t)}{\partial K} - \lambda_2 \tag{7.10}$$

$$\frac{\partial L}{\partial I} = -\phi(\hat{I}, t) + \lambda_0 + \lambda_3 - \lambda_4 = 0 \tag{7.11}$$

or:

$$\phi(\hat{I}, t) = \lambda_0 + \lambda_3 - \lambda_4 \tag{7.12}$$

$$\frac{\partial L}{\partial x} = P(\hat{x}, t) - \frac{\partial C(\hat{K}, \hat{x}, t)}{\partial x} + \lambda_1 - \lambda_2 = 0 \tag{7.13}$$

$$P(\hat{x}, t) = \frac{\partial C(\hat{K}, \hat{x}, t)}{\partial x} - \lambda_1 + \lambda_2 \qquad (7.14)$$

The complementarity conditions hold:

$$\lambda_1 x = 0, \lambda_1 \geqslant 0 \qquad (7.15)$$

$$\lambda_2 (K - x) = 0, \lambda_2 \geqslant 0 \qquad (7.16)$$

$$\lambda_3 I = 0, \lambda_3 \geqslant 0 \qquad (7.17)$$

$$\lambda_4 (M - I) = 0, \lambda_4 \geqslant 0. \qquad (7.18)$$

The transversality conditions hold:

$$\lambda_0(T) (K(T) - K_T) = 0, \lambda_0(T) \geqslant 0. \qquad (7.19)$$

The basic concept of the necessary conditions of optimal control theory is the following: in order that a solution be optimal to the optimal control problem, it is necessary that this solution is optimal in maximising the generalised Hamiltonian function (i.e. the Lagrangian function (7.9) at every instant of time $t \epsilon [0, T]$).

On the basis of the above theorem, we will derive optimal policies to Problem DPP. We assume throughout that the optimal solution $x(t)$ satisfies $\hat{x}(t) > 0$.

RESULT 7.2. Consider DPP. The optimal pricing policy satisfies:

$$(i) \quad P(\hat{x}, t) = \frac{\partial C(K, \hat{x}, t)}{\partial x}, \text{if } 0 < \hat{x}(t) < K(t) \qquad (7.20)$$

$$(ii) \quad P(\hat{x}, t) = \frac{\partial C(K, \hat{x}, t)}{\partial x} + \lambda_2(t), \text{if } 0 < \hat{x}(t) = K(t). \qquad (7.21)$$

(*Remark*: Note that these are the well-known marginal-cost pricing conditions for off-peak (i.e. (i)) and peak (i.e. (ii)) periods, where from (7.4) and (7.16) $\lambda_2(t)$ has the usual meaning of the shadow price of capital.)

Proof: By the assumptions $P(x, t) > 0$, $\partial P/\partial x < 0$, $\partial C/\partial x > 0$, and $\partial^2 C/\partial x^2 > 0$, so that Lagrangian function (7.9) is strictly concave in x. Hence there exists a unique $\hat{x}$ such that:

$$\left.\frac{\partial L}{\partial x}\right|_{x=\hat{x}} = P(\hat{x}, t) - \left.\frac{\partial C}{\partial x}\right|_{x=\hat{x}} + \lambda_1 - \lambda_2 = 0. \qquad (7.22)$$

There are two cases:

(i) If $0 < \hat{x}(t) < K(t)$ for t in the sub-interval $T_1 \subset [0, T]$, then $\lambda_1(t) = \lambda_2(t) = 0$ by complementarity conditions (7.15) and (7.16). Therefore, from (7.22), we obtain:

$$P(\hat{x}, t) = \frac{\partial C(K, \hat{x}, t)}{\partial x}. \tag{7.23}$$

(ii) If $0 < x(t) = K(t)$ for t in the sub-interval $T_2 \subset [0, T]$, then $\lambda_1(t) = 0, \lambda_2(t) > 0$ by (7.15) and (7.16). By (7.22) we have:

$$P(\hat{x}, t) = \frac{\partial C(K, \hat{x}, t)}{\partial x} + \lambda_2(t). \tag{7.24}$$

By inspecting Problem DPP we notice that control variables $x(t)$ and $I(t)$ are contained neither in the same function (i.e. $P(x, t), C(K, x, t), \phi(I, t)$) nor in the same constraints (7.2)–(7.6). Thus we can separate DPP into two problems. By so doing the structure of the optimal solution becomes clearer.

RESULT 7.3. An equivalent problem for DPP, assuming the optimal $x(t)$ and $I(t)$ piecewise continuous, can be formulated as below:

$$\underset{I(t)}{\text{Max}} \int_0^T e^{-rt}[F(K, t) - \phi(I, t)] \, dt, \tag{7.25}$$

subject to:

$$\dot{K}(t) = -\delta K(t) + I(t) \tag{7.26}$$

$$0 \leqslant I(t) \leqslant M(t) \tag{7.27}$$

$$K(0) = K_0, K(T) \geqslant K_T, K_0, K_T \text{ given,} \tag{7.28}$$

where $F(K, t)$ is the real-valued function given by:

$$F(K, t) = \text{Max}[\int_0^x P(y, t)dy - C(K, x, t)], \tag{7.29}$$

subject to:

$$0 \leqslant x \leqslant K. \tag{7.30}$$

Moreover, $F(K, t)$ is continuous if $P(x, t), C(K, x, t)$ and $K(t)$ are continuous. *Remark*: The essence of Result 7.3 is that, whatever the capacity, price is to be set so as to maximise instantaneous (short-run) welfare returns subject to the given capacity restriction. Of course, deter-mination of the optimal capacity requires the solution to (7.25)–(7.28) which balances instantaneous welfare returns against investment costs for maintaining and/or increasing capacity. Thus the static and the dynamic cases are the same, except that in the static case the time path of adjustment of capital stock is not considered.

Proof: The Lagrangian function of (7.29) and (7.30) is:

$$L_0(K, x, t) = \int_0^x P(y, t)dy - C(K, x, t) + q_1 x + q_2(K - x),$$
$$(7.31)$$

where q_1, q_2 are Lagrange multipliers. Comparing the Lagrangian func-tion of DPP (7.9) with (7.31) we note that it implies the same optimisa-tion problem with respect to $x(t)$. Thus the optimal solution of (7.31) is the same as the one obtained by (7.9) with respect to $\hat{x}(t)$, that is:

$$\hat{x}(t) = \begin{cases} G(K, t) \text{ if } \hat{x}(t) < K(t) \\ K(t) \quad \text{if } \hat{x}(t) = K(t), \end{cases} \qquad (7.32)$$

where $G(K, t)$ is obtained by solving (7.20) for $\hat{x}(t)$ in terms of $K(t)$ and t. For the problem defined by (7.25)–(7.28), the Hamiltonian and Lagrangian functions will be:

$$H_1(K, I, t, q_0) = F(K, t) - \phi(I, t) + q_0(-\delta K + I) \qquad (7.33)$$
$$L_1(K, I, t, q_0, q_3, q_4) = H(K, I, t, q_0) + q_3 I + q_4(M - I). \qquad (7.34)$$

Comparing (7.9) with (7.34), they both imply the same optimisation problem with respect to $I(t)$ only. Thus the optimal solution for DPP obtained from (7.34) is exactly the same as the one obtained from (7.9). Also, the optimal $K(t)$ obtained in both cases will be the same, because $K(t)$ is determined uniquely by (7.26). In addition $F(K, t)$ is continuous because $x(t) \in [0, K(t)]$, which is compact and non-empty, and all functions, including $K(t)$, are assumed continuous (see Kleindorfer and Glover, 1973, lemma 1, pp. 55–7).

To obtain the optimal trajectory of $I(t)$, we first look at the station-ary point $I_s(t)$ of the Langrangian (7.9). This yields:

$$\frac{\partial L}{\partial I} = -\phi'(I_s, t) + \lambda_0 = 0 \qquad (7.35)$$

$$\phi'(I_s, t) = \lambda_0 \tag{7.36}$$

$$I_s^- = {\phi'}^{-1}(\lambda_0, t). \tag{7.37}$$

Of course we need to consider the constraints (7.5) and (7.6), i.e. I_s may not be optimal. A simple analysis of boundary conditions, however, yields the following:

RESULT 7.4. Let $I(t)$ be the optimal solution of DPP. Then:

$$\hat{I}(t) = \begin{cases} M(t) & \text{if } {\phi'}^{-1}(\hat{\lambda}_0, t) \geqslant M(t) \\ {\phi'}^{-1}(\lambda_0, t) & \text{if } 0 < {\phi'}^{-1}(\hat{\lambda}_0, t) < M(t) \\ 0 & \text{if } {\phi'}^{-1}(\hat{\lambda}_0, t) \leqslant 0, \end{cases} \tag{7.38}$$

whenever $(I(t), t)$ is convex in $I(t)$. And:

$$I(t) = \begin{cases} M(t) \text{ if } (-\phi'(\hat{I}, t) + \hat{\lambda}_0) > 0 \\ 0 & \text{if } (-\phi'(\hat{I}, t) + \hat{\lambda}_0) \leqslant 0, \end{cases} \tag{7.39}$$

whenever $\phi(I(t), t)$ is concave in $I(t)$.

Proof: When $\phi(I(t), t)$ is convex in $I(t)$, (7.39) is obvious from (7.17)–(7.18) and (7.35)–(7.37). When $(I(t), t)$ is concave in $I(t)$, the solution will be on the boundary of $[0, M(t)]$. As long as (7.35) is positive the objective functional L will be increased by this amount by every unit increase of $I(t)$. Thus we should increase $I(t)$ as much as possible, i.e. to its upper bound $M(t)$; while if (7.35) is less than or equal to zero, we should reduce $I(t)$ as much as possible to its lower bound, i.e. to zero.

7.3 DISCUSSION

The above brief analysis of the dynamics of pricing and investment highlights the fact that the key to welfare-optimal behaviour continues to be pricing at *LRMC*. Result 7.1 provides the basic first-order conditions for Problem DPP. In particular the multipliers $\lambda_0(t), \ldots, \lambda_5(t)$ there can be understood, as in the static case, as shadow prices of their associated constraints. From these we derived in Result 7.2 the marginal-cost pricing conditions. Note that the only difference between these and the static results of previous chapters is that $\lambda_2(t)$ in (7.21) must be intepreted as *LRMC* at time t under an optimal capital trajectory (i.e. the cost of optimally adjusting capital stock and production to meet an additional unit of demand at time t, all of this as measured along an optimal trajectory). As such *LRMC* is somewhat harder to determine here as it depends explicitly on initial conditions and costs of maintaining and accumulating capital stock. Previously we took these latter costs (denoted by β_l) as given for each type of capacity. The realistic determination of these costs is complicated, of course, and is a major aspect of system planning.[4]

Additional insight on the relationship between optimal pricing and investment behaviour may be obtained from Result 7.3. This result indicates that, whatever the capital stock is, price should be set to maximise instantaneous welfare returns[5] subject to capital restrictions, i.e. price should equal *SRMC*. Of course, at optimum capital stock is adjusted so as to equate *SRMC* and *LRMC*. This result lays bare the structure of the optimal solution to the dynamic case. Optimal solutions are derived by trading off instantaneous welfare returns ($F(k, t)$) from a given capital trajectory against the (suitably discounted) costs of establishing and maintaining the given capital trajectory. Thus the optimal trade-off between these factors involves linking together, via optimal capacity planning (e.g. (7.25)–(7.28)), a number of static, welfare-optimal snapshots of the genre studied in Chapters 2–6 above.

Result (7.4) summarises the outcome of this trade-off between capital and investment costs and welfare gains. The optimal investment policy is characterised simply by equating marginal investment costs ϕ' and marginal benefits ($\lambda_0(t)$) from increases in the rate of capital accumulation at time t. Taken together with Result 7.2, these optimal investment results are analogous to the rule for capacity changes for the peak-load problem in comparative statics. In the event of demand changes whether capacity is increased depends upon whether price exceeds *LRMC*. If, for example, the change is a fall in demand, and price is less than *LRMC*, then capacity would be allowed to decline until equality between price and *LRMC* were re-established.

Summarising our introductory comparison of the static and dynamic cases, we see that they are structurally similar at optimum. Pricing is at *LRMC* and investment is set to equate *SRMC* and *LRMC*. The major difference between the static and dynamic cases is in the determination of *LRMC*. In the dynamic case this requires explicit recognition of initial conditions and the time path of adjustment of costs of maintaining and accumulating capital stock.

Part Three

Public Utility Regulation

8 Public Utility Regulation or Public Ownership

In Parts One and Two we discussed some of the background theory of the economics of public utilities. Our main concern to this point has been to determine policies which are in the public interest as embodied in the traditional social-welfare function. The purpose of Part Three is to examine and compare some of the institutional arrangements surrounding public utility pricing and investment planning. In this chapter we review briefly some historical and legal background to public utilities, particularly in the U.S. and the U.K., focusing on some of the important issues that have arisen. In Chapter 9 we examine the major theoretical issues associated with public utility regulation in the U.S. and relate these to our earlier discussion of peak loads and stochastic demands.

In this chapter, therefore, we first examine the origins, scope and nature of utility regulation in the U.S. and the U.K. Thereafter we discuss some alternative possibilities and considerations that have recently been raised for public utility regulation.

8.1 SOME ORIGINS OF REGULATION IN THE U.K. AND THE U.S.

The aim of maximising social welfare is not usually pursued by a monopolist. The traditional motivation for a monopolist is the maximisation of profit, which, in the absence of competition, is typically inconsistent with economic efficiency. The undesirable inefficiency of monopoly has been at least implicitly recognised in the institutional arrangements for public utilities in both the U.S. and the U.K. In both countries it was recognised that while it was desirable to achieve sometimes overwhelming scale economies (see Galatin, 1968) through a public utility monopoly, such a monopoly could not exist without a framework of government control. In the U.K. such control took the form of outright public ownership, while in the U.S. privately owned firms were controlled by various utility commissions.

119

The avowed aim of public ownership in the U.K. was, at least initially, consistent with economic-efficiency arguments. Private market arrangements were regarded, in certain respects, as unsuitable means for achieving the social good.[1] A desire to make utilities more sensitive to the common good, and a view that the previous arrangements involving private ownership had in some sense failed, comes over strongly in the debates on the original nationalising statues (see Morrison, 1933, p. 284).[2] Indeed, the Labour Party went further and extended its dissatisfaction with the existing economic institutions beyond public utilities to other industries. This conviction, exemplified by the Labour Party's constitution, which has as one of its aims the nationalisation of the means of production, was the driving-force behind bringing public utilities (and other industries such as transport, coal and steel) into public ownership in the years immediately following the Second World War. Political motives were important in this wave of nationalisation, but as outlined by Herbert Morrison (1933), a leading political figure and architect of nationalisation, many of the motives behind, and the justification for, nationalisation were also economic. The desire to avoid exploitation of consumers and workers and the desire to avoid monopoly profits were advanced as arguments for nationalisation. Similarly, Morrison argued that nationalisation would improve labour relations and that it could be the vehicle for cross-subsidisation, profitable activities subsidising unprofitable activities. Morrison also argued that nationalisation was a means of making certain industries, like public utilities, operate in socially more desirable ways. In particular he believed that nationalisation would lead such industries to be more efficiently and economically conducted. Unfortunately experience has not supported the high hopes behind the original nationalisation ventures.

The intention to serve the common good remained after nationalisation but this goal was not achieved easily. Some brave attempts to employ economic principles were made, but they never overcame fundamental problems involving changes in the incentive structure resulting from public ownership and control by politicians. A certain sensitivity to the latter problems was apparent in the statutes bringing the industries into public ownership.[3] For example, it was intended that public corporations should have some independence from the Government Minister to whom they were ultimately responsible. Except for certain matters specified in the statutes the public corporation is legally free to carry out its business in the way it sees fit. In practice, however, the government of the day has considerable powers to use the industries as instruments for its own policy. For example, the Conservative Government of 1970–4 used the nationalised industries as instruments of its anti-inflation policy, attempting to hold down the prices of the nationalised fuel and power industries at a time of fourfold increase in the world price of oil. In addition the power of the Minister to appoint the chief executives of public corporations also gives scope for considerable leverage, though on this there is evidence of Ministers, at least ostensibly, seeking the most able individual available rather than mere political appointees. Examples include the appointment by a Labour Minister of Lord Hyndley, a former colliery chairman, to the National Coal Board, and the appointment by Conservative Ministers of Lord Robens and Sir Richard Marsh, both former Labour Cabinet Ministers, to be, respectively, chairman of the National Coal Board and Chairman of British Rail.

As in the U.K. public utility regulation in the U.S. stems from the fact that while monopoly may be necessary to achieve the scale economies inherent in public utility operations, unrestricted monopoly power is undesirable from society's point of view. In the U.S. regulation by commisssion is the means adopted of controlling the undesirable features of monopoly and of making it more acceptable. Basically, through a number of devices, regulatory commissions in the U.S. seek to influence public utility prices in order to guard the public from monopolistic practices.[4] To the extent to which they are successful in getting utilities to price at marginal cost, as discussed in Chapter 2, the policy of regulation is consistent with economic efficiency. As we will see, the practice of regulation has not been strongly based in the theory of marginal-cost pricing, and only recently have utilities and regulatory commissioners paid much attention to the potential of marginal-cost pricing in the U.S. The institutional arrangements that have been adopted are discussed in the next section.

8.2 REGULATORY PRACTICES IN THE U.S. AND THE U.K.

In neither the U.S. nor the U.K. is regulation or public ownership confined to public utilities. In the U.K. many other businesses apart from public utilities are under public ownership.[5] In the U.S. also the scope for regulation extends far beyond public utilities.[6] From a practical point of view it is probably true that utility regulation is the most important type of regulation in the U.S. but it enjoys no special legal or constitutional status. Kahn (1970, p. 8) summed up the position as follows: 'As far as the United States Constitution is concerned, there is no longer any distinction between the public utilities and other industries.' This position arose when in 1934 the Supreme Court ruled that where the public interest was concerned it is not necessary to distinguish between particular categories of industries. In short the public interest could be said to affect all industries.[7]

In the U.S. and the U.K. the interests of the consumer and the desire to avoid monopoly exploitation are important aims of both regulation and public ownership. In the U.S. regulation attempts to achieve this by requiring the utilities to seek permission for price changes from a state regulatory commission in accordance with certain ground-rules. The main exceptions to this are fuel cost-adjustment provisions by which electric utilities are allowed to collect more or less automatically the extra costs which occur with increases in the prices of fuels they purchase. Otherwise the utilities must seek approval for their tariff structures. In the U.K. until the recent extensions of price control through the Price Commission to the peace-time economy, public utilities did not face any formal price regulatory machinery equivalent to the commissions of the U.S. General guidelines were provided from time to time by the government and requests for a price increase were discussed by the Consumers' Consultative Councils. However, these councils lacked the quasi-judicial powers, investigatory apparatus and other features of the U.S. regulatory commissions. Their main function was consultative and conciliatory, offering a right to hearing outside the courts for consumers in dispute with a public enterprise over what were, usually, rather small matters. However, like the regulatory commissions they were founded with a view to providing some protection of the consumers' interests when faced with a monopolist.[8]

In the operation of regulation and public enterprise economic principles have often been in the background of these activities. The principal consideration behind regulation and public enterprise has probably been the desire to avoid monopolistic exploitation (broadly defined) rather than promote economic efficiency. Hence the emphasis, until perhaps recently, has been on 'fairness', as exemplified primarily by the notion of a fair rate of return, but also in the rate structure itself.

Rate-of-return regulation is the centre-piece of U.S. regulation, and considerations of rate of return have taken on considerable importance in U.K. public enterprise as well. It is therefore appropriate for us now to examine some of the background to rate-of-return regulation. As we noted earlier, regulation is by a commission. The first thing to note about regulation by commission, whether at the federal or state level, is that attempts are always made to provide safeguards, in both a *de facto* and *de jure* sense, for the commission's independence. Commissioners are appointed for staggered terms. Not all commissioners may be from the same political party. They have a certain security of tenure during their term. However, their budgets are often handled by the executive branch and the legislative branch in framing statutes and writing appropriations.

Having been set up and provided with resources, the commission sets about its task of rate-of-return regulation. It has to provide facilities for 'hearings' where the utilities present their case, say, for a rate increase and to provide other facilities for dealing with customers' complaints. A number of guiding aims and principles underlie regulation. Commissions aim to prevent monopoly price and excessive price discrimination, to allow adequate earnings to maintain facilities in accordance with demand, and to ensure a high degree of public safety. The first two goals are difficult to achieve simultaneously. In keeping prices down to benefit present consumers a regulatory commission may find that insufficient capacity is provided to meet future demand, with the result that a higher price has to be charged in the future. The concern with public safety also may result in excessive reliability standards by public utilities. These issues will be examined further in Chapter 9. For the moment we want simply to describe the nature of rate-of-return regulation.

The typical regulatory framework can be illustrated by means of the familiar formula:[9]

$$R = O + (V - D)s, \tag{8.1}$$

where R = total revenue allowed, O = operating cost, s = allowed rate of return, V = gross value of rate base (the assets of the utility used in producing output), and D = accumulated depreciation.

In determining R the regulatory commission has an interest and control, to some degree, over all components of the right-hand side of (8.1). In general control exists by means of the accounting system. Utilities must use a system acceptable to the commission, and some uniformity in practice has developed over the years (see Phillips, 1969, pp. 143–77). Over s it has complete control. It is up to the commission to set the rate it feels is appropriate. It can influence O by disallowing certain expenses. It can influence $(V - D)$ and may attempt to avoid 'padding' it by adopting criteria like 'used and useful', or by its choice of asset-valuation criteria.[10] It could argue that only those assets that are used and useful in producing the output of the utility should be included in the rate base. It can also influence V and D by means of its choice of a valuation criterion, for example whether assets should be valued at original cost, or replacement cost, or whether depreciation should be based upon the straight-line method or some other method.

The above presents a simplified description of the task of rate-of-return regulation for the regulatory commission. Having determined the components of R in (8.1), the commission has of course to approve a corresponding rate structure.

In U.K. public enterprises rate-of-return considerations have taken on some significance, but they have not held the centre of the stage as they have in the U.S. Originally the financial obligation placed on the nationalised industries was to break even, or, to quote Robson (1962, p. 414), 'the legal obligation of the nationalised industries is only to conduct their undertakings in such a way as to avoid taking a loss, taking one year with another'. Thus, if a public corporation made a profit or surplus in any year, this was quite satisfactory; it could be used as a cushion for any future losses or to repay past losses.

Experience with the nationalised industries led to a change in attitude by government which invovled more precise criteria than the origial break-even constraint. Thus the government, in striving for more precise goals than break-even, was driven to examine rate-of-return considerations. In 1961 the government published its White Paper, *The Financial and Economic Obligations of the Nationalised Industries* (Cmnd 1337) and in 1967 published another White Paper, *Nationalised Industries: A Review of Economic and Financial Objectives* (Cmnd 3437), both of which dealt with the case of rates of return as a performance criterion for the nationalised industries. The 1961 White Paper set (over a five-year period) a target net rate of return for each public corporation, or a target gross rate of return. The former was defined as income before interest but after depreciation (at historic cost) as a percentage of average net assets, while the latter made no deduction of depreciation in arriving at the gross rate of return. The former ranged from 6 per cent for British European Airways to 12 per cent for the British Overseas Airways Corporation, and then later was 12.4 per cent for electricity supply. In addition the industries were given a 'financial ratio', which was actually the percentage which they were required to finance, of their estimated capital investment programmes. This financing ratio for the five-year period averaged 58.8 per cent over all the industries.

The 1961 White Paper was a crude document to which many objections could be made.[11] These were recognised in the 1967 White Paper, which made certain advances on pricing policy, in recognising the need to cover accounting costs (including adequate depreciation and servicing of capital), within, as far as possible, a framework of marginal-cost pricing. The White Paper recognised the need to take account of the capacity/demand relationships existing in the industries, i.e. the implications of potential excess demand for pricing policy. It asked all industries to use a common discount rate of 8 per cent (raised in 1969 to 10 per cent) in appraising major investment projects. Financial targets (rate of return) were still retained, however, in part in the belief that they encouraged managerial efficiency, despite their irrelevance or potential inconsistency with the first two criteria.[12]

Thus rate-of-return considerations play an important role in both the U.K. and the U.S. It is clear from the above brief description that their application leaves ample room for institutional differences. In the U.K., for example, rate of return acts primarily as a break-even constraint, thus giving rise to the second-best, constrained welfare analysis described earlier in this book. In the U.S, fair rate-of-return regulation gives rise to quite different issues, brought about by the separation of ownership and the instruments of regulatory control.

8.3 CONSIDERATIONS OF EFFICIENCY

In this section we want to broaden the scope to include considerations of dynamic X-efficiency. We first consider some of the relationships between regulation and X-efficiency. Second, we look at the implications of regulation for dynamic efficiency. Finally, we examine some alternative possibilities and aspirations for regulation, including an approach for evaluating alternative methods of regulation. The latter framework, developed by Williamson (1975), stresses the informational and transactions costs considerations of alternative contractual arrangements.

The interest in economic theory in the consequences on X-efficiency of regulation originated in the work of Averch and Johnson (1962), who noted that one consequence of rate-of-return regulation may be that utilities adopt excessively capital-intensive technologies. We will discuss the technical details of this in Chapter 9. Others have noted that regulation may have further effects on X-efficiency. For example, in his path-breaking theory of managerial discretion, Williamson (1964, pp. 57–9) indicates that expense preference, and therefore X-inefficiency, may be increased under profit regulation. At the level of practical policy in the U.K. there has been considerable concern with how to avoid X-inefficiency in public enterprise. The financial targets, which we noted in the previous section, were intended to provide incentives towards X-efficiency. Concern at this level has also been apparent in the U.S. Regulation has been criticised in general terms for its failure to promote X-efficiency. Wilcox (1966, p. 476) argued that it was unrealistic to expect regulation to be an effective substitute for competition, because 'regulation fails to encourage performance in the public interest by offering rewards and penalities'. Wilcox's basic idea has merit. Stated somewhat differently, regulation may offer rewards and penalties, but of the wrong kind.

The idea that regulation should have an effect on dynamic efficiency, in the sense of promoting growth or technological change, has come not only from economists but also from lawyers and others working in public utilities and regulatory commissions.[13] Amongst economists, probably the principal contribution on regulation and dynamic efficiency is the deliberate use of regulatory lag, the delay in decisions which follows from the fact that regulation cannot be instantaneous but, inevitably, takes time. In contrast to the position taken by traditional regulatory economists like Phillips (1969, p. 709), who argues that 'The Achilles heel of regulation is delay', some urge that regulatory lag be itself used as a policy instrument. The proponents of this deliberate delay in action argue that it is the *delay in regulation that can be beneficial*. The essence of the argument is found in a proposal by Baumol (1967), who argued that rates should be set only at periodic intervals, say three years, and in that interval the utility would normally absorb its losses or be allowed to keep all it made. The fact that any cost savings achieved by the company could be kept would give an incentive towards efficiency.

A further concern regarding regulation is that the process has high transactions costs. In the U.S. scarce managerial talent can be, and is, expended on rate cases. Similarly, in the U.K. managerial time can be wasted on tasks not directly related to the successful operation of the enterprise. These issues have spawned several recent proposals to reduce the transactions costs of regulation and simultaneously provide incentives toward dynamic and X-efficiency.[14] More radical suggestions still have been made by Demsetz (1968), who argues that certain utilities do not need regulation at all, and that a competitive bidding process, conducted at suitable intervals, could take the place of regulation. The winner of this bidding process would then be franchised to operate a monopoly at the 'bid price' over the agreed time interval until the next competitive bid. Clearly, for industries like electricity, with highly expensive and immobile capital, such a scheme is impractical. However, Edwards and Stevens (1976) imply that franchises offer an efficient means of regulation in areas like refuse collection where capital is more mobile.[15]

Such issues were very neatly pulled together by Williamson (1975, 1976) and Goldberg (1976). Williamson's basic argument is that an organisational form or a regulatory device must be judged on the basis of the extent to which it economises on bounded rationality and attenuates opportunism.[16] It is because of the existence of these two factors that transactions costs arise. Williamson (1976) examined competitive bidding for cable television franchises in Oakland and, in this case, indicated that competitive bidding had, on balance, many disadvantages. Williamson (1976, p. 102) summarises his findings as follows: 'Lest the argument appears unsympathetic to the franchise bidding approach, I should point out that there are circumstances where I suspect that regulation or public ownership can be supplanted by franchise bidding with net gains. Local service airlines and, possibly, postal delivery are examples.'

Thus there are a number of considerations regarding aspirations for regulation applying now which did not enter originally into the problem. These are well summarised by Commissioner Johnson, whose words on the broadened scope and role of regulation of telephone services would also apply more generally to public enterprise. In his view the following issues are typical of this expanded scope and role:[17]

What are the forces encouraging, or retarding, technological innovation in telephone equipment and service?

What are the most appropriate rates of change in making new equipment available to the subscriber?

What are the implications for national communications behavior of the ways in which we price telephone service?

What should be the standards by which some rate discrimination (or subsidies) are encouraged and others discouraged?

How should the pricing of telephone service respond as new techniques (satellites, wave guide, lasers) transform an industry of limited capacity into one of excess capacity?

In what ways would more, or less, competition in providing telephone service be useful?

By what procedures and institutional means can the needs and interests of both shareholders and subscribers best be formulated and translated into corporate or national policy?

9 Some Theoretical Considerations of Regulation

The purpose of this chapter is to provide an analytical framework for public utility regulation. Section 9.1 constructs a model of regulation from a simple examination of inputs to the regulatory process. In Section 9.2 we set out the Averch–Johnson effect for the deterministic case of a single product. Section 9.3 discusses the effects of regulation with stochastic peak loads. It shows the added potential provided with stochastic demands for Averch–Johnson effects or even gold plating. Section 9.4 explores some of the effects of behavioural assumptions other than profit maximisation on the part of the firm's management. Section 9.5 provides a brief discussion of dynamic effects and some remarks on the earlier results.

9.1 TOWARDS A GENERAL MODEL OF THE REGULATORY PROCESS

In this section we look at the inputs of the regulatory process in simple terms and formulate a general model which views the process as a system. The approach is meant to direct the reader's attention to the main forces at work, their possible magnitude and direction. The generality of the approach also complements our summary in the previous chapter of different theories of regulation.

Our approach draws, to some extent, upon recent contributions on informational and organisational problems in economics, for example Ross (1973) and Williamson (1975). Ross analysed the theory of agency, which is concerned with problems where a principal desires to accomplish a task but because of asymmetrical resource or informational endowments must rely on an agent to perform the task. The problem facing the principal is to choose appropriate incentives and set behavioural limits for the agent so as to balance the agent's better knowledge of uncertain states of the world against divergences in preferences between principal and agent.

129

Williamson is concerned with similar incentival and informational design problems in the context of complex organisations. His approach emphasises the coming together of bounded rationality and opportunism[1] with problems of uncertainty and small numbers. We now summarise his approach. The human mind has a limited capacity to solve problems (bounded rationality). As a result it is either very costly or impossible to identify *ex ante* future contingencies and the appropriate adaptations to them. Hence organisations may arise as alternatives to long-term contracts because of their ability to adapt and respond. Thus in the context of public utilities a possible explanation of regulation as being preferable to franchises is that franchising, as a form of long-term contracting, may lack the flexibility and adaptability of an organisational framework like regulation.

Following the above line of reasoning one may expect the behavioural consequences of bounded rationality and uncertainty to be important in regulation. However, the elaboration of a full-blown theory, for example Williamson's, encompassing such behavioural considerations is beyond the scope of this book. Indeed, only a few specific institutional arrangements for regulation have been analysed in any detail in the literature, rate-of-return regulation being the most common. The underlying (often implicit) assumption in any such specific analysis is that historical forces, in concert with the behavioural aspects just discussed, have led inexorably to the particular institutional form studied, at least in broad outline. Thus only minor variations (e.g. finding the socially optimal rate of return) on a theme (rate-of-return regulation itself) are studied. The more challenging task of understanding how history and human and economic forces have led or should lead to one institutional arrangement versus another is typically suppressed.

To illustrate the complexity of the incentival and informational interactions in a regulatory environment, we have depicted in Figure 9.1 a principal and agent formulation of the problem of regulation by commission. The principal is the regulatory commission representing the consumers. Another perhaps more realistic formulation would be to see the consumers as 'principal' and the commission as their agent, making the public utility a sort of sub-agency. This would be a reasonable approach to the extent that regulatory commissions develop motivation and objectives of their own which possibly diverge from the consumers' interests. However, for purposes of this simple diagram we will ignore such considerations and identify consumers exactly with the regulatory commission, the principal. The regulatory commission

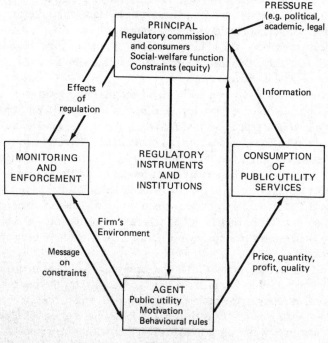

Fig. 9.1

attempts to achieve the desired vector of public utility services (right-hand box) by a number of regulatory instruments (vertical arrow) like rate-of-return and price regulation, moral suasion, threats and appeal to the public through the media. The public utility responds to these signals according to its motivation (e.g. whether or not it aims to maximise profit) with a set of behavioural rules and a resulting vector of prices, quantities, quality and profit. The commission attempts to see what effect its instruments are having on the public utility by monitoring and enforcement. The effect of this is that these get changed as they move through the monitoring and enforcement arrangements (see box and arrows on left). Information on prices, etc., also comes back directly (on the right-hand side of the diagram) from the actual vector of services made available for consumption. In addition there is exogenous pressure at work, shown in the top right-hand corner. This can come from a number of sources. A regulatory commission might find itself under pressure from the federal or state governments. For ex-

ample, in the U.S. the present Administration's (1978) energy programme puts pressure on commissions to at least take note of energy
conservation. There is also pressure from economists, lawyers and
political scientists, which has an effect on the quality, nature and
quantity of the research done by public utilities in their monitoring
and enforcement activities.

From the above we can see some of the main forces at work under
regulation. As noted earlier, little has been done at the level of general
theory to provide an integrated model of all of these. For example, the
interaction between monitoring and behaviour of the regulated firm has
received scant attention in the theoretical literature,[2] though this
interaction is clearly important in setting limits on firm behaviour, for
example on how far the firm may depart from cost-minimising behaviour. One would expect here some optimal trade-off between the
costs of monitoring and its social benefits. Similarly, only a few regulatory policies, for example rate-of-return regulation, have been studied
in detail.

We shall not attempt to fill in the lacunae in the literature here. Our
goal will be to illustrate in the following sections, on the basis of rate-
of-return regulation, the basic approach to analysing particular forms of
regulation. In general terms this approach assumes a given set of regulatory instruments or policies, say S, together with a behavioural model
of the regulated firm which would predict the firm's behaviour $x(s)$ as a
function of the regulatory policy $s \in S$ adopted. Finally, a welfare function $W(x(s), s, e)$ is specified in terms of the behaviour x of the regulated firm, the policy s chosen, and environmental variables e. The object
is to choose $s \in S$ so as to maximise $W(x(s), s, e)$ contingent on e. Of
interest would be optimal solutions for various classes of regulatory
policies as qualified by the firm's behavioural response function $x(s)$
and various technological and demand conditions. The next section
explores the approach just outlined for a very simple case.

9.2   THE AVERCH–JOHNSON EFFECT

In this section we will examine one of the major issues in the economic
theory of regulation, namely the Averch–Johnson (A–J) effect, referring to the inefficiency of rate-of-return regulation first analysed by
Averch and Johnson (1962). In describing this we will show that regulation need not lead to a maximisation of welfare as defined by the tradi-

tional social-welfare function. We confine our attention only to a simple presentation of the single-product case with two factors of production. We are not attempting to provide a thorough review of the literature, though the reader wishing to pursue this further may do so by following up the references and notes.

The Averch–Johnson effect has received more attention in the recent literature on the economic theory of regulation than any other topic,[3] and in our opinion probably more attention than its theoretical or practical significance justifies. For this reason our treatment will be brief. We start with the simple A-J model and then, in Section 9.3, proceed to the peak-load model of Bailey (1972).

We employ the following notation:

Π = profit.
x = output (measured in physical units).
K = capital.
L = labour.
r = firm's cost of capital.
w = unit cost of labour (wage rate).
$s(> r)$ = rate of return allowed by regulatory commission.
$x = F(K,L)$, where F is a quasi-concave neoclassical production function with positive marginal products and for which $F(0, L) = F(K, 0) = 0$ for all K, L.
$P = P(x)$ = inverse demand function.
$\theta = 0$ or 1, a variable explained below.
$R = Px$ = revenue.
c = cost of a physical unit of capital; henceforth we assume $c = 1$.
$\beta = rc$.

The firm is assumed to maximise profit subject to the regulatory constraint that its rate of return does not exceed the allowed rate s, that is:

$$\text{Max } \Pi = P(F(K, L)) \, F(K, L) - rK - wL, \qquad (9.1)$$

subject to:

$$\frac{PF(K, L) - wL}{K} < s. \qquad (9.2)$$

Assuming $s > r$, rewriting (9.1) and (9.2) and setting up a Lagrangian we have:

$$\Lambda = R - rK - wL - \lambda(PF(K, L) - wL - sK). \qquad (9.3)$$

Denoting MR = marginal revenue, the first-order conditions are:

$$\frac{\partial \Lambda}{\partial K} = (1 - \lambda)MR \, \frac{\partial F}{\partial K} - (1 - \lambda) \, r = \lambda(r - s) \qquad (9.4)$$

$$\frac{\partial \Lambda}{\partial L} = (1 - \lambda)MR \, \frac{\partial F}{\partial L} = (1 - \lambda)w. \qquad (9.5)$$

Thus (9.4)–(9.5) represent a solution to the problem of maximising profit subject to a regulatory constraint. Such a solution differs from the profit-maximising solution since, as we show directly, it is not a cost-minimising solution for the achieved level of output $x = F(K, L)$. Cost minimisation would require:

$$\frac{F_K}{F_L} = \frac{r}{w}, \qquad (9.6)$$

where $F_K = \partial F/\partial K$, $F_L = \partial F/\partial L$, the marginal products of K and L respectively. The reader may prove (9.6) for himself (see Exercise 9.1).

To see the difference between the regulated solution and a cost-minimising solution divide (9.4) by (9.5) to obtain:

$$-\frac{dL}{dK} = \frac{F_K}{F_L} = \frac{r}{w} - \frac{\lambda(s - r)}{(1 - \lambda)w} < \frac{r}{w}. \qquad (9.7)$$

If the regulatory constraint is binding, then $\lambda > 0$,[4] implying that the cost-minimising conditions (9.6) do not hold so that a regulated profit-maximising firm will not minimise costs. From (9.7) we see that the marginal rate of technical substitution $(-dL/dK)$ of capital for labour is lower for the regulated firm than for a cost-minimiser. Given the assumed convex shape of production isoquants (recall that F is assumed quasi-concave), it follows immediately that under regulation capital is overutilised and labour underutilised relative to any cost-minimising solution. This is called the A–J effect.

If this were, *ceteris paribus*, the only effect of regulation, then it would be an unambiguous disaster. If, however, regulation increased output and reduced price, then even though costs are not minimised there is the possibility of a welfare gain, to the extent that the added consumers' surplus exceeds the increase in costs. Unfortunately, it is not possible to say in general that output or capital intensity of the regulated firm will exceed that of pure monopoly.[5]

The implications of the above for our welfare framework can be noted by reference to a contribution of Sherman (1972, 1974), who used the same walfare framework in analysing the A–J effect. To simplify derivations we assume a constant-returns production function. To derive the welfare-maximising conditions and facilitate comparisons between the various cases it turns out to be easier to reformulate the Lagrangian (9.3) as follows:

$$\Lambda' = R - \theta wL - \lambda(R - wL - sK).\qquad(9.8)$$

For purposes of this analysis we must also assume that demand is elastic. Then setting $\theta = 0$ and $s = r$ it can be shown that the welfare-maximising solution results. With $\theta = 1$ and $s = r$ we have the equivalent of the A–J problem.[6] If we set $\theta = 1$ and $s = m$, where m is the pure monopoly return, we obtain the unregulated profit-maximising monopoly solution. We list below the first-order condition for (9.8):[7]

$$R_K = -\frac{\lambda}{1 - \lambda}s\qquad(9.9)$$

$$R_L = \frac{\theta - \lambda}{1 - \lambda}w\qquad(9.10)$$

$$R - wL - sK = 0.\qquad(9.11)$$

Table 9.1

	Regulated	Welfare maximisation	Pure monopoly
θ	1	0	1
s	r	r	m
Capital condition	$R_K = \dfrac{-\lambda}{1 - \lambda}r$	$R_K = \dfrac{-\lambda}{1 - \lambda}r$	$R_K = r$
Labour condition	$R_L = w$	$R_L = \dfrac{-\lambda}{1 - \lambda}w$	$R_L = w$
Rate of return	$R - wL - sK = 0$	$R - wL - rK = 0$	$R - wL - mK = 0$

The results are given in Table 9.1, where the effects of regulation are apparent. Regulation only changes the firm's rule for choosing its level of capital. It continues to adopt the same decision rule for determining the level of labour as the pure monopolist would, implying that the regulated firm would be inclined to use less than the welfare-maximising amount of labour. Thus the regulated firm produces a lower output than the welfare-maximising firm. In the case of the constant or increasing returns to scale production function the output of the regulated firm always exceeds that of the pure monopolist, though, as we noted earlier, this result is not true in general.[8]

The above is certainly useful in indicating the nature of the effect of rate-of-return regulation on a public utility's factor combination. Of equal interest is the effect of regulation on social welfare. Sheshinski (1971) and Bailey (1973) have explored this question. Using the traditional welfare function we may express the social benefits arising from regulation when the allowed rate of return is s as:

$$W(s) = \int_0^{F(K(s),\,L(s))} P(y)dy - rK(s) - wL(s), \qquad (9.12)$$

where $K(s)$ and $L(s)$ are the public utility's chosen capital and labour inputs when allowed rate of return is s, so that $X(s) = F(K(s), L(s))$ is the resulting output level.

From (9.12) we see that:

$$\frac{dW}{ds} = P(X(s))\left[F_K \frac{dK}{ds} + F_L \frac{dL}{ds} \right] - r\frac{dK}{ds} - w\frac{dL}{ds}, \qquad (9.13)$$

or, denoting $p = P(X(s))$:

$$\frac{dW}{ds} = (pF_K - r)\frac{dK}{ds} + (pF_L - w)\frac{dL}{ds}. \qquad (9.14)$$

If $s = m$, the pure monopoly rate of return, then $\lambda = 0$ in (9.4) and (9.5) and we may rewrite these conditions as:

$$pF_K - r = -P'FF_K \qquad (9.4a)$$

$$pF_L - w = -P'FF_L. \qquad (9.5a)$$

Substituting (9.4a) and (9.5a) in (9.14) yields:

$$\frac{dW}{ds} = -P'F\left(F_K \frac{dK}{ds} + F_L \frac{dL}{ds} \right) < 0, \qquad (9.15)$$

where the inequality follows from the fact that dK/ds and dL/ds are both negative when $r < s < m$ (see Exercise 9.1).

Thus the negative sign of dW/ds implies that if we reduce s from the monopoly return $s = m$, we increase the value of the social-welfare function. From this we see that some regulation is always desirable, unless marginal cost is zero.

To obtain the value of s for which W is maximised we set (9.14) to zero, obtaining:

$$p \frac{dX}{ds} = \frac{dC}{ds}, \tag{9.16}$$

where $C(s) = rK(s) + wL(s) = $ total costs.

Thus cost increases as s decreases, because output increases and inefficiency increases with decreases in s. From (9.16) we can derive the following optimality condition in terms of p:

$$p = \frac{dC}{dX}. \tag{9.17}$$

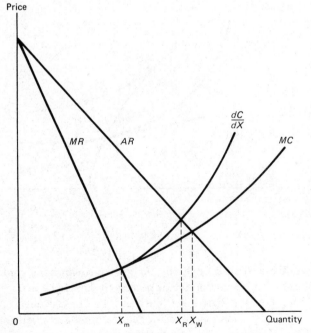

Fig. 9.2

Although (9.17) is similar to the standard welfare-optimality condition, it is not identical because dC/dX is higher as a result of the inefficient combination of inputs brought about by regulation. In terms of Figure 9.2 the effect of regulation is to cause a divergence of the (regulated) marginal-cost curve from the marginal cost of the pure monopolist. The different outputs of pure monopoly X_M, regulated monopoly X_R and welfare-maximising monopoly X_W are also shown. Thus for $r < s < m$ the value of s should be decreased until (9.17) is satisfied, to give optimal price and output as shown in Figure 9.2.[9]

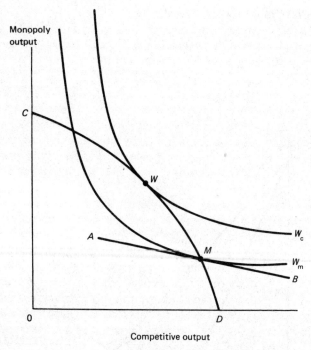

Fig. 9.3

While these results apply in the partial-equilibrium context, we should note that regulation is not necessarily beneficial in the general-equilibrium context. Figure 9.3 illustrates this for a two-sector model, one sector being a monopoly sector and the other a competitive sector. The effect of pure monopoly is to move the economy from the welfare optimum, point W on the transformation curve, to point M, the monopoly optimum. Point M is clearly on a lower social indifference curve (W_m).

If the regulation increases monopoly output, but only by using an inefficient combination of factors, the new transformation curve (or regulation possibility curve) diverges from the original one (CD) at M and offers lower levels of each output. However, as long as this curve is not below W_m, regulation is still beneficial because it offers the possibility of attaining a higher social indifference curve. Note that if regulation led to a point below the line AB it would be particularly undesirable; leading to a price higher than the monopoly price.[10]

9.3 PEAK LOADS AND REGULATION

After the introduction to A–J effects provided in Section 9.2, we aim in this section to relate regulation and A–J effects to our detailed analysis in Part Two of the peak-load problem. We are going to start with a simple deterministic mode similar to Bailey (1972, 1973) which we follow with our own stochastic model. The latter, as we shall see, opens up new dimensions in regulatory economics and provides even more difficulties than were apparent in the analysis of the last section.

We are going to confine ourselves to the simple case of one plant and two equal-length periods with independent demands. We start by recalling the simple welfare-maximising solution, contrasting it with the profit-maximising solution and comparing these with the regulated deterministic peak-load solution. We then compare the latter with the stochastic peak-load model.

The welfare-maximising two-period one-plant independent demand case has the following solution:

$$p_1 = b, \quad p_2 = b + \beta. \tag{9.18}$$

The corresponding profit-maximising case is where:

$$\frac{d}{dx_1}(x_1 P_1(x_1)) = MR_1 = b, \quad \frac{d}{dx_2}(x_2 P_2(x_2)) = MR_2 = b + \beta. \tag{9.19}$$

The regulated peak-load case may be formulated as follows:

$$\text{Max } \Pi = x_1 P_1(x_1) + x_2 P_2(x_2) - b(x_1 + x_2) - \beta \overline{q}, \tag{9.20}$$

subject to:

$$x_1 \leqslant \overline{q}, x_2 \leqslant \overline{q} \tag{9.21}$$

$$x_1 P_1(x_1) + x_2 P_2(x_2) - b(x_1 + x_2) - \beta\overline{q} \leqslant (s - \beta)\overline{q}. \tag{9.22}$$

Associate Lagrangian multipliers λ_i and μ with (9.21) and (9.22) respectively. The Kuhn-Tucker conditions are (9.21), (9.22) and:

$$(1 - \mu)MR_i - (1 - \mu)b - \lambda_i \leqslant 0, x_i \geqslant 0, i = 1, 2 \tag{9.23}$$

$$\sum_{i=1}^{2} \lambda_i \leqslant \beta - \mu s, \overline{q} \geqslant 0. \tag{9.24}$$

If we take the firm-peak case where $x_1 < \overline{q}$ and $x_2 = \overline{q}$, we have the following solution:

$$MR_1 = b \tag{9.25}$$

$$MR_2 = b + \beta - \frac{\mu(s - \beta)}{1 - \mu}. \tag{9.26}$$

The off-peak price (9.25) is derived easily from (9.23) since the constraint on capacity is non-binding in period 1, implying $\lambda_1 = 0$. This is the same as the monopoly price. Thus for the simple peak-load case the regulated firm sets off-peak price according to the pure monopoly pricing rule.[11] The peak price is derived by substituting (9.24) into (9.23) to yield (9.26) after a little rearrangement. The last term in (9.26) is positive if $0 < \mu < 1$. (This, of course, is true because μ, the Lagrange multiplier associated with the profit constraint, is the same as λ of note 4 and Exercise 9.1.)

Thus the effect of regulation in the firm-peak case is similar to the A-J effect. The regulated utility operates inefficiently by installing more peak-load capacity but not expanding off-peak use at all, thereby causing a poorer utilisation of capacity. In terms of the social-welfare function regulation nevertheless has increased welfare, because the gain in consumers' surplus in the peak period exceeds the increase in total costs brought about by the increase in capacity.[12]

Turning our attention now to the case of stochastic demand, we find a new dimension to regulation because of the need to come to terms with the issue of the reliability of service. We examined optimal reliability for the welfare-maximising firm in Chapter 5. When dealing with a regulated profit-maximising firm reliability provides a further problem for the regulators because it leaves an additional degree of freedom for the firm. As a result there may be additional 'effects' under stochastic demand beyond the simple A–J effect of the deterministic case.

For our basic framework we will retain our assumptions of Chapter 5 about additive independent stochastic demand. We will confine ourselves to the one-plant case, and of course we will drop the assumption of welfare maximisation in favour of expected profit maximisation. Thus we assume that the regulated monopoly's problem is as follows:

$$\text{Max } E\{\Pi(\mathbf{p}, z, \widetilde{\mathbf{u}})\}, \tag{9.27}$$

subject to:

$$E\{\Pi(\mathbf{p}, z, \widetilde{\mathbf{u}})\} \leqslant (s - \beta)z, \tag{9.28}$$

where $\mathbf{p} \geqslant 0$, $z \geqslant 0$, $s - \beta > 0$, where s and β are as above, and the disturbance term $\widetilde{\mathbf{u}}$ is a continuous random variable, with components $\widetilde{u}_i$ independent, and with $E(\widetilde{u}_i) = 0$. Thus there is some bounded interval $[u_{1i}, u_{2i}]$ such that $Pr\{\widetilde{u}_i \epsilon [u_{1i}, u_{2i}]\} = 1$. We define expected profits $E(\Pi)$ as follows:

$$E\{\Pi\} = E\left\{\sum_{i=1}^{2}(p_i - b)\, S_i(\mathbf{p}, z, \widetilde{u}_i) + r_i(D_i(p_i) + \widetilde{u}_i - z) - \beta z\right\}, \tag{9.29}$$

where $S_i(\mathbf{p}, z, \widetilde{u}_i)$ and $r_i(D_i(p_i) + \widetilde{u}_i - z)$ are exactly as defined in Chapter 5.

With this framework it turns out that optimal behaviour under regulation may be to treat capacity as if it were a free good, thus inducing an A–J effect with a vengeance. A more appropriate term might be 'gold plating', or more exactly gold plating on reliability, as we now show.[13] Let the maximum expected revenue obtainable when capacity is a free good be denoted by R^*. When capacity z is a free good the monopolist will set z high enough to ensure that demand is always less than z. Thus:

$$R^* = \underset{\mathbf{p} > 0}{\text{Max }} E\left\{\sum_{i=1}^{2}(p_i - b)\,[D_i(p_i) + \widetilde{u}_i]\right\}, \tag{9.30}$$

or, since $E\{\widetilde{u}_i\} = 0$, R^* reduces to the maximum obtainable deterministic revenue with capacity unconstrained:

$$R^* = \underset{\mathbf{p} \geqslant 0}{\text{Max }} \sum_{i=1}^{2}(p_i - b)D_i(p_i). \tag{9.31}$$

Letting $\mathbf{p}^*$ be the optimal pricing solution to (9.31), we show below that if:

$$\frac{R^*}{s} \geq \underset{i \in \{1,\,2\}}{\text{Max}} \, [D_i(p_i^*) + u_{2i}], \tag{9.32}$$

then the regulated monopolist will set price equal to $\mathbf{p}^*$, and $z^* = R^*/s$, thus achieving equality in the regulatory constraint. To establish the claim just made let $z^* = R^*/s$ and assume that optimal capacity z is less than z^*. Then:

$$E\{\Pi(\mathbf{p}, z, \widetilde{u})\} \leq (s-\beta)z < (s-\beta)z^* = E\{\Pi(\mathbf{p}^*, z^*, \widetilde{u})\}, \tag{9.33}$$

where the first inequality holds since any optimal solution $(\mathbf{p}, z)$ must satisfy (9.28), the strict inequality follows from $(s-\beta) > 0$, and the final equality holds by (9.32) and the definition of z^*. Thus, for any feasible price $\mathbf{p}$, z cannot be optimal. Suppose, likewise, that z is greater than z^*. Then:

$$E\{\Pi(\mathbf{p}, z, \widetilde{u})\} = E\{\text{Rev}(\mathbf{p}, z, \widetilde{u})\} - \beta z < R^* - \beta z^*$$
$$= E\{\Pi(\mathbf{p}^*, z^*, \widetilde{u})\}, \tag{9.34}$$

where the inequality follows by definition of R^* as the maximum obtainable net revenue. We see again that z is non-optimal. Clearly z^* is the optimal capacity and, since (9.32) holds, $\mathbf{p}^*$ is feasible and also optimal in (9.27)–(9.29).

One implication is that the regulated monopolist may set his reliability level to unity, which we can see from (9.31) and the definition of u_{2i}.[14] Thus regulation may induce excessive investment in capacity to achieve very high reliability levels. Consider a numerical example utilising the demand functions (6.1)–(6.2) with $b = 5$, and $\beta = 10$. We can easily show that (9.32) is satisfied for any s, β and γ satisfying $s/\beta < 7$ and $\gamma < 30$. For the case $s/\beta = 1.1$ and for any $\gamma < 30$ the solution to (9.27)–(9.29) is $p_1 = 142.5$, $p_2 = 58.5$, and $z = 431.4$. For this case, therefore, z^* is a massive fivefold multiple of the welfare-maximising optimal capacity. Thus A–J effects, reliability and 'gold plating' all work in the same direction, i.e. towards excessive capacity. Rate-of-return regulation with stochastic demand provides the opportunity, in certain instances, for unrestrained gold plating in the name of reliability. Very large excess capacity could result unless the regulatory commission applies some form of reliability constraint. Thus the analysis suggests that rate-of-return regulation should be coupled with some form of either specific reliability constraints or maximum reliability levels. Specifying minimal acceptable reliability levels may exacerbate the gold-plating effect, in that they may result in 'their being satisfied with a vengeance (i.e. more capacity is installed than that required to give reliability of unity). Indeed, the above example provides an illustration of gold plating if ever there was one.

A more detailed analysis of reliability and regulation is required before proceeding to general conclusions or implications for policy. However, a certain amount of pessimism about the efficiency of rate-of-return regulation without reliability constraints seems warranted, and is supported by the limited empirical evidence. Telson (1975) has argued that current levels of electricity reliability are far too high. He has supported this view with a cost–benefit analysis which indicates reliability levels far higher than his framework implies as reasonable. Regulatory commissions are also aware of these problems, and are attempting to arrive at a basis for checking the reasonableness of the reliability levels of the electricity utilities which they regulate.[15]

9.4 EXPENSE PREFERENCE AND REGULATION

Our analysis of the previous sections has been based upon the arguably naive notion that the firm maximises (expected) profit. As such it has ignored, along with most of the literature on regulation, some important developments in the theory of the firm. Recently Edwards (1977) has argued forcefully that under regulation some alternative motivation to profit maximisation might be appropriate. His evidence, based upon the banking industry, is supportive of the view that Williamson's (1964) notion of 'expense preference' is, for regulated companies, a plausible alternative to profit maximisation. In view of this we are now going to consider some of the implications of expense preference for the behaviour of firms subject to regulation.

From Williamson (1964), Bailey (1973) and Rees (1974) an expense-preference model of a regulated privately owned utility's behaviour would involve, in place of pure profit maximisation, the maximisation of the firm's preferences (which we represent by the function $U(S, \Pi)$) defined on pairs (S, Π) of staff expenditures S and profits Π. We define Π through:[16]

$$\Pi = xP(x, A) - wL - \beta K - A - S, \tag{9.35}$$

where A represents advertising expenditures, $P(x, A)$ is the inverse demand function, w, L, β and K are as in the A–J model of Section 9.2, and S is as defined above. We assume that x and S satisfy $x \leqslant F(K, L)$ and $S \geqslant S(x, A)$, where F is the production function and $S(x, A)$ represents minimal expenditures for staff sufficient to sustain an output x and advertising expenditure A.

If an expense-preference utility is subjected to rate-of-return regulation, a solution to the following problem would represent its behavioural response:

$$\text{Max } U(S, \Pi), \tag{9.36}$$

subject to the constraints:

$$S \geqslant S(x, A) \tag{9.37}$$

$$x \leqslant F(K, L) \tag{9.38}$$

$$\Pi = xP(x, A) - wL - \beta K - S - A \leqslant (s - \beta)K \tag{9.39}$$

$$x, K, L, A, S \geqslant 0, \tag{9.40}$$

where $s > \beta$ represents the allowed rate of return.

We associate Lagrange multipliers μ_1, μ_2, μ_3 with (9.37)–(9.39) and obtain the following Lagrangian:

$$L = U(S, \Pi) + \mu_1 (S - S(x, A)) + \mu_2 (F(K, L) - x)$$

$$+ \mu_3 ((s - \beta)K - \Pi). \tag{9.41}$$

Assuming that all variables are positive at optimum, the following first-order conditions result:

$$x: (U_2 - \mu_3)[P + xP_1] - \mu_1 S_1 - \mu_2 = 0 \tag{9.42}$$

$$A: (U_2 - \mu_3)[xP_2 - 1] - \mu_1 S_2 = 0 \tag{9.43}$$

$$K: (U_2 \beta - \mu_3)s - \mu_2 F_1 = 0 \tag{9.44}$$

$$L: (U_2 - \mu_3)w - \mu_2 F_2 = 0 \tag{9.45}$$

$$S: U_1 - U_2 + \mu_1 + \mu_3 = 0 \tag{9.46}$$

$$\mu_i \geqslant 0; \mu_1 (S - S) = \mu_2 (F - x) = \mu_3 ((s - \beta)K - \Pi) = 0, \tag{9.47}$$

where the numerical subscript i to a function indicates partial differentiation of the function with respect to its ith argument, for example $U_1 = \partial U/\partial S$. The first-order conditions for a profit-maximising firm, with staff expenditures, are obtained easily by setting $U_1 = 0$, $U_2 = 1$ in (9.42)–(9.47). For an expense-preference utility we assume $U_1 > 0$, $U_2 > 0$.

The first thing to note is that, whether regulated or not, the expense-preference firm has a higher level of staff expenditure and a lower level of profit than its profit-maximising counterpart. To verify this note that (9.46) implies $U_2 - \mu_3 = U_1 + \mu_1$, so with this substitution (9.43) implies:[17]

$$xP_2 - 1 - dS_2 = 0, \tag{9.48}$$

where $0 < d = \mu_1/(U_1 + \mu_1) \leqslant 1$. Now in the case of a profit-maximiser $U_1 = 0$ and $d = 1$, whereas for an expense-preference-maximiser $U_1 > 0$ and so $d < 1$. Thus it is clear from this essential difference in first-order conditions that an expense-preference-maximising solution can never be a profit-maximising solution, i.e. the expense-preference-maximising solution must entail strictly less profit than any solution to the profit-maximising problem. From this we see immediately that the expense-preference-maximising solution must then also entail strictly greater staff expenditure since otherwise it would be dominated (as evaluated by $U(S, \text{II})$) by the profit-maximising solution.

A little more effort (see Exercise 9.4) establishes that any solution (x, A) for an unregulated profit-maximiser must in fact satisfy $S = S(x, A) < S(x', A') \leqslant S'$, where (x', A') are the output level and advertising expenditure for the corresponding unregulated expense-preference utility and S and S' are the actual levels of (optimal) staff expenditure for the two firms. Assuming $S_1, S_2 > 0$, it follows from this that either $x' > x$ or $A' > A$ (or both).

Turning now to the A–J effects, assume $F_1, F_2 > 0$. Then, from (9.44)–(9.45):

$$\frac{U_2 - \mu_3 s}{F_1} = \frac{(U_2 - \mu_3)w}{F_2} = \mu_2. \tag{9.49}$$

Since $U_2 - \mu_3 = U_1 + \mu_1 > 0$ (see note 17), we see that:

$$\frac{\beta}{F_1} - \frac{(s - \beta)\mu_3}{U_2 - \mu_3} = \frac{w}{F_2}. \tag{9.50}$$

From (9.50) it follows that $F_1/F_2 = -dL/dK < \beta/w$ unless $s = \beta$ or $\mu_3 = 0$ and the regulatory constraint is inconsequential.[18] But $-dL/dK < \beta/w$ implies, just as in Section 9.2 above, that the A–J over-capitalisation effect persists for expense-preference utilities.

To get a clearer idea of the effects of expense preference under regulation consider the following example:

$$U(S, \Pi) = cS + (1 - c)\Pi \tag{9.51}$$

$$F(K, L) = K^{\alpha_1} L^{\alpha_2} \tag{9.52}$$

$$P(x, A) = \delta x^{-\zeta_1} A^{\zeta_2} \tag{9.53}$$

$$S(x, A) = x^{\epsilon_1} A^{\epsilon_2}, \tag{9.54}$$

where the parameters appearing above are all non-negative and satisfy:

$$c < 1, \alpha_1 + \alpha_2 \leqslant 1, \zeta_i < 1, \epsilon_i \leqslant 1 \ (i = 1, 2). \tag{9.55}$$

From this the reader may verify[19] that (9.42)–(9.47) yield the following first-order conditions:

$$(1 - c - \mu_3)(P + xP_1) - \frac{\mu_1 \epsilon_1 S}{x} = \mu_2 \tag{9.56}$$

$$(1 - c - \mu_3)(x\zeta_2 P - A) = \mu_1 \epsilon_2 S \tag{9.57}$$

$$(1 - c)\beta - \mu_3 s = \mu_2 F_1 = \frac{\mu_2 \alpha_1 x}{K} \tag{9.58}$$

$$(1 - c - \mu_3)w = \mu_2 F_2 = \frac{\mu_2 \alpha_2 x}{L} \tag{9.59}$$

$$1 - 2c = \mu_1 + \mu_3 \tag{9.60}$$

$$\mu_1 > 0, \mu_2 > 0, \mu_3 \geqslant 0, \mu_3 [(s - \beta)K - \Pi] = 0. \tag{9.61}$$

Since $\mu_1, \mu_2 > 0$, it follows from (9.47) that $S = S$ and $x = F$ at optimum. Note also from (9.60) and $\mu_1 + \mu_3 > 0$ that $c < 1/2$ must hold for a solution to exist. If c were greater than $1/2$, then (9.51) would imply that a pound of extra staff expenditure would always be preferred to an extra pound of profits. Since profits are not required to be non-negative, the utility would indulge its preference for staff beyond any bound.

A computer program was written to solve (9.56)–(9.60). Selected results are displayed in Tables 9.2 and 9.3. In Table 9.2 we vary the allowed rate of return s and compare the profit-maximising solution with the expense-preference solution for the parameter values indicated.

Table 9.2 Comparing profit-maximising and expense-preference behaviour

$s = $ *	10.2	10.6	11.0	11.4	11.8	∞†
x‡	12.66	12.08	11.54	11.04	10.58	5.14
x'	11.44	11.21	10.95	10.68	10.39	9.13
A	60.94	60.30	59.69	59.09	58.50	48.14
A'	106.75	103.72	100.81	98.03	95.38	85.58
P	43.88	44.69	45.48	46.26	47.03	61.23
P'	61.09	60.85	60.68	60.60	60.59	61.24
S	216.82	209.56	202.77	196.36	190.31	109.12
S'	361.10	347.22	333.60	320.30	307.45	258.53
K	18.93	17.67	16.54	15.51	14.58	5.14
K'	11.48	11.30	11.08	10.82	10.53	9.13
L	8.47	8.26	8.05	7.86	7.68	5.14
L'	11.41	11.12	10.83	10.54	10.26	9.13
Π	3.77	10.62	16.54	21.72	26.23	54.52
Π'	2.29	6.79	11.08	15.14	18.96	32.30
W	559.28	550.41	541.46	532.5	523.72	369.15
W'	701.09	688.8	675.47	662.34	649.47	591.39

*Parameters assumed (cf. equation (9.51)–(9.54): $c = 0.2$ or 0; $\alpha_1 = \alpha_2 = \zeta_1 = \zeta_2 = \epsilon_1 = 0.5; \epsilon_2 = 1; s = 20; w = \beta = 10$.

†$s = \infty$ yields the unregulated solution.

‡Profit-maximising solution ($c = 0$) is denoted x, A, P, S, K, L, Π. Expense-preference solution ($c = 0.2$) is denoted $x', A', P', S', K', L', \Pi'$.

Table 9.3　Comparing profit-maximising and expense-preference behaviour

$s = *$	10.2	10.6	11.0	11.4	11.8	$\infty\dagger$
$x\ddagger$	4.41	4.27	4.13	4.01	3.89	1.73
x'	4.00	3.98	3.97	3.94	3.89	2.53
A	34.10	33.96	33.82	33.68	33.55	28.90
A'	70.64	68.89	67.17	65.45	63.77	43.69
P	47.95	48.82	49.66	50.49	51.30	77.50
P'	73.23	72.43	71.72	71.13	70.65	75.76
S	71.62	70.14	68.75	67.41	66.14	37.97
S'	141.19	137.50	133.75	129.83	125.83	69.48
K	7.98	7.58	7.16	6.80	6.47	1.73
K'	4.03	4.09	4.13	4.15	4.15	2.53
L	2.44	2.41	2.39	2.36	2.34	1.73
L'	3.96	3.89	3.81	3.74	3.66	2.53
Π	1.58	4.54	7.16	9.52	11.64	32.36
Π'	0.79	2.47	4.11	5.79	7.47	27.86
W	319.67	317.23	314.72	313.03	310.86	283.22
W'	439.95	434.92	431.01	425.82	419.78	315.31

*Parameters assumed (cf. equations (9.51)–(9.54): $c = 0.2$ or 0;
$\alpha_1 = \alpha_2 = \zeta_2 = \epsilon_1 = 0.5; \zeta_1 = 0.6; \epsilon_2 = 1; s = 20; w = \beta = 10$.
$\dagger s = \infty$ yields the unregulated solution.
$\ddagger$Profit-maximising solution ($c = 0$) is denoted x, A, P, S, K, L, Π.
Expense-preference solution ($c = 0.2$) is denoted $x', A', P', S', K', L', \Pi'$.

The same is done in Table 9.3, but this time for more inelastic demands ($\zeta_1 = 0.6$, compared with $\zeta_1 = 0.5$ for Table 9.2).

The results in Tables 9.2 and 9.3 are intuitive for the most part. Output, advertising and staff expenditures all decrease as the regulatory constraint is relaxed. Of course profits increase as s is increased. The less elastic demands of Table 9.3 lead to higher prices and lower output. For the profit-maximiser, price increases steadily as s increases, while for the expense-preference firm price first decreases and then begins to increase. In a similar vein the capital–labour ratio, which for these examples should be unity for cost-minimising behaviour (since $\alpha_1 = \alpha_2$ and $w = \beta$), is always greater than unity except when regulation is inconsequential. Thus A–J effects are present. Interestingly, the capital–labour ratio always decreases as s increases for the profit-maximiser, whereas for the expense-preference utility this ratio starts at unity for $s = \beta$, increases over a certain range as s increases, and then decreases again to unity as s gets large enough for the unregulated solution to become feasible.[20]

The just-noted differences in price and capital–labour behaviour between profit-maximising and expense-preference utilities may be understood as follows. When the regulatory constraint is very tight, the profit-maximising firm has large incentives to over-capitalisation and thence to depressed prices. On the other hand, the expense-preference firm indulges its preference for staff expenditures as profits become more tightly constrained. In fact even though the expense-preference firm spends much more on advertising than the profit-maximiser in order to indulge these preferences, its price is so high that, for low values of s, its output is actually less than the profit-maximising utility.

Finally, we note some relevant values of the social-welfare function. In Table 9.2 we note that W decreases continuously from 559.28 to 369.15 and W' from 701.09 to 591.39, and where W and W' simply

Table 9.4 Optimal values of the decision variables for a welfare-maximising firm

| | Values of variables for parameters in | |
	Table 9.2	Table 9.3
$x = K = L$	98.25	26.75
A	330.05	227.45
$S = S$	3271.65	1176.36
P	36.65	41.98
Π	−1965.2	−815.75
W	1636.5	868.82

represent the value of the welfare function[21] for the profit-maximising and expense-preference firms respectively. Although not shown, the values of s which maximise W for the data of both Table 9.2 and Table 9.3 were $s = \beta + \epsilon$, where ϵ is small, for the profit-maximiser, and $s = 10 = \beta$ for the expense-preference utility. Thus, for these data, the welfare-maximising policy is to make regulation as tight as possible, and the closer the regulatory commission forces s to β the better.

To see how these results compare with a firm that maximised the traditional social-welfare function, we note in Table 9.4 the values of the variables for the parameters of Tables 9.2 and 9.3. We note that both the profit-maximiser and the expense-preference firm compare unfavourably with the welfare-maximiser.

Without being too zealous in extrapolating these illustrative results, it does seem clear enough that there are significant behavioural differences between profit-maximising and expense-preference firms in response to rate-of-return regulation. As indicated in Section 9.1, these differences could also entail substantive differences in designing appropriate regulatory mechanisms for such utilities. Although the above analysis suggests some important features of this design process, theoretical and empirical elaboration of these issues is still an open research question.

9.5 DYNAMIC ASPECTS OF REGULATION

To this point in our analysis of regulation we have assumed that regulatory constraints are imposed continuously. However, as noted in Chapter 8, in reality there is a time lag in adjusting prices to accommodate a rate-of-return constraint or to account for changing factor prices.[22] This section presents an introductory discussion of these dynamic issues with continued emphasis on rate-of-return regulation.

To begin our discussion let us return to the A–J model of Section 9.2. Following Bailey and Coleman (1971) we have drawn in Figure 9.4 the locus of points $R(s)$ for which the regulatory constraint is binding,[23] i.e. the (K, L) pairs for which:

$$P(F(K,L))F(K,L) - wL = P(x)x - wL = sK. \qquad (9.62)$$

Suppose that a regulated firm is currently operating at point A. Movement towards the A–J point D would increase profits, at least when

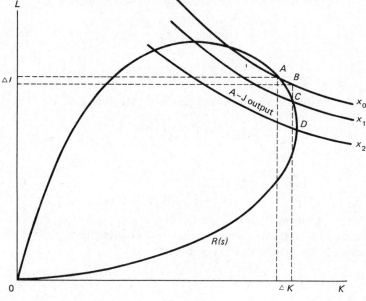

Fig. 9.4

such movement could proceed along $R(s)$. Suppose, however, that there is a regulatory lag of T periods before price changes can be enacted through the regulatory commission. In this case an increase in capital of ΔK will lead first to point B and then, after a lag of T periods, price is adjusted to allow movement to point C.

We consider two possibilities:

  (i) at A less capital is being used than is required for cost-minimising behaviour, implying that $r\Delta K \leqslant w\Delta L$; and

  (ii) increasing capital along the isoquant x_0 leads to increased costs, i.e. $r\Delta K - w\Delta L > 0$.

In case (i) profits are ever-increasing in going from A to B to C, so this adjustment path will be preferred by the firm to remaining at point A, and this irrespective of the lag T.

In case (ii), which is the more likely starting-point, a trade-off ensues. If the regulatory lag T is too large, then the discounted present value of increased costs in moving to point B are not offset by the present value of increased profits obtaining once point C is reached. More formally, suppose the firm is earning an annual profit of $\Pi = (s - r)K$ at point A.

Then the present value of the firm's profits if it remains at point A is:

$$\Pi_0 = \Pi + \Pi d + \Pi d^2 + \ldots = \frac{\Pi}{1-d}, \tag{9.63}$$

where $d = 1/(1 + r)$, taking the discount rate to be the firm's cost of capital.

On the other hand, discounted future profits along ABC are

$$\Pi_1 = [\Pi - (r\Delta K - w\Delta L)]\left(\sum_{t=0}^{T-1} d^t\right)$$

$$+ [\Pi + (s - r)\Delta K]\left(\sum_{t=T}^{\infty} d^t\right). \tag{9.64}$$

The first term in (9.64) represents discounted profits for the first T years and the second term represents discounted profits thereafter. Summing the series in (9.64) we obtain:

$$\Pi_1 = \frac{\Pi}{1-d} - \frac{(r\Delta K - w\Delta L)(1 - d^T)}{1-d} + \frac{(s - r)\Delta K d^T}{(1-d)}, \tag{9.65}$$

so that from (9.63):

$$\Pi_1 - \Pi_0 = \left[(s - r)\Delta K\frac{d^T}{1-d}\right] - \left[(r\Delta K - w\Delta L)\frac{1 - d^T}{1-d}\right]. \tag{9.66}$$

The trade-off involved is now clear from (9.66). Increments in capacity beyond the cost-minimising level are warranted when the discounted incremental profits after regulation (the first term) exceed the discounted incremental costs (the second term) accruing prior to regulatory adjustment. From (9.66) such over-capitalisation is clearly called for as T goes to zero or as d goes to unity (i.e. as r goes to zero). However, since by equation (9.7) $r\Delta K - w\Delta L > 0$ (for small enough ΔK) along isoquants in the vicinity of the A–J point D, we see that $\Pi_1 - \Pi_0$ is surely negative for large T when point A is close to D. A sufficiently large regulatory lag thus discourages over-capitalisation, i.e. an equilibrium capital input strictly less than point D will be maintained when T is large.

A special case of interest obtains in (9.66) when $\Delta L = 0$, which corresponds to the case where ΔK is added to the rate base but is left as idle capacity until regulatory adjustment. In this case (9.66) becomes:

$$\Pi_1 - \Pi_0 = \frac{s\Delta K}{1 - d} \left(d^T - \frac{r}{s} \right), \tag{9.67}$$

which has the same sign as $sd^T - r$, independent of ΔK. Thus, if $sd^T - r > 0$, the firm would move all the way to the A-J point D,[24] and otherwise would remain at point A.

The above developments can be extended in several ways (see also Bailey, 1973). Two interesting directions would be: (i) to models allowing explicitly for dynamic demand and technology (e.g. a rate-of-return regulated version of the model presented in Chapter 7); and (ii) to models dealing explicitly with the capital structure of the firm, an issue to which we now turn.

Davis (1970) has provided an interesting analysis of the complex interactions between capital markets, rate-of-return regulation and capital structure of regulated utilities. Starting with a regulated utility facing a binding rate-of-return constraint, Davis assumes that the utility attempts to maximise the present value of owners' holdings[25] through appropriate choices of levels of retained earnings, new outside equity and debt. Davis's basic concern is to understand the implications of the commonly accepted rate-setting principles[26] that the rate of return be set high enough (i) to provide comparable earnings for investments of the same risk class, and (ii) to attract capital compatible with growth requirements of the utility.

The main conclusion reached by Davis is that specifying a 'fair' rate of return, as embodied in the above principles, requires explicit recognition of the firm's capital structure and the characteristics of the capital market where the utility competes for investment capital. In particular setting the allowed rate of return on the basis of the current market rate of return alone without regard for capital attraction requirements may lead to perverse behaviour (e.g. shareholders block a needed new-equity issue to prevent a watering-down of their present equity). Similar comments on the importance of capital structure in regulated firms have been advanced by Lebowitz, Lee and Linhart (1976) in their study of the effects of inflation on 'fair' rates of return and by Sherman (1977) in his study of valuation theories for public utilities. We note, however, that a welfare analysis, along the lines of

Section 9.3 above, is lacking in the literature on dynamic aspects of regulation, with the result that vague guidelines, such as the principle of capital attraction, can easily be subverted to support a wide range of 'fair' rates of return. Measuarable and non-circular, welfare-based criteria accounting for the dynamics of the regulated firm have yet to be developed.

The discussion in this chapter, ranging from the general theoretical basis to some dynamic considerations of regulation, leads us to conclude that regulation is a promising area of theoretical research with many questions unanswered. On the empirical side there are a large number of studies complementing the above developments, many of these devoted to the A-J effect. Studies by Courville (1974), Hayashi and Trapani (1976), Petersen (1975) and Spann (1974) provide support for the A-J hypothesis. However, the Boyes (1976) and Smithson (1978) tests for the A-J effect were not significant. The ambivalence of these findings suggests that more complex models of firm behaviour and the institutional environments are required in understanding the effect of rate-of-return regulation on efficiency. The results presented above on the relationship between regulation and reliability and the effects of regulation under various alternatives to profit maximisation are in this spirit, and these should provide a reasonable starting-point for extensions of the A-J empirical literature.

EXERCISES

9.1 Consider the problem (9.1)-(9.2) of the regulated profit-maximising monopolist.

(i) Show that (9.6) is necessary for any minimum-cost solution by solving, for any fixed output level x, the problem $\text{Min}\{\beta K + wL \,|\, F(K,L) \leqslant x\}$. Thus verify that the solution to (9.1)-(9.2) is not cost-minimising.

(ii) Show that the Lagrange multiplier λ in (9.4)-(9.5) satisfies $0 < \lambda < 1$ whenever $r < s < m$, where m is the pure monopoly rate of return.

(iii) Show that when $r = s$, any solution yielding zero profit is optimal in (9.1)-(9.2), thus showing the indeterminacy of the solution to (9.1)-(9.2) when $s = r$.

(iv) Give an example to illustrate that the capital output ratio and output are not necessarily greater under regulation than they would be for the pure monopoly solution.

(v) Show from (9.4) that $\lambda = (r - F_K MR)/(s - F_K MR)$. Substitute this in (9.4) and use comparative statics to show that $dK(s)/ds$ and $dL(s)/ds$ are negative for $r < s < m$, where $K(s)$ and $L(s)$ are as in (9.12).

9.2   Verify the entries in Table 9.1 for the pure monopoly case.

9.3   Consider the following peak-load problem with demands and costs:

$$X_1(p_1) = 10 - p_1 ; X_2(p_2) = 30 - p_2 ; \beta = 2; b = 1.$$

Find the optimal unregulated profit-maximising solution and show that it has lower welfare than the regulated solution for any s satisfying $\beta < s < m$.

9.4   Following the same line of reasoning as that concerning equation (9.14) establish for unregulated profit-maximising and expense-preference utilities, under identical technology and demand conditions, that $S = S(x, A) < S(x', A') \leqslant S'$, where (x, A, S, K, L) and (x', A', S', K', L') are the respective solution behaviours for the two utilities.

9.5   Verify the first-order conditions (9.56)–(9.61). Check one of the entries in Tables 9.2 and 9.3 to see that there are appropriate multipliers for which these conditions are satisfied.

Part Four

Policy Implications for Electricity Supply

10 Electricity Supply

In Part Four we now explore some of the policy implications and applications of the analysis of the earlier parts. Chapter 10 will examine the general application of this analysis to electricity supply. We have chosen electricity supply for illustrating this analysis because of its obvious current importance and because of its classic status in the peak-load and public utility literature. Chapter 10 provides a perspective on the economic and technical characteristics of electricity supply as well as on the history of rate-making in the industry. Chapter 11 then examines the issue of energy conservation in greater detail, and in particular the use of peak-load pricing to promote energy conservation. Chapter 12 presents a concluding discussion of our analysis and its applications to electricity supply, with our view of needed future research.

The aim of this chapter is to examine some of the principles underlying the economics of electricity supply. We will show how our framework on peak-load pricing might be applied to the case of electricity supply, and how it differs from previous approaches to electricity pricing. In Section 10.1, we describe some of the institutional background to electricity supply. This will include an examination of the interesting technical and economic factors and a short review of some of the relevant historical developments in pricing that have taken place in the industry. Next in Section 10.2 we assess the core of the theoretical developments of the previous chapters in determining an optimal pricing policy for electricity supply, including an examination of present tarriff experiments. In Section 10.3 we will discuss the effects of regulation on electricity supply.

10.1 HISTORICAL, TECHNICAL AND ECONOMIC FEATURES OF ELECTRICITY SUPPLY

The electricity-supply industry was among the first high-technology industries and is of considerable importance in advanced economies, because electricity is required in every industry. It is a source of light, motive power and heat; it is also essential for certain chemical processes. Its growth has always been consistently faster than the average for the economy. Despite the 'energy crisis' there is ample reason to believe that growth in the energy sector will continue. In short electricity is a major industry of considerable interest and importance. From our point of view it is of further significance to the extent that its economic problems are amenable to analysis by the methodology of the earlier chapters. We now propose to provide a condensed description of some economic and technical features of electricity supply.

To produce the commodity electricity in a form that is usable by the consumer requires three basic processes: generation, transmission and distribution. Generation is the process of converting other forms of energy into electricity. It is usually performed by power-stations on a scale very large relative to the usage of individual consumers. This large scale means that generation can take place only on certain sites. Sometimes these are a considerable distance from consumers, necessitating the other two processes of transmission and distribution. Transmission consists of taking the electricity generated at the power-stations and sending it through wires at high voltage to sub-stations where it is transformed down to low voltage ready for distribution through low-voltage lines to individual meters (consumers).

There are four main methods of undertaking the generation of electricity:

(i) conventional thermal (i.e. coal, oil, gas);
(ii) nuclear;
(iii) gas turbine; and
(iv) hydro-electric (including pumped storage).

There are also many other ways of generating electricity, like solar power, wind, tides, diesel generation and geothermal power, to mention just a few. However, these are not currently feasible for generating large quantities, and it will be a number of years before they produce significant amounts of electricity. Realistically, for significant new investment in the near future, we can consider only (i)–(iii) above as the most economical. Hydro-electric projects have probably already been undertaken, and this source can therefore be expected to produce only a relatively small amount of future power needs. Accordingly our analysis in this chapter will be addressed to the problem of electricity supply where only methods (i)–(iii) are available.

Thus with a choice of plant types as described above an electricity utility has to generate, transmit and distribute electricity. It aims to generate, transmit and distribute a given quantity of electricity at a minimum cost. In view of the fact that electricity is economically non-storable and demand fluctuates periodically (and stochastically), we have a peak-load problem as described in Part Two above. As we noted in Chapter 5, to meet demand at any moment at minimum cost requires that plants be operated in ascending order of running costs. Thus as demand increases, plants of higher and higher running costs are operated. Thus in Figure 10.1 we rank plants according to marginal running costs (fuel plus costs of operating power-station auxiliaries like pumps and fuel-handling devices).

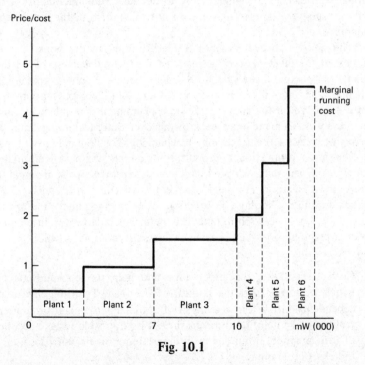

Fig. 10.1

When demand is 10,000 megawatts, plants 1–3 are operated. If demand increases slightly, plant 4 comes into operation. Clearly it is not cost-minimising to operate plant 5 for demands just over 10,000 megawatts. Similarly, if demand falls to 7000 megawatts, plant 3 would cease to operate. Thus at any moment plants are operated in ascending order of their marginal running costs to achieve cost-minimisation. In practice there are a few complications which mean that this rule does not apply absolutely. Transmission costs can cause departures from the rule. Plant 2 may have lower running costs than plant 3 but if most of the demand at a particular moment of time is occurring close to plant 3 and many miles away from plant 2, the transmission costs might cause a departure from the regime. Maintenance outage as well as unforeseen plant outages, or transmission failures, can also cause a departure from the regime of Figure 10.1. Thus, for example, if there is a transmission failure between plant 1 and where the demand is occurring, the system has to depart from the plan. Such considerations are of some operational significance to engineers but do not raise fundamental problems for our analysis. Accordingly we do not treat them in the rest of this chapter.

The above short-run analysis underlies long-run decisions like the nature of the plant type to be installed for the replacement of existing plants or to expand the system. Such problems are solved typically by engineers and are known as system planning, and there exists a considerable literature on the subject.[1] System planning is a problem in dynamic analysis. Demand may be growing over time, technology may be changing, relative fuel costs may be changing. The demand growth may not be simple proportionate growth. For example, if a peak-load pricing tariff were generally adopted, we would expect off-peak demand to grow most rapidly and peak demand to decline or stabilise. Thus detailed system planning is a function of the pricing policy, and optimally the two should be simultaneously determined. However, in practice system planning does not operate in this way, as Turvey (1968b, p. 13) notes:

> Costs depend on the programme and help to determine tariffs, which in turn affect the growth of the load. To bring this interdependence into a formal analysis of optimizing the plant programme would not be helpful, however, since it is impossible to take account of it in practice, simultaneously determining future tariff levels and the plant programme.

As a result system planners and engineers have produced simplifying devices which, while ignoring such problems, do provide an attempt to minimise long-run costs. The load curve is one such device; it plots demands in megawatts, say, over a given twenty-four hour period. In Figure 10.2(a) the daily load is plotted as a continuous curve. A load curve approximating very roughly a typical winter day in the U.K. is shown. A load curve for a typical summer day in the U.K. would be everywhere lower. (In the U.S. the situation would typically be some-what reversed, with the increased load in the summer brought about by air conditioning.) The load-duration curve of Figure 10.2(b) measures how long a level of demand 'lasts' over the year. Thus peak demand obtains for only a few minutes a year, as shown by the steepness of the load-duration curve in Figure 10.2(b). The load-duration curve is obtained by starting with the lowest value of demand on any day in the year. Since all demands were above this for the rest of the year, this demand was maintained for the whole year, giving point *A* in Figure 10.2(b). Similarly ranking demands in ascending order we are able to plot the whole load-duration curve *AB*. Thus at *C* load is main-tained for about half of the year.

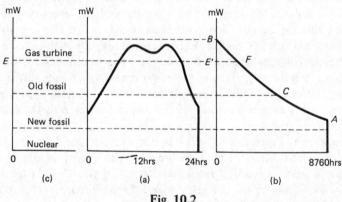

Fig. 10.2

Let us now consider how the load and load-duration curves can be used in solving the short-run and long-run problems of cost minimisa-tion. Let us imagine we have four types of plant: nuclear, new fossil-fired, old fossil-fired, and gas turbine. Nuclear plants have low running cost and high capacity cost (small *b* and large *B*) and gas turbines have high running cost and low capacity cost. The new fossil-fuel plants are in between these limits with intermediate running costs and intermedi-ate capacity costs. The new plant has lower running costs than the old because it is more efficient in its use of heat. If we rank these four types of plant in ascending order of fuel costs to the left in Figure 10.2(c), we can then derive the operating regime of the plants. Thus on a typical winter day gas-turbine operation is given by the area above the horizontal line *EF* in Figure 10.2(a), and during the year such plants operate for a total of *BEF* plant hours, from Figure 10.2(b). For the other types of plant similar areas may be examined to derive their annual operating hours.

It is clear (ignoring transmission costs) that Figure 10.2(a)–(c) provide a basis for short-run optimisation. If the plants are operated inversely to their marginal running costs, total running costs are minimised. Examination of Figure 10.2 reveals that this is indeed the case. Gas turbine operates for the shortest time and nuclear plants operate for the longest time. This short-run problem assumes, however, that capacity has been installed at quantities given by Figure 10.2(c). The long-run problem, as to what are the optimal quantities of each type of capacity, is still as yet unanswered.

Before examining an approach to the solution of the long-run problem, we will first examine some of the interactions involved. Let us assume that we are considering replacing an old fossil-fired plant with a nuclear plant. In this case capacity costs are higher but there are substantial fuel savings while the nuclear plant is operating instead of the old plant. It is the magnitude of these over time that determines whether or not to install the nuclear plant. In particular the nuclear plant would be installed if the present value of the cost savings exceeds the capital costs.

Looking at Figure 10.2(a)–(c) it is clear that the load-duration curve provides a basis for estimating the present value of cost savings. If the nuclear type is increased, then all other fossil-fuel plants will be 'pushed up' in the figure, causing them to operate for a shorter period (and the nuclear type to operate for an exactly corresponding longer period). The difference in the fuel costs for these periods are the fuel savings concerned. Thus Figure 10.2(a)–(c) provides a basis for least-cost operation in the short run; by providing a means for deriving the effect on running costs of different plant configurations, the figure also provides a basis for solving the long-run problem of the choice of cost-minimising plant mix for a given planned load profile. We return to this question below.

System planning and pricing are treated as separate processes. However, from the early days of electricity the peak-load problem has been present and the need to provide an appropriate pricing policy recognised. The grandfather of electricity rate-making was an English engineer Dr John Hopkinson. In 1892, in his presidential address to the Junior Engineering Society, he argued that costs are determined by peak demand and that 'The ideal method of charge then is a fixed charge per quarter proportioned to the greatest rate of supply the consumer will ever take, and a charge by meter for the actual consumption.'[2] Maximum-demand tariffs, which were to become so popular in the industry over the years, were born. Their original intent was apparently to come to terms with the peak-load problem to the extent that they aimed to improve utilisation or load factor.

Hopkinson's basic approach has dominated the thinking on electricity rate-making. Indeed, developments in the U.K. and the U.S. until recently have been in the spirit of Hopkinson.[3] The approach, as it evolved, entailed separating costs into three categories:

(i) consumer-related;
(ii) unit-related; and
(iii) demand-related.[4]

Prices were to be set so as to recover historical (accounting) costs over these three categories, with each of several customer classes paying its 'fair' share of the full costs. Let us now look at this proposal in more detail, starting with a description of the just-mentioned cost categories.

Consumer-related costs are those costs that are incurred no matter how large or how small the number of units consumed, for example billing, collection, connection and consumer service. Two-part and block tariffs would normally recover these costs in the fixed charge or in the first block of the tariff.

Unit-related costs are those which vary directly with the number of units used. Such costs are mainly fuel, some a small part of distribution costs, and certain other works' costs of generation and transmission. Very roughly they correspond to the b of our earlier analysis.

Demand-related costs vary with the speed and time with which users consume electricity.

Having divided up costs into these three categories, the rate analyst then divides the consumers into classes, the aim being that each class of consumer pays the total cost of supplying it, as defined in terms of the above categories. The idea behind this is an attempt to be fair to consumers as a class. The notion does not extend completely to individual consumers. An individual may pay more or less than the costs of supplying him, and this does not offend the notion of fairness applied in the industry.

Any procedure such as the above based on allocation of full histori-cal costs across customers will necessarily involve some averaging amongst individual consumers. In order for such a scheme to have any claim to logical consistency it would seem that the various consumer classes should each be reasonably homogeneous with regard to be-haviour. One aspect of this is the time at which consumers make their maximum demands. Lewis (1941, p. 252), among others, has noted that all consumers do not make their maximum demands at the same time, so that the system-diversity factor, which is defined as the ratio of the sum of individual maxima to the system maximum, typically differs from unity. Now homogeneous behaviour for a particular con-sumer group would mean that intra-group diversity is small compared with system diversity. Clearly the extent to which consumer groups can be homogeneously structured is crucial to the possibility of deter-mining and stably allocating their fair share of full historical running and capacity costs to them.

In fact experience has confirmed that stable consumer groups in terms of diversity and load factor can be determined.[5] The usual group-ings are residential, commercial and industrial. Almost invariably domestic consumers did not use enough to justify the maximum-demand-use metering used in industrial tariffs. Thus they were placed upon two-part or block tariffs while industrial consumers were charged according to maximum-demand (Hopkinson) tariffs. The maximum-demand tariff is roughly as discussed earlier, the charge per kW of maxi-mum demand being adjusted downwards according to class diversity factors so as not to over-collect costs. For domestic consumers the fixed charge collects the consumer-related costs and the unit charge collects the unit- and demand-related costs. The unit costs are derived by taking the total of such costs for the system and dividing by total outputs. (This figure corresponds to the unit charge in a maximum-demand tariff.) To the unit-related charge is added the demand-related charge in domestic tariffs. The demand-related charge per unit is based upon the load factor of the group (in the U.K. about 40 per cent) and the diversity and is simply added to the unit-related charge.[6] Two illustrative tariffs are given below in Table 10.1. Note that the unit of energy consumption is the kW-hour for any consumer, while maximum demand is expressed in terms of kilovolt-amperes (and not kW). This

Table 10.1

Domestic (residential) tariff		

Quarterly standing charge £5
Charge per kilowatt-hour (kWh unit) 3p

Industrial maximum-demand tariff	*High voltage*	*Low voltage*
Annual demand charge per kilovolt-ampere (kVa)		
For each of the first 300 kVa of maximum demand	£25	£26
For each of the next 200 kVa of maximum demand	£23	£24
For each of the next 400 kVa of maximum demand	£21	£22
For the remainder	£20	£21
Unit charge		
For each of the first 1752 units supplied per kVa of maximum demand in that year	2.0p	2.06p
For the next 1752	1.65p	1.7p
Remainder	1.6p	1.64p

difference is necessary to take into account the technical matter, familiar to electrical engineers, of power factor.[7]

The form of the tariffs in Table 10.1 is typical of tariffs employed in U.S. and U.K. utilities. The domestic tariff is sometimes in the form of a block tariff, for example 100 units at 8p and the remainder at 3p, which gives identical revenue to the tariff in Table 10.1 provided the consumption is not less than 100 units. The original justification of such tariffs in preference to two-part tariffs was based on the fact that consumers whose usage was so small that they did not even use all the units in one high block would pay less than under a two-part tariff.

For the most part rate-making in the U.S. still conforms rather closely to the above approach, though, as we indicate later, there has been some recent movement towards marginal-cost pricing. The main exception to the above approach in the U.K. has been the 'Bulk Supply Tariff' (B.S.T.), which is used by the Central Electricity Generating Board (C.E.G.B.) for the sale of electricity to the Area Boards. The C.E.G.B., with trivial exceptions, sells only to Area Boards, which are responsible for dealing with the final consumer. Its tariff has employed elements of time-of-day pricing since 1962. The 1962–3 B.S.T., as explained in Meek (1963), departed from the traditional Hopkinson approach by fixing a total capacity charge and sharing this out between Area Boards according to their share of system-peak rather than individual maximum demands. It priced units according to the time of day: between 07.00 hours and 23.00 hours the unit charge was about one and a quarter times that charge made in the night hours. In addition it embodied a fuel-cost adjustment factor which made provisions for increases (or decreases) in the unit rate if the price of coal changed from some given level.

In 1967 the C.E.G.B. introduced a major change in the tariff with three time-of-day unit charges and two capacity charges, one for peak capacity (about 10 per cent of system maximum demand) and one for 'basic' capacity. The peak-capacity charge was levied at a lower rate than the basic-capacity charge because of the fact the peak demands, as noted above, can be met at lower capacity costs by means of gas turbines. The procedure for measuring these charges, per kW, are to measure an Area Board's share of system maximum demand, to measure its share when system demand is about 90 per cent of system maximum demand, and to take the difference. This difference is expressed as a proportion of the sum of such differences for all Area Boards to give a Board's peak capacity charge. Similarly the proportions are taken at the 90 per cent level to obtain the basic-capacity charge. While no exact equivalent to the C.E.G.B. exists in the U.S., similar problems occur in various Regional Interchanges of Power. These interchanges are federations of utilities which co-ordinate their bulk pricing and dispatching decisions in ways similar to the C.E.G.B. procedures.

In short retail electricity tariffs in the U.K. and the U.S. have traditionally been based upon principles actively different from those outlined in Part Two to apply to situations with peak loads. Periodic variations in demand of the kind met in electricity supply would, according to the analysis of Part Two, be priced by tariffs where the price varied according to the time of day, so called time-of-day tariffs. Only within the last few years have such tariffs been offered generally as a matter of routine in the U.K.[8] In the U.S. they have usually been used only experimentally as part of widespread studies of load and market research that are currently being undertaken.[9] This is in contrast to the situation in France, where *Electricité de France* (E.D.F.) has approached the problem differently from the U.S. and the U.K. and has been responsible for innovations in time-of-day pricing and load-management devices. We will now comment briefly on some of these.

French tariffs clearly departed from the pattern of Hopkinson rates common in the U.S. and the U.K. some years after the nationalisation of the industry in 1946, when the industry apparently had no less than 13,000 different tariffs.[10] In 1958 perhaps the most significant development in electricity pricing was the introduction of *'le tarif vert'*, which applied to high-voltage customers. Other consumers, making up the vast majority (over 99 per cent), are charged on the universal tariff, either with ('double tariff') or without ('simple tariff') a time-of-day rate. We will briefly examine the latter before going on to look at *le tarif vert*.

The universal tariff has some novel features. The consumer must subscribe to a particular maximum kW load between 0.5 and 36 kW, for which he pays a fixed monthly charge. This subscribed demand is enforced by a circuit breaker, forcing the consumer to turn off some appliances and reset the breaker. The unit charges consist of two declining blocks.

Le tarif vert is rather complicated. As in the universal tariff, the consumer subscribes to a maximum demand. The kilowatt charge varies according to voltage size of load (e.g. loads over 10,000kW get a discount of 24 per cent) and according to where the maximum demand is at system peak. There are five energy charges, varying according to time of day and season. The energy charges do show a substantial

Table 10.2

	Winter			Summer	
	Peak 6¢	Full 3¢	Low 1¢	Full 2¢	Low 1¢
Time	0700–0900 and 1700–1900 Nov–Feb	0600–2200 (except peak) Oct–Mar	2200–0600 (and Sundays)	0600–2200	2200–0600 (and Sundays)
Periods					
Number of hours	408	2072	1864	2528	1888

differential between peak winter rate and lowest summer rate. Approximate rates for the most typical tariff *(tarif général)* in 1974 are given in Table 10.2, together with times in force. Variations also are incorporated into the tariff according to region, and these can be substantial, reflecting such factors as the proximity of cheap hydro-electric power.

Thus the picture emerging of electricity supply is different in several major respects to the models of Part Two. First, there is not the emphasis on time-of-day pricing to deal with the peak-load problem that we have in Part Two. Second, where there is time-of-day pricing it often incorporates kW demand charges and unit charges, an apparently redundant procedure on the basis of the models of Part Two. Third, there is some concern for equity or some notion of fairness. Fourth, problems of cost minimisation and pricing are separated in the two functions of system-planning and rate-making.

10.2 PEAK-LOAD PRICING IN ELECTRICITY SUPPLY

Wenders (1976) has probably got closest to relating the theory of peak-load pricing to the pricing problem in electricity supply. In this section we review his results and compare them with our analysis of Part Two.

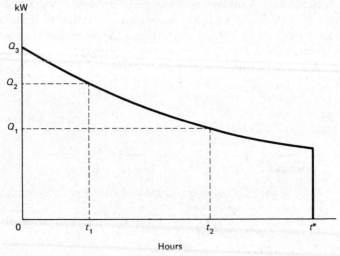

Fig. 10.3

His approach is particularly interesting for its ability to combine system planners' tools like the load-duration curve in an analysis of peak-load pricing that very simply solves the problem of unequal-length periods.

He assumes three types of plant with annual (marginal) capacity costs per kW of β_1, β_2 and β_3. Wenders (1976, p. 233) defines 'marginal and average energy cost of production a kW of electricity *for one year*,' as b'_1, b'_2 and b'_3. These variables are of course not the same as our definitions of b_i. We will, however, at the moment proceed using Wender's notation, leaving until later in the section the reconciliation of his results with ours.

Using a load-duration curve like the one used in Figure 10.2, Wenders first notes that optimal plant mix depends on the slope of the load-duration curve. In Figure 10.3 the year is divided into three periods which represent the following fractions of the year: $w_1 = t_1/t^*$, $w_2 = (t_2 - t_1)/t^*$, $w_3 = (t^* - t_2)/t^*$, where $t^* = 8760$ hours, where $Q_1 = q_1$, $Q_2 = q_1 + q_2$ and $Q_3 = q_1 + q_2 + q_3$, with q_1, q_2, q_3 the installed capacities of base, intermediate and peaking plant.

If the firm has built q_1 units of base-load capacity and considers increasing by one unit, it has to consider the alternative of intermediate capacity and can compare the following marginal costs:

$$MC_1 = \beta_1 + (t_2/t^*)b'_1 \tag{10.1}$$

$$MC_2 = \beta_2 + (t_2/t^*)b'_2. \tag{10.2}$$

If $MC_1 < MC_2$, base load rather than intermediate capacity should be used and this would apply until $MC_1 = MC_2$, or:

$$t_2/t^* = w_1 + w_2 = \frac{\beta_1 - \beta_2}{b'_2 - b'_1}. \tag{10.3}$$

Similarly, intermediate capacity should be added until $MC_3 = MC_2$, or:

$$t_1/t^* = w_1 = \frac{\beta_2 - \beta_3}{b'_3 - b'_2}. \tag{10.4}$$

Finally, since $w_1 + w_2 + w_3 = 1$:

$$w_3 = 1 - \frac{\beta_1 - \beta_2}{b'_2 - b'_1}. \tag{10.5}$$

We note from (10.3)–(10.5) that w_1, w_2, w_3 depend only on the relative capital and running costs and not on the slope of the load-duration curve, though the *amounts installed of each kind of plant* depend on the shape of the load-duration curve.

Using a simplified version of the load-duration curve of Figure 10.2 and the above analysis of marginal cost, Wenders places the problem in the context of the familiar welfare-maximising framework used elsewhere in this book. The simplified load-duration curve is shown in Figure 10.4. The demand periods are indicated by t_1', t_2' and t^*. Thus period 1 covers a fraction of one year given by $v_3 = t_1'/t^*$, $v_2 = (t_2' - t_1')/t^*$ and $v_1 = (t^* - t_2')/t^*$. Period 3, the peak period, is serviced by q_1 of base capacity, q_2 of intermediate capacity and q_3 of peak capacity, period 2 by q_1 of base, and q_2 of intermediate and period 3 by q_1 of base capacity, as in Chapter 4.

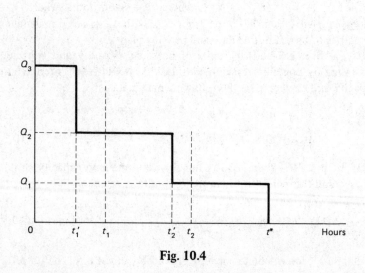

Fig. 10.4

The dashed lines at t_1 and t_2 are the same as the t_1 and t_2 of Figure 10.3. Thus $v_3 < w_1$, $v_3 + v_2 < w_1 + w_2$. We can proceed to illustrate the optimal pricing policy using v_1, v_2, v_3 as weights in the social-welfare function (recall that prices and costs are based on the complete cycle here as in Williamson's analysis in Chapter 3 above):

$$W = \sum_{i=1}^{3} v_i \int_0^{x_i} P_i(y_i) dy_i - C_r - C_c, \qquad (10.6)$$

where C_r = running cost and C_c = capacity cost, that is:

$$C_r = b'_1 q_1 + b'_2 (v_2 + v_3) q_2 + b'_3 v_3 q_3 \tag{10.7}$$

$$C_c = \beta_1 q_1 + \beta_2 q_2 + \beta_3 q_3. \tag{10.8}$$

Maximising w with respect to q_l, while noting that $x_3 = q_1 + q_2 + q_3$, $x_2 = q_1 + q_2$, $x_1 = q_1$, yields the following optimal prices for the situation depicted in Figure 10.4:

$$P'_3 = b'_3 + \beta_3/v_3 \tag{10.9}$$

$$P'_2 = \frac{(v_2 + v_3)b'_2 - v_3 b'_3 + \beta_2 - \beta_3}{v_2} \tag{10.10}$$

$$P'_1 = \frac{b'_1 - (v_2 + v_3)b'_2 + \beta_1 - \beta_2}{v_1} \tag{10.11}$$

The above results are similar to those of Chapter 4, to the extent that capacity costs are included in the off-peak periods. We will discuss this similarity further after noting that Wenders also offers another case, without any capital costs in the off-peak periods, namely:

$$P_1 = b'_1, \text{ and } P_2 = b'_2. \tag{10.12}$$

The result (10.12) occurs, Wenders contends, only if $v_3 = w_1$, $v_2 = w_2$. This implies from (10.3) and (10.4), in the case of three equal-length periods (i.e. $w_i = v_i = 1/3$, for $i = 1, 2, 3$):

$$\beta_2 - \beta_3 = 1/3(b'_3 - b'_2) \tag{10.13}$$

$$\beta_1 - \beta_2 = 2/3(b'_2 - b'_1). \tag{10.14}$$

This violates Lemma A on page 42, implying that plant 2 *need* not be used.[11] Thus Wenders's result (10.12) refers to a special case and a situation that need not occur. We do not wish, however, to overemphasise such criticism.[12] Essentially Wenders provided a very lucid demonstration of some of the major results of peak-load pricing applied to electricity supply which enables him to solve rather simply the problems of multiple plants and unequal-length periods.

10.3   REGULATION OF ELECTRICITY SUPPLY

In Section 10.1 and 10.2 we indicated some of the important technological and economic features of electricity supply and showed briefly how some of the peak-load pricing theory of Part Two might be applied to the industry's pricing problem. As such the approach was general, having applicability beyond electricity supply in the U.K. or the U.S. In this section we take a different approach, examining some of the effects of regulation on the U.S. and U.K. electricity-supply industries.

As we stated in Chapter 8, the approach to public utilities has been very different in the U.S. and the U.K. The publicly owned electricity-supply industry in the U.K. has been subject to certain government intervention not present in the U.S. The main problem in this regard in the U.K. has been the attempt by government to use the industry as a device for achieving its macroecnomic policy objectives like control of inflation and/or economic growth. It would have been surprising if such efforts had been successful as macroeconomic policy instruments. The attempts have taken two forms: control of pricing and control of investment. Even before the attempt by the Conservative government under Heath to freeze electricity prices while energy costs were sky-rocketing, there had been a long history of price regulation and control of electricity prices. Just after 1945 the energy-pricing policy during the period of acute coal shortage led Little (1953) to attack the policy of keeping prices down and argue for a time-of-day tariff for electricity. Macroeconomic policies of planning investment in electricity supply have also been practised. In part this interest arose because of the substantial amount of investment being undertaken in electricity supply.[13] The size of the investment and the potential for using such a large amount of investment for purposes like stabilisation prompted general intervention and control of electricity investment. This policy was apparently not successful in achieving its macroeconomic objectives, its main effect probably being to impose an added restriction in the industry.[14]

The macroeconomic objective of price control was not successful. However, there were some aspects of the price control that, arguably, provided a positive contribution. We are thinking of the activities of the National Board for Prices and Incomes (N.B.P.I.) which was established on 8 April, 1965, and which produced some 170 reports over the period to 29 April, 1971.[15] These reports included a number of public utilities, including coal, gas, electricity and the telephone service.[16] On balance we think these served a useful purpose. It is true that they did have a high cost in terms of managerial effort by executives and other staff in the public utilities in providing data, informing civil servants ignorant of the relevant technical and economic features of the industry under review, and in arguing and presenting their case. There was also a tendency for the N.B.P.I. to try to cover too much ground. The 170 reports in about five years speaks for itself in this regard. One consequence of this is that its impact in individual cases might have been reduced. For example, the threat of a N.B.P.I. inquiry, if it were known that such inquiries were highly rigorous, might be a spur towards X-efficiency. However, this impact would be reduced if it were felt that inquiries were brief and superficial. Fells (1972, p. 247) argues this in part:

> 'If the N.B.P.I. were purely an efficiency stimulating body, with no role in prices and incomes policy, there is little doubt in the writer's mind that it would have been preferable to have conducted fewer, deeper studies, of six months' duration, on average using interdisciplinary teams of managers, industrial relations experts, economists, statisticans, accountants, and the Enquiring Team'.

On the other hand, the N.B.P.I. did improve information and did provide a means, through press and radio coverage, of making the public better informed on economic problems of the industries. Moreover, the level of microeconomic analysis was usually reasonable and the reports themselves informative.[17] While we do not wish to evaluate the role of the N.B.P.I., we do feel that it represented an advance on the macroeconomic tinkering with the nationalised industries that happened before and after the N.B.P.I.

By contrast, the regulation of electricity supply in the U.S. has been less ambitious. Generally speaking the guidelines discussed in Chapter 8 have applied. There are a number of innovations and adaptations in U.S. regulation, however, which warrant some attention – such as reliability levels, 'life lines' and fuel-adjustment clauses.

As noted in Chapter 9, the presence of stochastic demand leaves a potential for excessive reliability in public utilities. Bates (1963) argued that electricity supply in the U.K. was excessively reliable.[18] Telson (1975) made a similar argument for U.S. electric utilities. Recently the problem of reliability has become subject to regulatory attention in the U.S. While it is not possible on the basis of current research to say much more about the reliability issue, the indications are that it is going to be increasingly important.

As we indicated earlier in this book, the basic problem in determining efficient solutions to the reliability problem is in assessing and apportioning the social costs of excess demand and associated rationing schemes. Although we hesitate to suggest additional tasks for regulatory commissions, it seems clear that they will have to deal with these issues if excess capacity is to be controlled.

The increase in utility prices and the desire of politicians to do something for lower-income groups have resulted in proposals to introduce 'life lines'. A 'life line' is an attempt to provide a subsidy to low-income groups so that they can purchase a minimum of light and heat for basic survival. One idea is to incorporate this welfare aim into the tariff by making it more expensive for medium and large consumers and less expensive for the small consumers. One method might be an increasing block tariff, for example xp for the first 100 units a month and $(x + 3)$p for the remainder plus fuel adjustments. Such devices warrant further study.

The fuel-adjustment clause is a device which allows a utility to pass on its increased fuel costs almost instantaneously to the consumer and not have to go for a formal regulatory hearing. Thus, if the price of coal increases by 20 per cent and other fuels stay constant, the electricity energy cost will increase, the precise increase depending upon the proportion of coal used, the place in the merit order of the coal plants (see Figure 10.1) and the load. Clearly the energy cost will usually not increase by anything like 20 per cent. This figure for increased energy cost is calculated by the company and then sent to the regulatory commission for approval. In New Jersey this was done with a three-month delay and the Public Utility Commission had to disallow the increase within a week or it became approved automatically. Because of the instability of this fuel cost in consumers' monthly bills, both the companies themselves and the Public Utility Commission have introduced devices to reduce instability. Some of the companies had found consumer resistance and misunderstanding when faced with a large additional item on the bill called 'fuel adjustment'. One of the devices introduced to ensure stability is called 'levelising'. The fuel-adjustment clause is fixed for a period of, say, six months. If the charge over-collects the companies' fuel costs, they have to return them over the next six months with 10 per cent interest. Such fuel-adjustment charges differ from the fuel cost-adjustment charges in the context of U.K. electricity tariffs. The latter, which are indexed with the price of fuel, may over-collect or under-collect depending on the load and merit order. The fuel-adjustment charges in the U.S., as we noted, reflect such factors as load and operating mix and therefore apparently offer no scope for the companies to make windfall losses or profits as they would if some simple formula were used. While reserving judgement, we would assess the contribution of U.S. fuel-adjustment clauses rather favourably, to the extent that they reduce the transactions costs of regulatory hearings in a period of rising fuel prices. They also have the feature of presumably reducing risk. An electric utility's cost of capital is presumably lower, to the extent that risk is reduced by its being sure of its ability to pass on increases in fuel costs outside of its control. Against this is the possibility that the opportunity of fully recovering costs may dull incentives to cost minimisation.

In the U.S. and in the U.K. more is now expected of electric utilities. The interest in life lines and reliability are examples of this. A further important example of this interest is the use by government of the utilities as instruments for government policy, particularly in the area of the environment and energy conservation. Utilities are being used as instruments of energy conservation in that they advertise electricity-saving ideas, give advice on how to save electricity by improved building insulation, and act as lenders to their consumers who wish to improve their insulation. It is not immediately obvious how well-suited utilities are to perform these tasks; nor is it clear that this is the best way to achieve government objectives on energy conservation. If the utilities have no incentive (e.g. in terms of profit) to perform these activities, it seems likely that they will under-perform them in some respects. Involving the utilities in these areas probably also serves to raise the transactions costs of regulation. While it is not possible to be conclusive, objectives of energy conservation could probably better be achieved by the construction of an optimal pricing policy, as we discuss in Chapter 11.

EXERCISES

10.1 Let $v_i = \frac{1}{3}$ for all i; reconcile Wenders's (10.9)–(10.11) results in terms of the results in Chapter 4.

10.2 Using the following table of 'annualised' capacity and energy costs from Wenders's paper, calculate the price per kW-hour for the Wenders solution using the 'values' of v_2 of Exercise 10.1:

Plant type	β_l	b_l
1	£100	£20.81
2	£40	£175.20
3	£20	£240.90

Comment on your results. (*Hint*: What did you notice about Wenders's prices in Example 10.1.)

10.3   Given that the peak demand lasts 438 hours, the intermediate demand 2628 hours, and the off peak the remainder of the year, derive 'optimal' prices using the cost data of Exercise 10.2. (*Note*: the above figures ignore transmission and distribution costs, whose marginal costs would be added to these prices.)

10.4   Costs are given in the following table:

Plant type	1	2	3
b_l	5	10	15
β_l	20	10	5

Demand and supply periods coincide, i.e. $t_1' = t_1$, $t_2' = t_2$, implying $v_3 = w_1$, and $v_3 + v_2 = w_1 + w_2$ and are of equal length.

(i) Using Lemma A and Proposition A of Chapter 4, derive optimal price and minimum total cost if demand is given by $x_1 = 30, x_2 = 40$, $x_3 = 50$.

(ii) How many solutions did you derive in solving (i)? Comment.

11 Peak-load Pricing and Energy Conservation

Over recent years the idea of an energy shortage has become a reality. The indications are that governments are likely to consider various policy alternatives increasingly in terms of their effects on energy usage. In view of such considerations it is clear that peak-load pricing will be regarded by government and regulators in terms of its contribution to energy conservation. Indeed President Carter's energy policy (1977–8) proposes time-of-day pricing and various rate reforms as devices for energy conservation. The energy shortage, and the desire for conservation, thus seems to have provided a catalyst for the reform of rate structures and the adoption of peak-load rates. A key question in this regard is therefore whether peak-load pricing contributes to energy conservation or not.

Accordingly the purpose of this chapter is to examine some of the effects that peak-load pricing might have on energy conservation. The traditional Steiner peak-load pricing theory has stressed the capacity-saving nature of the peak-load pricing solution compared to a uniform pricing policy. Indeed, this may be the only saving in the one-plant Steiner case as it is possible for more running costs to be incurred under peak-load pricing, particularly in a shifting-peak case. However, in the multi-plant case there may be substantial energy savings as a result of peak-load pricing. In Section 11.1 we explore in elementary terms some of the effects of peak-load pricing on energy conservation. In Section 11.2 we examine some of the effects of relaxing the simplifying assumptions of Section 11.1 and discuss some of the problems of incorporating peak-load pricing into electricity tariffs, including the relationship with maximum-demand charges.

11.1 A SIMPLE ANALYSIS OF PEAK-LOAD PRICING AND ENERGY CONSERVATION

Let us illustrate the role of peak-load pricing in energy conservation by means of the simplest case of two demands and two plants ($n = m = 2$).[1] We will add an additional constraint to the problem (4.2)–(4.5) of

179

Chapter 4, namely that prices are uniform over time:

$$P_1(\mathbf{x}) - P_2(\mathbf{x}) = 0. \tag{11.1}$$

Adding this constraint and forming the Lagrangian in the usual way, we obtain:

$$L = W + \sum_{i=1}^{2} \lambda_i \left(\sum_{l=1}^{m} q_{li} - x_i \right) + \sum_{i=1}^{n} \sum_{i=1}^{m} \mu_{li}(q_l - q_{li})$$
$$+ \eta(P_1(\mathbf{x}) - P_2(\mathbf{x})). \tag{11.2}$$

From (11.2) we obtain first-order conditions:

$$\mu_{l1} + \mu_{l2} \leqslant \beta_l; q_l(\mu_{l1} + \mu_{l2} - \beta_l); q_l \geqslant 0, \text{ for } l = 1, 2 \tag{11.3}$$

$$\lambda_i - \mu_{li} \leqslant b_l; q_{li}(\lambda_i - \mu_{li} - b_l) = 0; q_{li} \geqslant 0, l, i = 1, 2 \tag{11.4}$$

$$\mu_{li}(q_l - q_{li}) = 0; \mu_{li} \geqslant 0, \quad l, i = 1, 2 \tag{11.5}$$

$$P_i(\mathbf{x}) - \lambda_i + \eta \left(\frac{\partial P_1}{\partial x_i} - \frac{\partial P_2}{\partial x_i} \right) = 0, \quad i = 1, 2. \tag{11.6}$$

Assuming a firm peak with $x_2 > x_1 > 0$, Proposition A in Chapter 4 applies:

$$Q = (q_{11}, q_{21}, q_{12}, q_{22}, q_1, q_2)$$
$$= (x_1, 0, x_1, x_2 - x_1, x_1, x_2 - x_1), \tag{11.7}$$

as does Lemma A for both plants to be used, that is:

$$\frac{\beta_1 - \beta_2}{2} < b_2 - b_1 < \beta_1 - \beta_2. \tag{11.8}$$

Now from (11.7) and (11.4) we obtain:

$$\lambda_i - \mu_{li} = b_l, \text{ for all } (l, i) \text{ except } (l, i) = (2, 1). \tag{11.9}$$

From (11.7) and (11.3) we obtain:

$$\mu_{l1} + \mu_{l2} = \beta_l. \tag{11.10}$$

Since $q_{21} = 0 < q_2 = x_2 - x_1$ (11.5) implies $\mu_{21} = 0$, so that (11.9)–(11.10) yield:

$$\lambda_1 = 2b_1 + \beta_1 - (b_2 + \beta_2); \quad \lambda_2 = b_2 + \beta_2. \tag{11.11}$$

We now denote the peak-load pricing solution (i.e. the solution to the above problem (11.2) without the uniform pricing constraint (11.1)) by $\hat{p}_i$ for $i = 1, 2$. As shown in Chapter 4 and in Crew and Kleindorfer (1971), $\hat{p}_i = \lambda_i$, $i = 1, 2$, with λ_i, as in (11.11) we may rewrite (11.6) as:

$$\overline{p} - \hat{p}_1 = -\eta\left(\frac{\partial P_1}{\partial x_1} - \frac{\partial P_2}{\partial x_1}\right); \overline{p} - \hat{p}_2 = \eta\left(\frac{\partial P_1}{\partial x_2} - \frac{\partial P_2}{\partial x_2}\right),$$

(11.12)

where $\overline{p}$ is the optimal uniform price.

As $\partial P_i/\partial x_i < 0$ it follows that, if $|\partial P_i/\partial x_i| > |\partial P_i/\partial x_k|$ for $k \neq i$, $\eta > 0$ (since otherwise (11.12) implies $\hat{p}_2 < \overline{p} < \hat{p}_1$, which violates (11.8) and (11.11) since these imply $\hat{p}_1 = \lambda_1 < \lambda_2 = \hat{p}_2$).[2] In particular $\hat{p}_1 < \overline{p} < \hat{p}_2$.

Comparing uniform and peak-load pricing it is clear that welfare is less under the former than under the latter. In addition since $\overline{p} < \hat{p}_2$, it also follows that total capacity will be greater under uniform pricing, though capacity of type (e.g. nuclear) will be less under uniform pricing than under peak-load pricing.

To get an idea of the relative running and capacity costs under the two pricing schemes, suppose the demand curves are linear of the form:

$$x_1 = D_1(p_1, p_2) = d_1 - c_1 p_1 + a p_2 \tag{11.13}$$

$$x_2 = D_2(p_1, p_2) = d_2 - c_2 p_2 + a p_1, \tag{11.14}$$

where $d_2 > d_1 > 0; c_1, c_2 > 0; 0 < a < \text{Min}(c_1, c_2)$.

We note in passing that peak-load prices:

$$\hat{p}_1 = 2b_1 + \beta_1 - (b_2 + \beta_2)$$
$$\hat{p}_2 = b_2 + \beta_2$$

(11.15)

are optimal if and only if $x_2 > x_1$, i.e. if and only if:

$$d_1 - c_1[(2b_1 + \beta_1) - (b_2 + \beta_2)] + a[2(b_2 + \beta_2)$$
$$- (2b_1 + \beta_1)] - d_2 + c_2(b_2 + \beta_2) < 0. \tag{11.16}$$

Note the special case where $c_1 = c_2 = c$, $x_2 > x_1$ if and only if:

$$d_2 - d_1 > 2(a + c)[(b_2 + \beta_2) - (b_1 + \beta_1)]. \tag{11.17}$$

As we regard (11.16) as the general case and the case of practical application to energy conservation, we will now examine in detail its solution and its implications for energy conservation.

To examine the properties of the solution, we need to rewrite (11.13)–(11.14) in inverse form, i.e. as:

$$P_1(x) = \frac{c_2}{\Delta}(d_1 - x_1) + \frac{a}{\Delta}(d_2 - x_2) \tag{11.18}$$

$$P_2(x) = \frac{c_1}{\Delta}(d_2 - x_2) + \frac{a}{\Delta}(d_1 - x_1), \tag{11.19}$$

where $\Delta = c_1 c_2 - a^2 > 0$. We now rewrite (11.6), substituting for $\partial P_i / \partial x_j$ from (11.18)–(11.19), to give:

$$P_1(x) - \lambda_1 + \eta\left(\frac{-c_2}{\Delta} + \frac{a}{\Delta}\right) = 0 \tag{11.20}$$

$$P_2(x) - \lambda_2 + \eta\left(-\frac{a}{\Delta} + \frac{c_1}{\Delta}\right) = 0. \tag{11.21}$$

Now $p_1 = p_2 = \bar{p}$ and (11.11) imply:

$$\bar{p} - \hat{p}_1 = \eta\frac{c_2 - a}{\Delta} \tag{11.22}$$

$$\bar{p} - \hat{p}_2 = \eta\frac{a - c_1}{\Delta}. \tag{11.23}$$

From (11.22) and (11.23) we can note again that $\eta > 0$; otherwise (11.22)–(11.23) would imply that $\hat{p}_1 < \hat{p}_2$. For completeness we note the solution for η and $\bar{p}$:

$$\eta = \frac{\Delta}{c_1 + c_2 - 2a}(\hat{p}_2 - \hat{p}_1) \tag{11.24}$$

$$\bar{p} = \frac{c_1 - a}{c_1 + c_2 - 2a}\hat{p}_1 + \frac{c_2 - a}{c_1 + c_2 - 2a}\hat{p}_2 \tag{11.25}$$

We can easily examine the relationship between uniform price $\bar{p}$ and the interdependent demand term l. First, we substitute optimal $\hat{p}_1$ and $\hat{p}_2$ from (11.15) to (11.25) to give:

$$\bar{p} = \frac{c_1 - a}{c_1 + c_2 - 2a} \left[2b_1 + \beta_1 - (b_2 + \beta_2)\right]$$

$$+ \left[1 - \frac{c_1 - a}{c_1 + c_2 - 2a}\right](b_2 + \beta_2). \tag{11.26}$$

This reduces to:

$$\bar{p} = (b_2 + \beta_2) + \left(\frac{c_1 - a}{c_1 + c_2 - 2a}\right)[2b_1 - \beta_2 - 2(b_2 + \beta_2)].$$

$$\tag{11.27}$$

We note that the last term in (11.27) is negative by (11.8). If we differentiate (11.27) with respect to a we have:

$$\frac{\partial \bar{p}}{\partial a} = \left(\frac{c_1 - c_2}{(c_1 + c_2 - 2a)^2}\right)[2b_1 - \beta_2 - 2(b_2 + \beta_2)]. \tag{11.28}$$

The first term in (11.28) may be negative or positive. The second term is always negative, as noted above. If, however, we assume typically that $c_2 > c_1$ –as period 2 is the peak period this does not seem too unreasonable – we can argue that usually:

$$\frac{\partial \bar{p}}{\partial a} > 0, \tag{11.29}$$

which implies that as interdependence (as denoted by a) increases, the uniform price (p) will increase. This in turn implies that in the case of linear demand the benefits of peak-load pricing are more the greater the interdependence.

We may now note the implications of all this for energy conservation for the two-plant case.[3] We want the difference between running costs in the uniform and peak-load pricing cases, namely:

$$\Delta RC = [2b_1 \bar{x}_1 + b_2(\bar{x}_2 - \bar{x}_1)] - [2b_1 \hat{x}_1 + b_2(\hat{x}_2 - \hat{x}_1)]$$

$$= (2b_1 - b_2)(\bar{x}_1 - \hat{x}_1) + b_2(\bar{x}_2 - \hat{x}_2)$$

$$= (2b_1 - b_2)\left(\frac{\bar{p} - \hat{p}_1}{c_1'}\right) + b_2\left(\frac{\bar{p} - \hat{p}_2}{c_2'}\right), \tag{11.30}$$

where $c_1' = (c_1 - a)/\Delta$ and $c_2' = (c_2 - a)/\Delta$ and where barred (respectively, hatted) quantities refer to uniform (respectively, peak-load) pricing.

From (11.30) the following can be derived:[4]

$$\Delta RC = 2(b_2 - b_1)\frac{\Delta}{c_1 + c_2 - 2a}(\hat{p}_2 - \hat{p}_1) > 0. \qquad (11.31)$$

Thus running costs are greater under uniform pricing with these linear interdependent demands and, of course, with independent demands ($a = 0$). By similar reasoning it is possible to show the effects on capacity costs. The difference in capacity costs is:

$$\Delta CC = (\beta_1 - \beta_2)(\overline{x}_1 - \hat{x}_1) - \beta_2(\overline{x}_2 - \hat{x}_2) = (2\beta_2 - \beta_1)\eta \qquad (11.32)$$

Noting (see note 4) that $\hat{x}_1 - \overline{x}_1 = \overline{x}_2 - \hat{x}_2$ for all linear demands, we can see that running costs always decrease with peak-load pricing but that capacity costs may increase, decrease, or stay the same depending on the sign of $2\beta_2 - \beta_1$. This is an important result raising the possibility that capacity costs may be higher under peak-load pricing when a diverse technology is present. This contrasts strongly with traditional Steiner one-plant models (see Exercise 11.1 in this regard).

11.2 PRACTICAL TARIFFS AND ENERGY CONSERVATION

The analysis of the last section, including the linear-demand model, is useful to the extent that it raises significant questions. The results there, however, may be sensitive to changes in the basic assumptions, for example non-linearities in demand and cost structure. In this section we consider some extensions of this analysis as well as the practical implications of all of this for electricity supply.

Referring to (11.30) we note that (in this two-period case) if $2b_1 \leqslant b_2$, then peak-load pricing will always result in energy savings irrespective of whether demands are linear. The only assumption required for this to be so in the independent demand case is that demands be negative sloping. This automatically guarantees $\overline{x}_2 - \hat{x}_2 > 0, \overline{x}_1 - \hat{x}_1 < 0$. Where demands are interdependent, slightly more assumptions are required to guarantee the signs of $\overline{x}_i - \hat{x}_i$ above.[5]

We can easily illustrate the above remarks with an example of two periods and two plants, where peak demand is linear and off-peak demand is concave. This arrangement has the potential for making

$\hat{x}_1 - x_1 > \overline{x}_2 - \hat{x}_2$, because the peak decreases linearly but the off-peak increases exponentially with a rise in peak price and a fall in off-peak price. We have two demand curves:

$$P_1(x_1) = 100e^{-0.25x_1} \tag{11.33}$$

$$P_2(x_2) = 200 - 10x_2. \tag{11.34}$$

We have costs of $b_1 = 1.4, b_2 = 2; \beta_1 = 3, \beta_2 = 2$. These imply peak-load prices of $p_1 = 1.8, p_2 = 4$; uniform price $\overline{p} = 2.68$, and outputs of $\hat{x}_1 = 16.07, \hat{x}_2 = 19.60, \overline{x}_1 = 14.47, \overline{x}_2 = 19.73$. We note that x_1 increases substantially and x_2 only decreases by a small amount with peak-load pricing. The net effect is that running-cost savings are negative with peak-load pricing. (This can be seen by plugging in the above figures in (11.30) to give $\Delta RC = -1.014$.) On the other hand, even with these demands, if costs had been different, for example, $b_1 = 8, b_2 = 2$, $\beta_1 = 4, \beta_2 = 2$, then peak-load pricing would have led to savings in running costs.

Accordingly peak-load pricing would seem to offer the prospect of energy conservation in a wide variety of situations. There are problems, however, with its practical implementation in electricity supply. One problem is the fact that there are not just two price–demand periods of equal length but many, leading to the problems of pricing complexity discussed in Chapter 4. These theoretical problems are simple, however, compared with the problems of metering such complex tariffs. Currently, time-of-day tariffs have got to be relatively simple, having only two or three periods during the day, with seasonal differentials, and perhaps week-end differentials. With the advance in semi-conductors, electronic metering may permit more sophistication, but in the immediate future relatively simple tariffs have to be assigned because of limitations in metering technology. In addition consumer acceptance and/or understanding might be a problem if the new tariffs were more complicated.

The need to keep tariffs fairly simple creates problems in itself; these we illustrate with a simple case. Imagine that there are three equal-length periods, but that constraints on complexity require that only two prices for two equal-length periods be used. This is illustrated in Figure 11.1, where the solid line shows demands given uniform pricing. The effect of, say, charging a peak price for 0–12 hours is to reduce both peak and off-peak demand in kW.

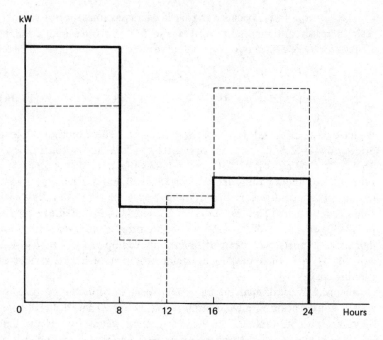

Fig. 11.1

The demand is shown by the dashed line. By having an off-peak price in period 12–24 hours we get an increase in off-peak demand from 12–16 hours and an increase in 'shoulder' demand from 16–24 hours to the level above the peak. It is this kind of problem that could occur and that worries electric utilities. Indeed, when there are more demand periods than pricing periods, the phenomenon known as 'needle-peaking' can occur, namely a peak of short duration within the peak period. It is concern with problems like this that has prompted the Virginia Electric and Power Company (VEPCO) to introduce maximum-demand rates into their tariffs. VEPCO's argument is as follows:

> as to the inclusion of a demand charge in the prototype rate, such a charge is theoretically desirable for two reasons: first, the cost-causation element of load factor should be recognised, and, second, without such a charge, the per-kilowatt-hour 'inclusive rate' would be so high as to foster needle-peaking, i.e., reducing peak-season usage without materially reducing peak demand on the hot, hot day (Electric Utility Rate Design Study, 6 June 1977).

Thus, even if energy conservation is served via peak-load pricing, this could well be at the cost of poor capacity utilisation relative to, say, uniform pricing with maximum-demand charges (or peak-load pricing with maximum-demand charges). However, the desirability of maximum-demand charges is not generally agreed upon. For example, Wenders and Taylor (1976), p. 535 presented the following views recently:

We shall consider two different tariff structures, namely:
(1) A fixed customer charge plus a charge for peak kW for capacity costs plus a kWh charge for energy.
(2) A fixed customer charge, plus a single kWh charge for energy and capacity that varies by time of day.

Of the two pricing schemes, the second is clearly [more] desirable in the abstract since it is a direct approximation of peak-load pricing. The first is non-optimal in that it does not take into account the fact that individual peak demands are not necessarily coincident with the system peak. Indeed whether it leads to welfare improvement over the present practices is problematical.

We show below that maximum-demand charges are efficient in certain cases and, moreover, not levying maximum-demand charges may be inefficient, so that the efficiency of such charges does not rest on distributional considerations alone. While we note that all of this is diametrically opposed to the Wenders and Taylor position cited above, we hasten to add that little research has been done on this issue and that our results are merely illustrative, leaving room for justifiable caution in implementing maximum-demand tariffs.

We will proceed by way of example. Given the controversy surrounding maximum-demand charges and the lack of general results, we felt it desirable to work out some examples in detail. Our first example considers three consumer classes having demands for electricity in three periods. The preferences for these different classes are in terms of electricity supplied in each of the periods (x_1, x_2, x_3) and money (m) spent on other goods. These preferences are represented by the utility functions:

$$\text{Class 1: } U_1(x_1, x_2, x_3, m) = (\sqrt{x_1} + c\sqrt{x_2})m \qquad (11.35)$$

$$\text{Class 2: } U_2(x_1, x_2, x_3, m) = (\sqrt{x_1} + c\sqrt{x_3})m \qquad (11.36)$$

$$\text{Class 3: } U_3(x_1, x_2, x_3, m) = (\sqrt{x_2} + c\sqrt{x_3})m \qquad (11.37)$$

where $c > 1$ is a parameter identical for all classes. We see from (11.35)–(11.37) that there is a certain degree of substitution between electricity consumption and m (which enters linearly).

We now assume that the following tariff structure obtains. Price p_1 per unit is charged in period 1; price p_2 per unit is charged throughout periods 2 and 3; and a maximum-demand charge of K per unit of each individual's maximum demand may be charged. We are interested in deriving efficient prices p_1, p_2, K for the above classes of consumers and for a profit-maximising producer. To do this we first need the indirect utility functions $V_j(p_1, p_2, K, M)$ for each class, where M represents the budget constraint, and:

$$V_j(p_1, p_2, K, M) = \{\text{Max } U_j(x_1, x_2, x_3, m) | K \max[x_1, x_2, x_3]$$

$$+ p_1 x_1 + p_2(x_2 + x_3) + m \leqslant M\}. \tag{11.38}$$

The solution to (11.38) is obtained readily for U_j, i.e., as given in (11.35)–(11.37), and is provided by the following (see Exercise 11.2):

$$V_1(p_1, p_2, K, M) = V_2(p_1, p_2, K, M)$$

$$= \tfrac{2}{9} M^2 \left(\frac{3(c^2 p_1 + p_2 + K)}{M p_1 (p_2 + K)} \right)^{1/2}$$

$$\text{if } c p_1 \geqslant p_2 + K$$

$$= \tfrac{2}{9} M^2 \left(\frac{3(p_2 + c^2(p_1 + K))}{M p_2 (p_1 + K)} \right)^{1/2}$$

$$\text{if } c(p_1 + K) \leqslant p_2$$

$$= \tfrac{2}{9} M^2 \left(\frac{3(1 + c)^2}{M(p_1 + p_2 + K)} \right)^{1/2}$$

$$\text{if } \frac{p_2}{c} - K \leqslant p_1 \leqslant \frac{p_2 + K}{c}, \tag{11.39}$$

and:

$$V_3(p_1, p_2, K, M) = \tfrac{2}{9} M^2 \left(\frac{3(p_2(1 + c^2) + K)}{M p_2 (p_2 + K)} \right)^{1/2}$$

$$\text{if } cp_2 \geqslant p_2 + K$$

$$= \tfrac{2}{5}M^2\left(\frac{3(1+c)^2}{M(2p_2 + K)} \right)^{1/2}$$

$$\text{if } cp_2 \leqslant p_2 + K \tag{11.40}$$

To obtain the profit function we assume a simple technology with proportional running and capacity costs b and β respectively. Profits for the above preference structure may then be expressed as:

$$\Pi(p_1, p_2, K) = (p_1 - b)\left(\sum_{j=1}^{3} x_{1j} \right) + (p_2 - b)\left(\sum_{j=1}^{3}(x_{2j} + x_{3j}) \right)$$

$$+ K \sum_{j=1}^{3} \text{Max}\,[x_{ij}, x_{2j}, x_{3j}] - \beta \,\text{Max}\left[\sum_{j=1}^{3} x_{1j}, \sum_{j=1}^{3} x_{2j}, \sum_{j=1}^{3} x_{3j} \right],$$

$$\tag{11.41}$$

where $x_{ij} = x_{ij}(p_1, p_2, K, M)$ is the demand from class j in period i and can be verified to be (see Exercise 11.2):

$$x_{31} = x_{22} = x_{13} = 0 \tag{11.42}$$

$$x_{11} = x_{12} = \begin{cases} \dfrac{M}{3p_1}\left[\dfrac{p_2 + K}{c^2 p_1 + p_2 + K} \right] & \text{if } cp_1 \geqslant p_2 + K \\[2ex] \dfrac{M}{3(p_1 + K)}\left[\dfrac{p_2}{p_2 + c^2(p_1 + K)} \right] \\[1ex] & \text{if } c(p_1 + K) \leqslant p_2 \\[2ex] \dfrac{M}{3(p_1 + p_2 + K)} & \text{if } \dfrac{p_2}{c} - K \leqslant p_1 \\[2ex] & \leqslant \dfrac{p_2 + K}{c} \quad (11.43) \end{cases}$$

$$x_{21} = x_{32} = \begin{cases} \dfrac{M}{3(p_2 + K)} \left[\dfrac{c^2 p_1}{c^2 p_1 + (p_2 + K)} \right] \\ \qquad\qquad\qquad\qquad \text{if } cp_1 \geqslant p_2 + K \\[2ex] \dfrac{M}{3p_2} \left[\dfrac{c^2(p_1 + K)}{c^2(p_1 + K) + p_2} \right] \text{if } c(p_1 + K) \leqslant p_2 \\[2ex] \dfrac{M}{3(p_1 + p_2 + K)} \qquad \text{if } \dfrac{p_2}{c} - K \leqslant p_1 \\[2ex] \qquad\qquad\qquad\qquad \leqslant \dfrac{p_2 + K}{c} \qquad (11.44) \end{cases}$$

$$x_{23} = \begin{cases} \dfrac{M}{3p_2} \left[\dfrac{p_2 + K}{p_2(1 + c^2) + K} \right] \text{if } cp_2 \geqslant p_2 + K \\[2ex] \dfrac{M}{3(2p_2 + K)} \qquad\qquad \text{if } cp_2 \leqslant p_2 + K \end{cases}$$

$$(11.45)$$

$$x_{33} = \begin{cases} \dfrac{M}{3(p_2 + K)} \left[\dfrac{c^2 p_2}{p_2(1 + c^2) + K} \right] \\ \qquad\qquad\qquad\qquad \text{if } cp_2 \geqslant p_2 + K \\[2ex] \dfrac{M}{3(2p_2 + K)} \qquad\quad \text{if } cp_2 \leqslant p_2 + K \end{cases}$$

$$(11.46)$$

To determine efficient prices we must solve the following problem for pre-specified weights $\alpha_1, \alpha_2, \alpha_3, \alpha_4 > 0$:

$$\max_{p_1, p_2, K \geqslant 0} \left(\sum_{j=1}^{3} \alpha_j V_j(p_1, p_2, K, M_j) + \alpha_4 \Pi(p_1, p_2, K) \right),$$

$$(11.47)$$

where V_j and Π are as in (11.39)–(11.41).

Although it may not be apparent, the functions V_j and Π, as well as the consumer demands x_{ij}, are all continuous and well-behaved and readily allow numerical solutions for the problem (11.47). For example, for the case:

$$M_1 = M_2 = 1, M_3 = 2, c = 2, b = 1, \beta = 3, \alpha_i = 0.25, \text{ for all } i,$$
$$(11.48)$$

the optimal solution to (11.47) is:

$$p_1 = 1.306, p_2 = K = 1.389, z = 0.242 \qquad (11.49)$$

$$x_{31} = x_{22} = x_{13} = 0; x_{11} = x_{12} = x_{21} = x_{32} = 0.082;$$

$$x_{23} = x_{33} = 0.16 \qquad (11.50)$$

As a second example consider the following utility functions in place of (11.35)–(11.37):

$$U_1(x_1, x_2, x_3, m) = m \sqrt{(x_1 + cx_2)} \qquad (11.51)$$

$$U_2(x_1, x_2, x_3, m) = m \sqrt{(x_1 + cx_3)} \qquad (11.52)$$

$$U_3(x_1, x_2, x_3, m) = m \sqrt{(x_2 + cx_3)}. \qquad (11.53)$$

Substitutability across periods is now increased. Indeed (as we ask the reader to verify in Exercise 11.3), when $K = 0$ and $cp_1 < p_2$, consumer classes 1 and 2 only make demands in period 1, while consumer class 3 makes demands only in period 3 (since price p_2 is uniform in periods 2 and 3 and $K = 0$). When, however, $K = 0$ and $cp_1 > p_2$, consumer classes 1 and 2 only make demands in period 2 and 3 respectively, while consumer class 3 only makes demands in period 3. Thus needle-peaking occurs when $K = 0$. For $cp_1 < p_2$ nothing is demanded in period 2, while $cp_1 > p_2$ implies nothing is demanded in period 1. (When $cp_1 = p_2$ there is a certain indeterminacy which we do not discuss here.) By considering different income distributions the size of the needle peak can be made arbitrarily large. Clearly $K = 0$ is not Pareto efficient in this case. Energy conservation is also served here by having $K > 0$, since otherwise more inefficient peaking plant will be kept available to meet needle peaks with resulting energy losses.

The above examples indicate that maximum-demand charges may not be ruled out as inefficient, especially when diversity and substitution possibilities are large. In effect maximum-demand charges allow each consumer group to self-select their peak period while none the less providing the right signal to each group as to the social costs of peak demand. In the absence of such maximum-demand charges, however, one or other of these groups could avoid the peak charge by shifting demand to their next most preferred period, with possibly deleterious aggregate effects. Of course, if there were no diversity (identical preferences), or if demands were time inelastic (no period substitution effects), then one could accomplish the same efficient demand manipulation via simple peak-load pricing. Such empirical evidence[6] as there is available on European experience with peak-load pricing suggests, however, that while significant changes in system utilisation can take place with peak-load pricing, controlling the time shifts in demand in response to peak-load pricing is also a problem. From the point of view of recovering costs as well as in providing appropriate price incentives to consumers, therefore, it may well be that maximum-demand charges are desirable ingredients of practical peak-load tariffs.

The above analysis hardly scratches the surface with respect to either energy conservation or the theory of maximum-demand charges. For example, analyses of uncertainty and dynamic effects would be interesting extensions of the above discussion. All of this awaits further research. In any case the energy-conservation effects of peak-load pricing, whether alone or in combination with maximum-demand charges, result from increasing the system load factor, thus increasing the running efficiency of the corresponding optimal plant mix as we discussed in Chapter 10. According to recent European experience such efficiency increases can be substantial (see Acton, Manning and Mitchell, 1978).

EXERCISES

11.1 For independent linear demands $p_i(x_i) = c_i x_i + d_i$, $i = 1, 2$, and costs as in (11.8), answer the following:

(i) Solve for η and $\bar{p}$.

(ii) Show that η is positive.

(iii) Note that this is a special case of (11.24)–(11.25).

(iv) Show that running costs are greater under uniform pricing.

(v) What happens to capacity costs under uniform pricing?

(vi) If we have only plant 1, how do capacity and running costs compare under peak-load and uniform pricing?

11.2 Verify equations (11.39)–(11.46) by solving the following problem, using Kuhn–Tucker theory:

$$\text{Max}\,[m\,\sqrt{x} + c\,\sqrt{y})]\,,$$

subject to:

$$Kz + p'x + p''y + m = M$$

$$0 \leqslant x \leqslant z, 0 \leqslant y \leqslant z.$$

(The constraints $x \leqslant z$, $y \leqslant z$ will at optimum imply $z = \text{Max}(x, y)$.) Note that, for example, for consumer class 1 translation of these results in deriving demands and indirect utility functions would have $x = x_1$, $y = x_2$, $p' = p_1$, $p'' = p_2$, while for consumer class 3 the appropriate translation would be $x = x_2$, $y = x_3$, $p' = p'' = p_2$.

11.3 Consider the utility functions (11.51)–(11.53). Analogously to Exercise 11.2, derive the indirect utility functions for each class and analyse efficient pricing policies by solving the corresponding problem to (11.47) for this case. Show, in particular, that the consumer demands are given by:

$$x_{13} = x_{22} = x_{31} = 0, \text{always}$$

$$x_{11} = x_{12} = x', x_{21} = x_{32} = 0, \text{if } c(p_1 + K) < p_2$$

$$x_{11} = x_{12} = 0, x_{21} = x_{32} = x'', \text{if } cp_1 < p_2 + K$$

$$x_{11} = x_{12} = x_{21} = x_{32} = x''', \text{if } \frac{p_2}{c} - K < p_1 < \frac{p_2 + K}{c}$$

$$x_{23} = 0, x_{33} = x'', \text{if } p_2 + K < cp_2$$

$$x_{23} = x_{33} = y, \text{if } p_2 + K > cp_2,$$

where:

$$x' = \frac{M}{3(p_1 + K)}, x'' = \frac{M}{3(p_2 + K)}, x''' = \frac{M}{3(p_1 + p_2 + K)},$$

$$y = \frac{M}{3(2p_2 + K)}.$$

Thus verify that 'needle-peaking' occurs in this case.

12 Concluding Remarks

Our treatment of public utilities has been more analytical than most previous studies. As a result we have been able to develop and extend the theoretical basis of several major problem areas like the peak-load problem and the problem of regulation. Our treatment, in aiming to achieve depth in certain areas, meant that we had to sacrifice some of the broadness in coverage that tends to typify previous texts on public utilities. In these concluding remarks we mention some of the areas which we have not covered and discuss the significance of our approach for their future study.

In Section 12.1 we summarise the peak-load pricing theory and discuss some of its applications. In Section 12.2 we discuss briefly our treatment of regulation and our views of the regulatory problem. In Section 12.3 we suggest some avenues for future research. Throughout this chapter we are presenting our personal views of the subject and not attempting to assess alternative approaches and possibilities.

12.1 THEORY AND APPLICATIONS OF PEAK-LOAD PRICING

In Part Two we provided a rigorous treatment of the theory of peak-load pricing. We described the major contributions and were able to extend the treatment of unequal-length periods and other detailed matters. Our substantive contributions concerned multiple-plant operation and stochastic demand. This enabled us to deal with more complicated and important peak-load problems, as well as to answer several important questions. For example, we were able to indicate the extent to which stochastic problems could be approximated by deterministic models. We were able to focus on the problem of reliability including its implications for efficient pricing and regulation. Our treatment indicated the importance of peak-load pricing and the prospects of its widespread application.

Currently the use of peak-load pricing is increasing in utilities and elsewhere. Telephone utilities, at least in the U.S. and the U.K., have had in use a fairly sophisticated system of peak-load pricing. In the U.S. it applies most strongly to inter-state calls where three rates prevail, with the peak rates applying during daytime on weekdays. In the U.K. the system is more developed, with peak-load pricing applying to all calls, whether local or long distance, and with, on weekdays, day time being divided into a peak rate (currently from 09.00 hours to 13.00 hours) and a standard rate, with a cheap rate from 18.00 hours to 08.00 hours. Telephone utilities have begun to develop a certain sophistication over rates as a result of such tariffs and are aware of factors like elasticity according to time of day. No doubt this sophistication in telephone rates will continue, in view of the potentially great benefits it offers, and the rather low metering costs compared to other utilities. In the U.S. it seems that extensions of peak-load pricing to inter-state and local calling are also likely.

Peak-load pricing will be extended to electricity utilities and, possibly, gas utilities. As we indicated in Chapters 10 and 11, a major effort is currently being undertaken to introduce peak-load pricing on a more general basis in electricity supply. In view of the contribution that peak-load pricing can make to energy conservation, government and regulatory commissions are likely to encourage this trend. In addition it may have substantial advantages for the utilities themselves, especially those that have invested heavily in nuclear energy, with the resultant need to raise load factors. On the negative side the utilities will have to overcome some high metering costs if peak-load pricing is adopted, and this could stall its widespread extension in the U.S. This is especially true if the technology in alternative metering and monitoring increases more rapidly than the peak-load metering technology. For example, ripple control or some other method of controlling the consumer's load on major appliances like air-conditioning or water-heating may provide an alternative to peak-load pricing.

There is also scope for application of peak-load pricing in other industries. Airlines have some of the characteristics of public utilities and are increasingly turning to forms of peak-load pricing and price discrimination in an effort to improve load factors. Possiblilities for peak-load pricing also exist amongst other service industries, like hotels and car-rental firms. With the growth of the service sector these applications may be of increasing importance. Another application is peak-load pricing in computer systems and related telecommunications systems.

Currently some combination of peak-load pricing and queuing operates on such systems. Alternative possibilities for peak-load pricing systems with stochastic demands seem likely to offer further benefits in this area.

Peak-load pricing has thus arrived and it promises significant potential for improving efficiency of capacity utilisation and energy conservation. This will make it of increasing interest to utilities, other industries and to government, as well as providing a fertile area for applied economic research.

12.2   THE FUTURE OF REGULATION

Our analysis of regulation was mainly concerned with the current state of the regulatory economic theory as embodied in the Averch–Johnson effect, the effects of peak load, stochastic demand and reliability on regulation, and the theoretical consequences of alternative motivational assumptions on the regulated firm. We also looked at some new perspectives in regulation, particularly some elementary considerations of the theory of incentives, and the organisational-failures framework. The approach led to some dissatisfaction on our part with the current state of regulation, with the feeling that the issues surrounding regulation are highly complex and the current framework is ill-suited to deal with the demands placed upon it.

The emphasis of both regulatory research and policy seems possibly to be misplaced. In examining the issues of reliability and managerial motivation in the regulated public utility we hope that we have indicated the desirability of turning away from increasing refinements of the A–J effect to more pressing problems of public utilities. The problem of reliability warrants further attention by regulators and researchers as it clearly offers scope for utilities to escape some of the consequences of regulation. Recent interest by regulatory commissions in reliability seems to bear this out.

Our concern with regulation is not just at the academic level but is also at the level of policy. Too much seems to be expected of the regulatory apparatus with conflicting ends that are not adequately dealt with in the existing structure. Government is not clear what it expects of regulation. While we are not in favour of considerations of fairness and equity being placed outside the role of commissions, we think that the primary aim of regulation should be to provide an alternative to the efficiency provided by the spur of competition. We have stressed, along with others like Averch and Johnson, that inefficiency is a problem in public utility monopolies, and that this inefficiency can take many forms. It is here that commissions have a primary role to play. They should be spared that political interference which turns them away from the primary task of improving efficiency. For example, some politicians are in favour of so-called 'life-line' tariffs. These are an attempt to have the small consumer subsidised by the large consumer. In some cases it may mean that consumers face increasing block tariffs, whereby the price they pay rises as their consumption increases. Apparently this offers an almost painless way for politicians to help those on low incomes avoid some of the increased energy charges by making the larger consumers pay more. Unfortunately such cross-subsidisation may have inefficiency consequences which make it undesirable. It may be inconsistent to offer life-line rates and pursue a policy of energy conservation. More needs to be known about the load pattern of small consumers compared with those who are to subsidise them. It may be that the effect of such a rate, in the absence of peak-load pricing, is to exacerbate the system peak. Small consumers may consume more at the peak and the large consumers may make most of their reduction in demand in off-peak periods, depending on the elasticity. Moreover, some large consumers may have low incomes. This could occur with electricity if low-income consumers used electric water-heating, which seems possible in veiw of the low capital cost of electric water-heating. Thus such rates may fail the test of equity as well as efficiency. In this case commissions could be concerned with fairness to the extent that they provide government with information on the alternatives, like income subsidies, on loans and grants towards home insulation to help persons on low incomes with increasing energy costs.

Our suggestion that commissions make efficiency their main concern is not our only problem with regulation. We are concerned about the effect it has on incentives and the rather high transactions costs of the present system. It consists basically of approving, disapproving or (more usually) modifying proposals by companies for a rate structure that aims to produce a rate of return approved by the commission. This approach has the high transactions costs of hearings, expenditure by companies on making a case, including top-management time, and it is not clear that it results in the gains in efficiency, equity or whatever that is expected of it. We would therefore like to see an effort to reduce the transactions costs of regulation and increase the incentives towards efficiency by the utilities. This might be done by first having the commissions concentrate on efficiency. Second, the present structure should be modified; the hearing system currently in operation should become a last resort. In its place a system of targets set by the commission for prices, taking into account the technological change expected, could be adopted. The companies would be free to set their prices within these targets. Where the companies achieved better than average performance, they would be free to continue without a hearing. The commission would meanwhile monitor the performance of the utilities and have some system of putting 'on notice' utilities not performing according to the targets. Setting targets would be difficult, particularly at first. They could be fraught with errors. If they were too high, then the utilities would be able to some extent to expolit their monopoly power. If they were too low, then the utilities would seek a hearing. While either situation would be unsatisfactory, it would have the main difference from the current situation of getting away from rate of return as the centre-piece of regulation with its resulting unfavourable effects on incentives and efficiency.

12.3 DIRECTIONS FOR FUTURE RESEARCH

We see public utility economics as a potentially fruitful area of research, particularly in terms of empirical work and application. We list below a few of the promising possibilities:

(1) Peak-load pricing would appear to offer considerable benefits in terms of energy conservation. This would include some theoretical research to determine, for example in terms of elasticities and cost functions, the benefits that will ensue from peak-load pricing. In addition the role of extensions like maximum-demand charges also seem to be a promising area of theoretical study.

On the applications side, measuring demands, elasticities and costs will be an important input in the design of peak-load rate structures. It is hoped that the studies now being undertaken will provide significant advances in this area.

(2) Alternatives to peak-load pricing, like interruptable supplies and central control of individual loads, warrant theoretical study, especially in dealing with the problem of stochastic demand and reliability. Reli-

ability, itself, is a fruitful area of study, particularly for its interaction with regulation.

(3) It has long been recognised that technological change is of considerable importance. As a result of recent work employing the organisational failures framework and the theory of incentives, the importance of innovation in organisations is becoming increasingly recognised. Regulation provides an opportunity for organisational innovation to be put to good use. Arguably the current system has not kept pace with the advances in the utilities it aims to regulate. The task would be formidable, requiring extensions to theory as well as to empirical work, but the rewards could be significant. In a more traditional framework the dynamic theory of the regulated firm is still very much in its infancy. This would also offer some promising possibilities. However, it seems desirable that much research should proceed in tandem with the developments in the organisational-failures/incentives framework.

In this concluding chapter we have been free with our personal views on public utility economics, especially our views on policy. We expect them to be fairly controversial. Time and more research will make it possible to judge their significance.

Mathematical Appendix

This appendix provides an introduction to, and a summary of, key mathematical tools used in this book. Three sections are provided: (i) set theory and probability; (ii) mathematical programming; and (iii) control theory. Intentionally the treatment is very brief, and the reader who finds some discomfort with the results or examples here should consult more exhaustive treatises, for example Feller (1966, 1968) for probability theory, Zangwill (1969) for mathematical programming, and Arrow and Kurz (1970, ch. 2) for control theory.

SET THEORY AND PROBABILITY

Let $X, Y, N, \ldots$ denote sets. A set X may be specified exhaustively (e.g. $X = \{x_1, x_2, x_3\}$ is the set containing the elements x_1, x_2, x_3) or through some defining property (e.g. $X = \{x \mid x$ satisfies $P\}$ means X is the set of all x satisfying the property P). The following standard notation is used:

$x \in X$ (respectively, $x \notin X$) means x belongs (respectively, does not belong) to the set X;

$X \subset Y$ Means the set X is a subset of the set Y;

The set of (respectively, non-negative) real numbers is denoted by the symbol $\mathcal{R}$ (respectively, $\mathcal{R}_+$);

The set of (respectively, non-negative) m-vectors is denoted by the symbol $\mathcal{R}^n$ (respectively, $\mathcal{R}^n_+$); for $\mathbf{x} = (x_1, \ldots, x_n) \in \mathcal{R}^n$ we denote:

$$\sum_{i=1}^{n} x_i = x_1 + x_2 + ,,, + x_n.$$

For $a \in \mathcal{R}, b \in \mathcal{R}, a < b$, we denote the sets:

$$[a, b] = \{x \in \mathcal{R} \mid a \leqslant x \leqslant b\}$$
$$[a, b) = \{x \in \mathcal{R} \mid a \leqslant x < b\}$$
$$(a, b] = \{x \in \mathcal{R} \mid a < x \leqslant b\}$$
$$(a, b) = \{x \in \mathcal{R} \mid a < x < b\}.$$

For sets X, Y we denote a function f from X to Y by $f\colon X \to Y$; we assume the reader's familiarity with the concepts of continuity and differentiability; when $f\colon \mathcal{R} \to \mathcal{R}$, we denote the derivative of f by f' (i.e. $f'(x) = df(x)/dx$).

Turning to probability theory, when $\widetilde{u}$ is a (real-valued) random variable, we use the notation: $F(u) = \mathrm{Prob}\{\widetilde{u} < u\}$, for $u \in \mathcal{R}$, is the cumulative distribution function (C.D.F.) of $\widetilde{u}$; $f(u)$ is the probability density function (P.D.F.) of $\widetilde{u}$ (if such exists) so that $F(u) = \int_{\infty}^{u} f(y)dy$ and $f(u) = F'(u)$;

The expected value $E\{\widetilde{u}\}$ is usually written in Laplace–Stieltjes form as $E\{u\} = \int_{-\infty}^{\infty} u \, dF(u)$; when $\widetilde{u}$ has a P.D.F., which the reader may assume throughout, we also write $E\{\widetilde{u}\} = \int_{-\infty}^{\infty} u f(u)du$, an ordinary integral;

When $g\colon \mathcal{R} \to \mathcal{R}$ we note the following rule for computing the expected value of the random variable $g(\widetilde{u})$:

$$Eg(\widetilde{u}) = \int_{-\infty}^{\infty} g(u)dF(u) = \int_{-\infty}^{\infty} g(u)f(u)du.$$

Example: Let $D(p, \widetilde{u}) = \widetilde{u} X(p)$ be a demand function depending on mean demand $X(p)$ (p is price) and a random variable $\widetilde{u}$. Let z represent capacity. A typical problem is to compute the expected excess demand, call this ED, for given p and z. From above:

$$ED = E(\mathrm{Max}\,[D(p, \widetilde{u})] - z, 0)$$

$$= \int_{-\infty}^{\infty} (\mathrm{Max}\,[D(p, u) - z, 0])f(u)du$$

$$= \int_{-\infty}^{\infty} \mathrm{Max}\,[uX(p) - z, 0]\,f(u)du$$

$$= \int_{z/X(p)}^{\infty} [uX(p) - z]\,f(u)du,$$

since $\mathrm{Max}\,[uX(p) - z, 0] = 0$ precisely when $u \leqslant z/X(p)$. When, for example, $\widetilde{u}$ is a uniform random variable on $[1 - r, 1 + r]$ ($r \leqslant 1$), we have $f(u) = 1/2r$ for $u \in [1 - r, 1 + r]$ and $f(u) = 0$ elsewhere, so the above reduces to:

$$ED = \begin{cases} X(p) - z & \text{if } z/X(p) \leqslant 1 - r \\[2mm] \int_{z/X(p)}^{1+r} \dfrac{(uX(p) - z)}{2r}\,du & \text{if } 1 - r < z/X(p) \leqslant 1 + r \\[2mm] 0 & \text{if } z/X(p) > 1 + r. \end{cases}$$

Frequently it is useful to be able to differentiate integrals like ED above with respect to variables other than the variable of integration (e.g. with respect to p and z). We recall the following result: let $f(u)$ be bounded and $a(t)$, $b(t)$ and $g(u, t)$ be continuously differentiable with respect to t for almost every $u \in \mathcal{R}$ (i.e. for $u \in U \subset \mathcal{R}$, where the set U satisfies $Pr\{\tilde{u} \in U\} = 1$) with $\partial g(u, t)/\partial t$ bounded whenever it exists. Then:

$$\frac{d}{dt}\left(\int_{a(t)}^{b(t)} g(u, t)f(u)du\right) = \int_{a(t)}^{b(t)} \frac{\partial g(u, t)}{\partial t}f(u)du$$

$$+ b'(t)g(b(t), t)f(b(t)) - a'(t)g(a(t), t)f(a(t)).$$

In particular:

$$\frac{d}{dt} E\{g(\tilde{u}, t)\} \frac{d}{dt} \int_{-\infty}^{\infty} g(u, t)f(u)du = \int_{-\infty}^{\infty} \frac{\partial g(u, t)}{t}f(u)du$$

$$= E\left\{\frac{\partial}{\partial t} g(\tilde{u}, t)\right\}.$$

Example: For the above example with $\tilde{u}$ uniformly distributed, the reader may compute:

$$\frac{\partial ED}{\partial z} = \begin{cases} -1 & \text{if } z/X(p) \leqslant 1 - r \\ \frac{1}{2r}\left(\frac{z}{X(p)} - (1 + r)\right) & \text{if } 1 - r \leqslant z/X(p) \leqslant 1 + r \\ 0 & \text{if } z/X(p) \geqslant 1 + r. \end{cases}$$

Note here that $g(u, t) = \text{Max}[uX(p) - z, 0]$ is not everywhere differentiable, but only *almost* everywhere differentiable.

MATHEMATICAL PROGRAMMING

Let $X \subset \mathcal{R}^n$, $f: X \to \mathcal{R}$, $g: X \to \mathcal{R}^n$. Then the general problem of interest in mathematical programming is the following:

$$\text{Max}\{f(\mathbf{x}) | \mathbf{x} \in X, g(\mathbf{x}) \geqslant 0\}. \tag{A.1}$$

The meaning of (A.1) is that an $\mathbf{x}$ is to be found which maximises $f(\mathbf{x})$ in the class of all $\mathbf{x} \in X$ which satisfy $g(\mathbf{x}) \in \mathcal{R}^n_+$. An important sub-class of such problems are 'linear programmes' where $X = \mathcal{R}^n_+$ and f and g are linear. Another important class of optimisation problems is that of unconstrained optimisation theory where X is all of $\mathcal{R}^n$ and g is identically zero (i.e. effectively there are no constraints). In this case the well-known necessary conditions for a point $\hat{x} = (x_1, \ldots, x_n) \in \mathcal{R}^n$ to be optimal are that $\partial f(x)/\partial x_i$ (i.e. $\partial f/\partial x_i$ evaluated at $\hat{x}$) should be zero for all $i = 1, \ldots, n$.

By far the most important result from mathematical programming for this book is the Kuhn-Tucker theorem, which we state here for reference.

KUHN-TUCKER THEOREM. Consider the problem:

$$\text{Max } f(\mathbf{x}), \tag{A.2}$$

subject to:

$$g_i(\mathbf{x}) \geqslant 0, i = 1, \ldots, m \tag{A.3}$$

$$h_j(\mathbf{x}) = 0, j = 1, \ldots, k \tag{A.4}$$

$$\mathbf{x} = (x_1, \ldots, x_n) \geqslant 0, \tag{A.5}$$

where $\mathbf{x} \in \mathcal{R}^n$ and where all functions are real-valued and continuously differentiable.

Let $\hat{x}$ be an optimal solution to the above problem and assume the constraint qualification holds (this is discussed below). Then the following three conditions hold:

$$\hat{x} \text{ satisfies (A.3), (A.4), (A.5).} \tag{A.6}$$

There exists real numbers $\lambda_i \geqslant 0$, $i = 1, \ldots, m$, and $\mu_j, j = 1, \ldots, k$ (sometimes called Lagrange multipliers) such that:

$$\lambda_i g_i(\hat{x}) = 0, i = 1, \ldots, m \tag{A.7}$$

$$\frac{L(\hat{x}, \lambda, \mu)}{\partial x_i} \leqslant 0, x_i \left[\frac{\partial L(\hat{x}, \lambda, \mu)}{\partial x_i} \right] = 0, i = 1, \ldots, n, \tag{A.8}$$

where $L(\hat{x}, \lambda, \mu)$ is defined by:

$$L(\mathbf{x}, \lambda, \mu) = (f(\mathbf{x}) + \sum_{i=1}^{n} \lambda_i g(\mathbf{x}) + \sum_{j=1}^{k} \mu_j h_j(\mathbf{x})). \tag{A.9}$$

Remarks: The Kuhn-Tucker constraint qualification (C.Q.) referred to above essentially rules out 'cusps' in the constraint set. It is always satisfied when the constraint functions g_i and h_j are linear, or at least define a convex region with non-empty interior. We will always assume C.Q. to be satisfied.

A further point of interest is the important theorem that the multipliers λ_i and μ_j may be interpreted as shadow prices, in the sense that $c\lambda_i$ (respectively, $c\mu_j$) measures the difference between the optimal solution value for (A.2)-(A.5) as is and the optimal solution which would obtain in (A.2)-(A.5) if the constraint $g_i(x) \geqslant 0$ (respectively, $h_j(x) = 0$) were replaced by the constraint $g_i(x) \geqslant c$ (respectively, $h_j(x) \geqslant c$), where c is some small number.

When the objective function f is concave (or at least a monotonic transformation of a concave function, i.e. quasi-concave), and the constraint region defined by (A.3)-(A.5) is convex, then the Kuhn–Tucker conditions are also sufficient, and this without assuming C.Q.). Finally, the function $L(x, \lambda, \mu)$ is usually referred to as the Lagrangian.

Example: Let $P(x)$ be the inverse demand function for a commodity x, whose supply is constrained by capacity z. Let production costs be represented by $C(x, z)$. Then (see Chapter 2) we may represent the problem of choosing x and z so as to maximise welfare as follows:

$$\text{Max } W(x, z) = (\textstyle\int_0^x P(y)dy - C(x, z)), \tag{A.10}$$

$$\text{Subject to: } 0 \leqslant x \leqslant z. \tag{A.11}$$

To solve this using the Kuhn–Tucker theorem, first form the Lagrangian:

$$L(x, z, \lambda) = W(x, z) + \lambda(z - x), \tag{A.12}$$

where the constraints (A.3) are, in this case, only $z - x \geqslant 0$, and where (A.4) is vacuous. The Kuhn–Tucker theorem thus states that any optimal solution $(\hat{x}, \hat{z})$ to (A.10)-(A.11) must satisfy (A.11) and, for some $\lambda > 0$:

$$\frac{\partial L}{\partial x} = P(x) - \frac{\partial C}{\partial x} - \lambda \leqslant 0, \quad x\frac{\partial L}{\partial x} = 0 \tag{A.13}$$

$$\frac{\partial L}{\partial z} = -\frac{\partial C}{\partial z} + \lambda = 0, \quad z\frac{\partial L}{\partial z} = 0. \tag{A.14}$$

If, for example, it can be shown that $0 < \hat{x} = \hat{z}$ at optimum, then (A.13)-(A.14) imply price $P(x)$ should be set so that:

$$P(x) = \frac{\partial C}{\partial x} + \lambda = \frac{\partial C}{\partial x} + \frac{\partial C}{\partial z}, \tag{A.15}$$

i.e. marginal-cost pricing should prevail.

CONTROL THEORY

Control theory essentially provides Kuhn–Tucker-like conditions for dynamic problems, especially when there are constraints on the decision variables involved. The basic problem of control theory may be stated as follows:

$$\text{Max} \int_0^T e^{-rt} F(\mathbf{x}, \mathbf{u}, t) dt, \tag{A.16}$$

subject to:

$$x_i = f_i(\mathbf{x}, \mathbf{u}, t), x_i(0) = \text{known}, i = 1, 2, \ldots, n \tag{A.17}$$

$$g_j(\mathbf{x}, \mathbf{u}, t) \geqslant 0, j = 1, 2, \ldots, m \tag{A.18}$$

$$x_i(t) \geqslant 0, i \in M \subset \{1, 2, \ldots, n\} \tag{A.19}$$

$$x_i(T) = \overline{x}_i, i \in N_1 ; x_i(T) \geqslant \overline{x}_i, i \in N_2, N_1, N_2 \subset \{1, 2, \ldots, n\} \tag{A.20}$$

where x_is are state variables, u_ks are control variables, r is a discount factor, the $\overline{x}_i$ in (A.20) are fixed constants, and T is the planning horizon. The Hamiltonian and Lagrangian functions are defined as:

$$H(\mathbf{x}, \mathbf{u}, \mathbf{p}, t) = F(x, u, t) + \sum_{i=1}^{n} p_i(t) f_i(x, u, t) \tag{A.21}$$

$$L(\mathbf{x}, \mathbf{u}, \mathbf{p}, \mathbf{q}, r, t) = H(x, u, p, t) + \sum_{j=1}^{m} q_j(t) g_j(x, u, t)$$

$$\qquad + \sum_{i \in M} s_i(t) x_i(t). \tag{A.22}$$

·where the p_is are adjoint variables, and the q_js and s_is are Lagrange multipliers. Then the necessary conditions for optimality are provided by the Pontryagin Maximum Principle, which we now state:

THEOREM. Assume a piecewise continuous solution to the above problem exists. Denote this solution by $\hat{x}(t)$ and $\hat{u}(t)$. If the constraint qualification holds for (A.18)–(A.19), then there exist adjoint trajectories $p_i(t)$, $i = 1, 2, \ldots, n$, and Lagrange multipliers $q_j(t)$, $j = 1, 2, \ldots, m$, and $s_i(t)$, $i = 1, 2, \ldots, n$, such that (A.23)–(A.29) below obtain:

$$\frac{dp_i}{dt} = rp_i - \frac{\partial L}{\partial x_i}, i = 1, 2, \ldots, n \tag{A.23}$$

$$\frac{\partial L}{\partial u_k} = 0 \text{ for all } k, \tag{A.24}$$

where the functions $\partial L/\partial x_i$ and $\partial L/\partial u_k$ are evaluated along the optimal trajectory $(\hat{x}(t), \hat{u}(t))$.

The complementarity conditions hold:

$$q_j(t)g_i(\hat{\mathbf{x}}, \hat{\mathbf{u}}, t) = 0, q_j(t) \geqslant 0, j = 1, 2, \ldots, m \tag{A.25}$$

$$s_i(t)\hat{x}_i(t) = 0, s_i(t) \geqslant 0, i \in M. \tag{A.26}$$

The transversality conditions hold (note $N_1, N_2 \subset \{1, \ldots, n\}$ in (A.20)):

$$p_i(T) = \text{no condition if } i \in N_1 \tag{A.27}$$

$$p_i(T) \geqslant 0 \text{ and } p_i(T)(x_i(T) - \overline{x_i}) = 0 \text{ if } i \in N_2 \tag{A.28}$$

$$p_i(T) = 0 \text{ if } x_i(T) \text{ is free, i.e. if } i \notin N_1 \text{ and } i \notin N_2. \tag{A.29}$$

Notice that constraint (A.18) could involve either x_is or u_ks, or both. The reader should recognise that the above necessary conditions (A.24)-(A.26) are in fact the Kuhn-Tucker conditions for maximising (A.21) subject to (A.18)-(A.19). The maximality of the Hamiltonian (A.21) at each instant of time is what gives this theorem its name. Interested readers may consult a more detailed discussion of this theorem in Arrow (1968), Arrow and Kurz (1970) and Takayama (1974).

A further important point is that, just as in the Kuhn-Tucker theorem, the optimal multipliers p, q, s above may be interpreted as discounted shadow prices of their respective constraints. For example, $ce^{-rt} q_j(t)$ represents the marginal change in the objective function at optimum as the right-hand side of (A.18) is changed from zero to c at time t and then allowed to return to zero again. Similarly, it can be shown that $cp_i(t)$ is the present value (measured from time t to time T) of the marginal change in the objective function at optimum due to disturbing the ith state x_i slightly at time t (say, by external action) from its optimal value $x_i(t)$ to $x_i(t) + c$, and then, given this perturbation, following an optimal path to the end of the time horizon.

Readers should be aware that analytical solutions for optimal control problems are usually impossible. This is because of the so-called two-point boundary-value problem which arises through the above theorem in that initial values of state variables are known and the terminal values of state or adjoint variables are given by one of the transversality conditions. Such constrained systems of differential equations are generally very difficult to solve and the use of the computer to obtain numerical solutions becomes the only resort when explicit solutions are desired. Of course, qualitative insights, as in Chapter 7, are possible without numerical methods.

Solutions and Hints to Selected Problems

2.4 (i) $L = W[u^1(x_1^1, x_2^1), u^2(x_1^2, x_2^2)] + \lambda F(y_1, y_2) + \sum_{i=1}^{2} \mu_i(y_1 - x_i)$.

(ii) Derive optimality conditions and solve for the following:

$$\frac{\partial u^j}{\partial x_1} \bigg/ \frac{\partial u^j}{\partial x_2} = -\frac{\partial F}{\partial Y_1} \bigg/ \frac{\partial F}{\partial Y_2}, \text{ for } j = 1, 2.$$

this is simply $MRS_{x_1 x_2}^j = MRT_{x_1 x_2}$.

(iii) The marginal-cost pricing rate is derived by noting the equivalence of the MRT and the ratio of the marginal costs. Similarly, the equivalence of MRS and the price ratio is also noted to give the desired result, $MC_1/MC_2 = p_{y_1}/p_{y_2}$ (the marginal-cost rule) (for further details, see a textbook on microeconomics, e.g. Ferguson and Gould, 1975).

3.1 The solution is obtained via Figure 3.2.

3.2 For the Williamson approach convert to units with $L = 1$. For the Steiner approach convert to units with $L = 4$ and subdivide period 1 into three equal periods of length six hours each. In $L = 1$ units we obtain $b = 24$, $\beta = 10$, and for demands (see note 3 to Chapter 3) $D_1(p) = D_2(p) = \frac{6}{5}(4 - p/24)$. The optimal solution is then $q = 6.4$, $p_1 = 24, p_2 = 64$ (in £/cap-day).

4.1 Note that the solution to both (4.1) and (4.2)–(4.5) is price equals long-run marginal cost.

4.3 No. The β_l do not change and the b_l are all divided by 2. More generally, the efficient frontier and Lemma A are independent of n when units are properly accounted for.

4.4 The proof is facilitated by noting that (4.1) consists of two parts, the non-linear consumers' surplus S and linear costs. Thus it suffices to show that S is concave. We can show this by noting that $\partial D_i/\partial x_i = \partial^2 S/\partial x_i^2 = S_{ii} < 0$, which implies strict concavity of the consumers' surplus function S.

4.5 The proof is by contradiction. For example, set $p_1 \geqslant p_2$ and substitute into Lemma A, i.e. $3b_1 + \beta_1 < 3b_2 + \beta_2$, to yield the desired contradictions $b_2 + \beta_2 \leqslant b_3 + \beta_3$.

4.6 Consider the case $n = 3$, where $x_1 < x_2 < x_3$. Then if $\{\overline{x}_i\}$ is flatter than $\{x_i\}$, we have $x_1 \leqslant \overline{x}_1 \leqslant \overline{x}_2 \leqslant \overline{x}_3 \leqslant x_3$. Since k_i in (4.35) are unaffected by the x_i schedule, the same number of plants is used in meeting $\{x_i\}$ (less if there are more shifting peaks in $\{\overline{x}_i\}$).

4.7 Answer: $p_0 = 1$ and $p_p = 1.324$.

5.1 The function $\overline{w}(\mathbf{x}, \mathbf{q})$ may be written when $m = 1$ (costs $= b, \beta$) as:

$$\overline{w}(\mathbf{x}, \mathbf{q}) = E\Big\{ \sum_{i=1}^{n} \text{Min } [(\int_0^{x_i + \tilde{u}_i} (p_i(y_i - u_i) - b)dy_i),$$

$$(\int_0^z (p_i(y_i - u_i) - b)dy_i)] - \sum_{i=1}^{n} r_i(x_i + \tilde{u}_i - z)\Big\} - \beta z.$$

Now show for any fixed $\mathbf{u}$ that the expression in $\{\ \}$ is concave. Note that the pointwise minimum of two concave functions is concave, and the expected value of a concave function is concave.

5.4 Use the implicit function theorem in (5.35)–(5.36) to derive comparative-static results $\partial z/\partial c$, $\partial x/\partial c$. It is easier to do this in terms of capacity rather than price and capacity (but do not forget to substitute $p = P(x)$ in (5.35) if you do use x and z). The only trick is to show under the given assumptions that the derivative of (5.36) with respect to z is more negative than the derivative of (5.36) with respect to x.

9.4 First define the 'normal profit function' $\Pi(x, A, K, L)$ as profits from (x, A, K, L) when minimal staff expenditures are used, i.e. $\Pi(x, A, K, L) = \Pi(x, A, \mathbf{S}(x, A), K, L)$. Now $\mathbf{S} = \mathbf{S}(x, A)$ is easily established for the profit-maximiser. Since (see note 17) $\mu_1 > 0$ for the profit-maximiser, (9.42) becomes for him $x p_2(x, A) = 1 + S_2(x, A)$, a condition on (x, A) alone. But (9.48) must hold for the expense-preference utility for some $c < 1$. Noting for any fixed c that (9.48) is a function of only (x', A'), it then follows that (x', A') cannot be a part of any profit-maximising solution for any $S' \geqslant \mathbf{S}(x', A')$, in particular not for $S' = \mathbf{S}(x', A')$. Thus $\Pi(x, A, S, K, L) = \Pi(x, A, K, L) > \Pi(x', A', K', L')$.

From this verify that if $\mathbf{S}(x', A') \leqslant \mathbf{S}(x, A)$, then the solution

$\Pi(x'', A'', S'', K'', L'')$ given by $x'' = x', A'' = A', K'' = K', L'' = L'$, and $S'' = [\Pi(x, A, K, L) - \Pi(x', A', K', L')] + [S' - S(x', A')] + S(x, A)$ is feasible and yields the same profits as, and higher staff expenditures than, the assumed optimal solution (x', A', S', K', L'). This contradiction establishes the desired result $S(x', A') > S(\dot{x}, A)$.

10.1 $P_3' = b_3' + \beta_3/\beta_1 \nu_1$.

As $\nu_i = \frac{1}{3}$, multiply both sides by $\frac{1}{3}$ to yield:

$$\tfrac{1}{3}P_3' = \tfrac{1}{3}b_3' + \beta_3$$

$$\tfrac{1}{3}P_3' = P_3 = b_3 + \beta_3, \text{ i.e. } \tfrac{1}{3}b_3' = b_3.$$

Similarly,

$$P_2' = \tfrac{2}{3}b_2' - \tfrac{1}{3}b_3 + \beta_2 = \beta_3$$

$$P_2 = \tfrac{1}{3}P_2' = 2b_2 - b_3 - \beta_2 - \beta_3$$

Finally,

$$P_1 = \tfrac{1}{3}P_1' = 3b_1 - 2b_2 + \beta_1 - \beta_2 \text{ (recall } b_1' = 3b_1).$$

10.2 These are annualised prices as they all need to be divided by 8760:

$$kWh_1 = \frac{P_3'}{8760} = \frac{60 + 240.90}{8760} = 3.435p$$

$$kWh_2 = \frac{(116.8 - 80.3 + 40 - 20)3}{8760} = 1.935p$$

$$kWh_3 = \frac{(20.81 - 116.8 + 100 - 40)3}{8760} = -1.233p$$

The negative price of kWh_3 indicates that one of the plants should not be used. Reference to Lemma A indicates that only plants 1 and 2 are used. In this case the optimal prices are $p_3 = b_2 + \beta_2, p_2 = 2b_1 + \beta_1 - (b_2 + \beta_2)$, $p_1 = b_1$, as the reader will recall from Chapter 4. These results do not imply that the real-world plants providing Wenders's data are a non-optimal configuration. All that is implied is that when periods are of equal length that this plant mix is non-optimal.

10.3 $\dfrac{\beta_1 - \beta_2}{b_2' - b_1'} = \dfrac{60}{154.39} = 0.3886 = w_1 + w_2$

$$\frac{\beta_2 - \beta_3}{b_3' - b_2'} = \frac{20}{65.7} = 0.3044 = w_1$$

$$0.6114 = w_3$$

$$v_1 = 0.65, v_2 = 0.3, v_3 = 0.05$$

$$P_3 = \frac{400 + 240.90}{8760} = 7.316p$$

$$P_2 = \frac{(0.35)\,(175.2) - 0.05(240.9) + 40 - 20}{0.3(8760)} = \frac{230.92}{8760} = 2.636p$$

$$P_1 = \frac{20.81 - (0.35)\,(175.2) + 100 - 20}{0.65(8760)} = \frac{29.98}{8760} = 0.3423p$$

10.4   We first note that by Lemma A plant 3 *need* never be used. Cost-minimising solutions are given by the following:

Plant type	1			2			3		
	I	II	III	I	II	III	I	II	III
q_{l1}	30	30	30	0	0	0	0	0	0
q_{l2}	40	30	40	0	10	0	0	0	0
q_{l3}	40	30	40	10	10	0	0	10	10
q_l	40	30	40	10	10	0	0	10	10

Total cost = 1550; $p_1 = 5, p_2 = 10, p_3 = 20$. Notice that Wenders would compute these as, using our notation, $p_1 = b_1, p_2 = b_2, p_3 = b_3 + \beta_3$. On the other hand, we would, using Lemma A, eliminate plant 3 and solve the Kuhn–Tucker conditions to give:

$$p_1 = b_1, p_2 = 2b_1 + \beta_1 - (b_2 + \beta_2), p_3 = b_2 + \beta_2.$$

11.1   First of all place appropriate restrictions on c_i and d_i:

(i) $\eta = \dfrac{-1}{c_1 + c_2}(p_2 - \hat{p}_1)$ and $\bar{p} = \dfrac{c_2}{c_1 + c_2}\hat{p}_1 + \dfrac{c_1}{c + c_2}\hat{p}_2$.

(ii) From (11.12) $p - \hat{p}_1 = -\eta(\partial p_1/\partial x_1)$. Proof by contradiction if $\eta < 0$ then above implies $\bar{p} < \hat{p}_1$. Similarly, if $\eta < 0$, $\bar{p} - \bar{p}_2 = -\eta(\partial p/\partial x_2)$ implies $\bar{p} > \hat{p}_2$. Together these imply $\hat{p}_1 > \bar{p} > p_2$, which is excluded by (11.5).

(iii) Note $\eta = \dfrac{-1}{c_1 + c_2}(\hat{p}_2 - \hat{p}_1)$ and, noting (11.30), $\Delta RC = (2b_1 - b_3)(-\eta) + b_2\eta > 0$.

(iv) See (11.32).

(v) $\Delta RC = 0$, $\Delta CC = \beta_1(\bar{x}_2 - \hat{x}_2) = \beta_1\eta > 0$.

11.2 The problem stated is equivalent to:

$$\text{Max } (M - Kz - p'x - p''y)(\sqrt{x} + c\sqrt{y}),$$

subject to:

$$0 \leqslant x \leqslant z. \, 0 \leqslant y \leqslant z.$$

Form the Lagrangian with the remaining two constraints ($z - x \geqslant 0$, $z - y \geqslant 0$). Eliminate the case $x = 0$ or $y = 0$ as uninteresting and then use Kuhn–Tucker theory to obtain the solution.

11.3 Do a similar conversion to that suggested for Exercise 11.2. In this case, however, $x = 0$ *or* $y = 0$ *can* obtain.

Notes

CHAPTER 1

1. In a multi-service environment Baumol (1977) has recently argued that the appropriate criterion is 'cost subadditivity'. 'Cost subadditivity' requires that the cost level of meeting a given demand of services by one firm will be smaller than the total cost associated with providing the same servcies by two or more firms. For a detailed discussion see Baumol (1977).

CHAPTER 2

1. See Arrow and Scitovsky (1969) and Mishan (1971) for an introduction to this literature.

2. Notably Samuelson (1947) and Little (1957). As we will see, much of their criticism has since been blunted by Willig (1976).

3. We will usually distinguish the variable of integration (y in (2.2)) from the variable limits of integration (x in (2.2)).

4. This definition and related analysis are due to Hotelling (1932). See also Pressman (1970) for a more recent discussion.

5. A review of line integrals and consumers' surplus is included as an appendix to this chapter.

6. See the appendix to this chapter.

7. When the budget constraint has to be met exactly the following looser conditions can be applied in place of (2.6)–(2.7). For all i, j, k:

$$p_k\left(\frac{\partial P_i}{\partial q_j} - \frac{\partial P_j}{\partial q_i}\right) + p_i\left(\frac{\partial P_j}{\partial q_k} - \frac{\partial P_k}{\partial q_j}\right) + p_j\left(\frac{\partial P_k}{\partial q_i} - \frac{\partial P_i}{\partial q_k}\right) = 0.$$

When all income elasticities are equal across goods and individuals these latter conditions are easily shown to hold whether budgets are fixed or not.

8. See, for example, Katzner (1970) for definitions.

215

9. As Willig notes, these bounds are only approximate, but for most realistic values of income elasticities η and ratios S/m', he found these bounds to hold within a tolerance of 0.5 per cent. See also Exercise 2.2 in this regard.

10. The literature is not unanimous on the definitions and origins of the various compensation criteria. For example, compare Henderson and Quandt (1971, p. 279), Baumol (1972, p. 402), Hicks (1941, pp. 328-9), Kaldor (1939) and Scitovsky (1941, p. 86). We have followed Scitovsky in our definitions.

11. The rationale for weighting these surpluses equally is related to the Pareto principle fot the extent that *ex post* redistribution of income amongst producers and consumers is allowed. See, for example, Williamson (1966).

12. For the reader who wishes to recall briefly the rationale for marginal-cost pricing a modest exercise (Exercise 2.4) is included. An excellent graphical analysis is included in Bator (1957). See also Mohring (1970) and Turvey (1969).

13. See Comanor and Leibenstein (1969) and Crew (1975) for a development of these issues.

14. The importance of this issue might be noted by reference to the 'early' literature, for example Coase (1946), Farrell (1958), Henderson (1948), Hotelling (1938), Ruggles (1949), Tyndall (1951) and Wiseman (1957). For some recent restatements, see Dreze (1964), Marchanu (1973), Feldstein (1972), Ng and Weisser (1974).

15. Let $C(x)$ represent total costs at output level x. Let $AC(x)$ denote average costs $C(x)/x$ and let $MC(x)$ denote marginal costs $dC(x)/dx$. The reader can easily verify that $dAC(x)/dx = [MC(x) - AC(x)]/x$, so that, for any positive output level x, if $dAC(x)/dx < 0$, then $MC(x) < AC(x)$. It can also be verified that if $MC(x)$ is everywhere decreasing (concave costs), then, assuming $C(x) \geqslant 0$, $MC(x) < AC(x)$. Thus either decreasing marginal or average costs leads to the result that marginal cost will be less than average cost. There are reasons other than scale economies that can cause observed average costs to exceed marginal costs. Feldstein (1972, pp. 183-4) states: 'Although there are now several econometric studies showing approximately constant returns to scale in the production of electricity, the very substantial distribution costs imply that long run marginal cost is much less than long run average costs.' This is possibly true, but such differences could arise from the fact that an inefficient pricing policy is employed with the effect that capacity is not utilised to the full. As will become apparent

in the next and subsequent chapters, such under-utilisation could mean that *LRAC* (defined as *LRTC* divided by total output) is greater than *LRMC*, ignoring distribution costs.

16. A further problem, with which we are not concerned, is the income-distributional consequence of marginal-cost pricing under decreasing costs in that it implies a subsidy of users by non-users.

17. An introductory discussion of optimisation is given in the Mathematical Appendix (pp. 201–8).

18. This argument about least distortion applies only to the case of increasing returns. When decreasing returns obtain a symmetric argument could be applied with a *maximum* profit constraint replacing (2.22). But such a case could also be handled by setting $p_i = MC_i$ and imposing a lump-sum tax to absorb surpluses without introducing allocative inefficiencies.

CHAPTER 3

1. The reader is encouraged to demonstrate his understanding of this point by solving Exercise 3.1.

2. If we were to start Figure 3.3 at the origin, we would have to replace β, β' and β'' with $b + \beta$, $2b + \beta'$ and $3b + \beta''$.

3. For example, unit = kW-hr, L = 24 hours, b = £ per kW-hr, β = £ per kW. For a comprehensive discussion of unit compatibility issues, see Wilson (1972).

4. Contrast the complications of using these definitions in the Steiner–Hirshleifer analysis. In Steiner's case we have *LRMC* represented by the horizontal line at β. In Hirshleifer's case he has to represent *LRMC* in the two-period firm-peak case by $b + \beta$ and by $2b + \beta$ in a two-period shifting-peak case. In a three-period case it would be more complicated. For example, for the cases (i), (ii) and (iii) discussed in Figure 3.3 we would have *LRMC* as follows: (i) $b + \beta$, (ii) $2b + \beta$, (iii) $3b + \beta$ (for details see Hirshleifer, 1958, especially pp. 452–7).

5. The corresponding quantities for $D_1^{L_1}(p_1) = x_1^{L_1} = 4$ and $D_2^{L_2}(p_2) = x_2^{L_2} = 4\frac{3}{8}$.

6. In converting from units based on L to units based on kL (here $k = 3$) we have $\hat{x} = kx$, $\hat{p} = p/k$, and $x = D(p)$, where p, x are in L units and $\hat{p}$, $\hat{x}$ in kL units. Thus $\hat{x} = kx = kD(k\hat{p})$, i.e. the demand curve in new units is $\hat{x} = \hat{D}(\hat{p}) = kD(k\hat{p})$.

CHAPTER 4

1. See, for example, Hotelling (1932), Dreze (1964) and Nelson (1964).

2. We use the term 'plant' throughout this book to refer to the various types of capacity available. It is hoped that this will not detract from interpreting the results in areas where 'plant' is not the usual designation of capital equipment (e.g. in transportation).

3. See Turvey (1969) for a discussion of the determination of b_l, β_l. For b_l this is a straightforward allocation of operating costs once units have been fixed. For β_l this consists essentially of pro-rating the annuitised cost of building and maintaining the plant over its useful life. Thus, if the basic cycle is 1 year and the life of a plant l of size 100 is 50 years, then β_l would equal 1/100th of the annuity sufficient to maintain and replace the given plant after 50 years.

4. See also Exercise 4.1 in this regard.

5. Of course, when cost minimisation cannot be assumed, for example under regulation of a profit-maximising firm (as in Chapter 9), then the various problem specifications lead to different possibilities for describing departures from cost-minimising behaviour. Note that economies of scale are not treated via (4.2)–(4.5), as we discuss in Section 4.3.

6. On pp. 42–7 we rigorously establish (4.19)–(4.20) as necessary conditions for using both plant types.

7. The convexity of the technological frontier is only a necessary condition that plants on it will be used. See also Exercise 4.3 and the discussion in the next chapter on this point.

8. The reader is encouraged to prove this himself in Exercise 4.4.

9. This result contrasts somewhat with Dansby (1976), who finds for continuously varying demand that peak price may exceed $b_1 + \beta_1$. Dansby's result assumes that the total length of the peak pricing period is unity (i.e. $N_p = (i)$ for some i) with demand varying with time within N_p. This is clearly orthogonal to our formulation.

10. This follows essentially because the trade-offs determining k_l in Proposition A are not affected by the shape of the supply schedule (see also Exercise 4.6).

11. Let $W(\pi)$ superscript refer to welfare-(profit-) maximising solution. Then $p_i^W = \partial R(x^\pi)/\partial x_i < P_i(x^\pi) = p_i^\pi$ as asserted. Of course, if the $LRMC_i = \lambda_i$ were different for x^W and x^π, then $p_i^W = \lambda_i^W = \lambda_i^\pi = \partial R/\partial x_i$ would no longer hold. Here we assumed $x_2 > x_1$, so Proposition A implies that $\lambda_i^W = \lambda_i^\pi$, for all i. More generally, of course, one would

expect price–output distortions under profit-maximising pricing to be higher in periods with relatively more inelastic demand (see later in the text).

12. More generally, multi-part tariffs are specified through break-points $O = \bar{x}_0 < \bar{x}_1 < \ldots < \bar{x}_k$ and prices $p_{1i}, p_{2i}, \ldots, p_{ki}$, where the marginal unit x in $\bar{x}_{j-1} \leqslant x < x_j$ is sold at price p_{ji} in period i. The two-part tariff in the text is obtained by specifying p_{1i} so that $p_{1i}\bar{x}_1 = F$ and letting $\bar{x}_1$ approach zero.

CHAPTER 5

1. In general it can be established for the deterministic case that excess demand is optimal only when demand varies within pricing periods (as in Section 4.1, p. 52). Even here, however, one would expect that the zero excess-demand condition (imposed in the previous chapters) is a close approximation to reality, especially when demand uncertainty is low. See also Dansby (1976) on this point.

2. The reader can easily verify this solution from (4.10)–(4.13) for the case of $m = n = 1$.

3. The analysis of this section was developed originally in Crew and Kleindorfer (1976). Copyright © 1976, The American Telephone and Telegraph Company. Reprinted with permission from the *Bell Journal of Economics*.

4. See Carlton (1977) for further discussion on this point.

5. On pp. 80–7 we also discuss the multiplicative $D(p, \widetilde{v}) = \widetilde{v}X(p)$, with $E(\widetilde{v}) = 1$. It should be noted that equation (5.1) and the non-negativity of x imply that $\widetilde{u}$ should actually depend on p. In equations (5.26) and (5.27) we show that $b_1 \leqslant p_i \leqslant b_1 + \beta_1$ for all i. Thus (5.1) need only be a good approximation of demand in this range.

6. Given the regularity conditions above (see (5.2)), one condition whch assures the existence of $\bar{W}$ is that $\widetilde{u}$ have a compact range, i.e. there is some closed and bounded set $\Omega \subset R^n$ such that $Pr\{\widetilde{u} \in \Omega\} = 1$.

7. Strictly speaking, these are first-order conditons. It can be shown, however, that these conditions are also sufficient (see Exercise 5.1 in this regard).

8. When taking expected values with respect to a random variable, say $\widetilde{u}$, we use the notation $\int u dF(u)$, where $F(u)$ is the cumulative distribution function of $\widetilde{u}$. The reader who wishes may substitute $dF(u) =$

$f(u)du$ everywhere, where $f(u)$ is the density function of $\tilde{u}$ (see also the Mathematical Appendix for a discussion).

9. If rationing costs are strictly monotonic (i.e. $r'_i(y) > 0$ when $y > 0$), then $F_i(z - X_i(p_i)) > 0$ is certainly satisfied since $F_i(z - X_i(p_i)) = 0$ implies $F_i(Q_l - X_i(p_i)) = 0$, for all $l = 1, \ldots, m$. Moreover, $F_i(z - X_i(p_i)) = 0$ implies $E\{r'_i(X_i(p_i) + \tilde{u}_i - z)\} > 0$. From (5.11) these two conditions would violate $\partial \overline{W}/\partial p_i = 0$, which is a necessary condition (except in the uninteresting case $p_i = 0$).

10. See the note on Proposition A (p. 43) indicating that $k_1 = 0$ (and thus $q_l = 0$) is possible. This is clearly a knife-edged case, however, and Result 4 is the one to heed in practical planning.

11. This contrasts with the recent results by Carlton (1977), to which we return in Section 5.3. Carlton finds that price may exceed $b_1 + \beta_1$ if rationing is sufficiently inefficient (e.g. if rationing is random).

12. We will be coming back to this point again in Section 5.3. In passing, we note that this was not always thought to be the case. Salkever (1970, p. 488), for example, argued that 'when demand is random, peak load pricing is simply not efficient'. He did, however, go on to hint at the optimality of peak-load pricing where the marginal running cost function is upward-sloping.

13. Alternatively, the reader may think of the following analysis as being restricted to the peak period, where all off-peak periods are such that demand is less than optimal capacity with probability 1, with the consequence (see (5.17) for $m = 1$) that price = b in off-peak periods. See Crew and Kleindorfer (1978) and Sherman and Visscher (1978) for a discussion of the multi-period case.

14. This statement assumes that (5.11)–(5.12) (or their equivalents, (5.35)–(5.36)) are sufficient for optimality (see Exercise 5.1).

15. See Billingsley (1968, p. 24) for a proof of this; assuming that $\tilde{u} \rightarrow 0$ means convergence in distribution to a random variable having a degenerate distribution centred at the origin.

16. See also the more extended discussion of these issues in Crew and Kleindorfer (1978).

17. See Exercise 5.4 for details (see also Sherman and Visscher, 1978).

18. These costs could well be borne by the producer, even if they are just surplus losses. For example, for a utility employing a two-part tariff, the utility might agree to pay (by reduced entry fees) those con-

sumers who will be cut off in the event of excess demand (see also Dansby, 1977, in this regard).

19. For a more detailed discussion, see Sherman and Visscher (1978).

20. See note 18 in this regard.

CHAPTER 6

1. We have used this approach before (see Crew and Kleindorfer, 1976, 1978). What follows in Chapter 6 is based upon the examples of the above papers. All of the results involve simple iterative search procedures to solve the appropriate first-order conditions.

2. The reader will note than any price between 0 and 15 would be optimal. However, in line with our assumption of Chapter 5 we are disregarding any 'optimal' prices which do not at least recover operating expenses.

CHAPTER 7

1. See, for example, Nerlove (1974) for a discussion of scale economies in electricity generation.

2. See the Mathematical Appendix (pp. 201-8) for some introductory remarks on optimal control theory.

3. See the Mathematical Appendix (pp. 201-8) for details.

4. See, for example, Anderson (1972) for details of the economics of systems planning.

5. Note that if price could not be adjusted instantaneously, then some averaging of the optimal marginal-cost conditions would occur, as discussed in Section 4.1 (pp. 39-53).

CHAPTER 8

1. Even prior to the wave of public ownership that took place in the U.K. just after the Second World War there was a long history of public ownership. Interestingly, public ownership is traced back to the reign of Henry VIII, who granted a charter to Trinity House to provide lighthouses, a classic case of a public good!

2. For the details and discussion of the background by one of the leading authorities on public enterprise, see Robson (1962). For much more critical discussion, see Kelf-Cohen (1961, 1969), who discusses Morrison's views as set forth in Morrison (1933).

3. The electricity and gas industries were brought into public ownership with the creation of 'public corporations' through the Electricity Act, 1947 and the Gas Act, 1948. For a discussion see Robson (1962, pp. 46–77).

4. Posner (1974) is highly critical of this basis of regulation. He surveys a number of possible theories of regulation, including the 'public-interest' theory. Of most significance are the 'captive' theory, which originated with political scientists, and the 'economic' theory, developed by Stigler (1971) following the work in the economics of politics by Downs (1957), Buchanan and Tulloch (1962) and Olson (1965). The economic theory is of more interest, to the extent that it is able to provide testable implications. It argues that regulation can be analysed within the apparatus of supply and demand. Regulation can confer benefits to the regulated by providing barriers to entry that are not otherwise available. However, there are costs associated with obtaining legislation for regulation and running the regulatory apparatus. The theory does not as yet have substantial empirical support. For example, Stigler's (1971) study of occupational licensing, while interesting and supportive of this, is hardly conclusive.

5. Many activities that could just as well be carried on by private capital are public enterprises. In many cases they compete in the product market with private businesses. A list of most of the public enterprises in the U.K. together with the date they were nationalised is given as follows: Central Electricity Board (1926, the industry being fully nationalised in 1947), the Port of London Authority (1909), The Forestry Commission (1921), the National Coal Board (1947), the British Transport Corporation (1947), the General Post Office (1659), the Gas Boards (1949), the White Fish Authority (1951), the British Broadcasting Corporation (1926), Rolls-Royce (1971), the British Steel Corporation (1967). The U.S. also is not without its public enterprises, for example, the Post Office, the Pennsylvania State Liquor Control Board, liquor monopolists in other states, and more recently Conrail and Amtrak.

6. A complete description of the extent of industries regulated in the U.S. is beyond the scope of this work. Besides, it varies according to state. For a comprehensive list, see Phillips (1969, pp. 92–5). In New

Jersey, for example, regulatory commissions exist not just for public utilities but for such diverse commodities as refuse collection, insurance, milk and liquor.

7. For example, *Nebbia* v. *New York*, 2.91 U.S. 502 (1934). Mr Nebbia, a Rochester grocer, defended his right to sell cut-price milk on the grounds that milk was a competitive industry with none of the characteristics of a public utility. For a good summary of the case and its background and consequences, see Phillips (1969, pp. 45-82).

8. It may be putting it too strongly to say that the Consumer Consultative Councils have no teeth. David Coombes's (1971, p. 148) summary of the position is worth noting: 'It is fairly safe to make a generalization and say the role of consumer's organizations in the nationalized industries is essentially *consultative* in that consumers' representatives *have the right to make complaints and suggestions of their own and at the same time the boards are obliged in most cases to hear those representatives*' (italics added).

9. For a detailed discussion based upon this formula, see Phillips (1969). An interesting contribution by Joskow (1972) attempts to predict the rate of return a commision will allow. His predictions were good. His work also indicated consistency of behaviour by the New York Public Service Commission, whose positions he studied.

10. For the moment to understand the 'used and useful' criterion we need not go beyond the literal meaning of the words. Regulatory commissions might concern themselves that the capital equipment making up $(V - D)$ is both 'used and useful'. We will return to this again in Chapter 9. For an interesting comment on this, see Westfield (1965, p. 440).

11. This matter will be raised again from time to time. For a flavour of some of the most common objections, see Webb (1973, pp. 153-60). For some indication of its operational significance for the electricity-supply industry, see Crew (1966).

12. Presumably using a specified discount rate together with marginal-cost pricing will uniquely determine the rate of return.

13. For a good survey of these issues, see Phillips (1969, pp. 691-726). Some doubts about the dynamic effects on efficiency of plant scale are raised in Peck (1977).

14. See, for example, H. J. De Podwin and Associates (1974), *Regulation of Utility Performance: A Proposed Alternative to Rate Base Regulation*, report prepared for the Federal Communications Commission under Contract FCC-0071 (July 1974). The main features of

the scheme are a rate of return on equity and a measure of productivity based upon net income per unit of output. A range of acceptable values for these is derived and regulatory intervention will not occur if its performance falls within these ranges. Incentives are therefore provided to the utilities to avoid the transactions costs of reviews. Additionally, by means of various methods provided to allow the utilities to share with their consumers the benefits of cost savings, the scheme hopes to provide incentives for dynamic and X-efficiency.

15. However, Edwards and Stevens (1976) conclude: 'the particular sub-institutional arrangements used to implement collectivization (i.e. to set up the monopoly), such as competitive bidding and price regulation, are not important compared to the decision to collectivize'. The extent to which this conclusion is robust is important, leaving the way open to comparing only the government transaction costs of, for example, price regulation or franchise bidding.

16. To the reader unfamiliar with Williamson's work in this area, 'bounded rationality' refers to that part of 'human behavior that is intendedly rational but only limitedly so' (Simon, 1961, p. xxiv); opportunism extends the usual self-seeking assumptions of economic theory to include some allowance for strategic behaviour. Thus presumably some contracts are written with this in mind. Moral hazard in insurance might prompt the insured to make a high claim for damages and the insurance company to respond with a low figure for compensation, with obvious implications for transactions costs. Williamson's contribution was to show how these considerations can be extended to a wide variety of situations.

17. See Commissioner Nicholas Johnson's statement, *Re American Telephone and Telegraph Co.*, 70 P.U.R. 3d, 233–4 (F.C.C., 1967).

CHAPTER 9

1. Let us recall the nature of opportunism in Williamson's (1975, p. 9) words: 'Opportunism refers to a lack of candor or honesty in transactions, to include self-interest seeking with guile.' Presumably this includes misrepresentation, for example, as in the tactics of an unscrupulous used-car salesman. To be significant, however, opportunism need not be so strong or as morally reprehensible as misrepresentation. A public utility has information not available to a regulatory commission. There is no reason why it should reveal such information without a

specific request by the commission and the commission may lack the information to make such a request.

2. See, however, Harris and Raviv (1976, 1978) for an extension of principal and agent problems to cover monitoring, and the earlier discussion by Alchian and Demsetz (1972) and Crew (1975).

3. A list of some of the major contributions is: Bailey (1973), Baumol and Klevorick (1970), El Hodiri and Takayama (1973), Kafoglis (1969), Takayama (1969), Westfield (1965), Zajac (1970, 1972).

4. It is possible to show that $0 < \lambda < 1$ if (9.2) is binding, as Baumol and Klevorick (1970) have done, and as the reader may do in Exercise 9.1.

5. For a formal proof of this, see Baumol and Klevorick (1970).

6. In fact this is Westfield's (1965) formulation. It gives the same solution as A-J. However, we note that the A-J formulation will result in indeterminancy when $s = r$ (see Averch and Johnson (1962, p. 1055) and Exercise 9.1).

7. Except for the profit-maximising problem, which the reader is encouraged to address in Exercise 9.2.

8. This follows from the fact that while the price monopolist and the regulated firm will use the same *rule* for determining the quantity of labour, they each use different amounts of capital. This could imply a smaller optimal amount of labour, and thus even a smaller output, by the regulated firm (see Exercise 9.1).

9. Bailey (1973, p. 107) criticises Sheshinski (1971) on the grounds that 'he neglected . . . to point out the possibility that the solution $s = r$ may be optimal; instead he left the reader with the impression that an interior $s(s > r)$ will always maximise social welfare'. However, her criticism seems to rely on resolving the indeterminacy that results when $s = r$ by assuming that 'the regulated firm operates efficiently when $s = r$'. Klevorick (1971) also discussed several possibilities for the firm when $s = r$. However, to assume at $s = r$ that the firm will become efficient surely serves only to add a *deus ex machina* to the regulator's inadequate tool-box. We have not dealt with, and at this stage will not deal with, the issue of when $s = r$ is welfare optimal (see, however, Section 9.4).

10. For an introduction to the use of general equilibrium in the analysis of regulation, see Bailey (1973, pp. 107-9) and Peles and Stein (1976, pp. 287-9).

11. This result was first noted by Wellisz (1963).

12. See Exercise 9.3 for a numerical example illustrating this point.

13. We regard gold plating as synonymous with rate-base padding. This is probably not the usual use of the term. For example, Zajac (1972, p. 311) notes: 'In the past, rate base padding allegations have generally been of two forms: (1) that regulated firms 'gold plate', i.e., use unnecessarily expensive materials and designs or (2) that they maintain excessive spare capacity.' Our analysis will be concerned with the second of these components of rate-base padding.

14. We can see this by noting that $u_{2i} = \text{Max } \tilde{u}_i$, by definition, implying from (9.32) and $z^* = R^*/s$ that demand cannot exceed capacity.

15. For example, see the New Jersey Public Utility Commission Docket 762-194 *In the Matter of the Board's Order of Inquiry into the Reasonableness of Electric Utilities Construction Program* (1976).

16. One might also investigate tax effects in (9.35), as Williamson (1964) does. We ignore such considerations here.

17. The reader may verify that $U_1 + \mu_1$ is always positive as long as $U_2, F_1, F_2 > 0$ and $s > \beta$, which we assume. This follows from (9.44)–(9.45) and the just-noted equality $U_1 + \mu_1 = U_2 - \mu_3$.

18. If $\mu_3 = 0$, then the optimal solution obtained from the first-order conditions (9.42)–(9.47) is the same as that obtained from first-order conditions corresponding to maximising (9.36) subject to (9.37), (9.38) and (9.40), i.e. paying no heed to (9.41). Assuming the appropriate convexity conditions, these first-order conditions are then also sufficient for optimality, so that (9.39) is inconsequential.

19. See also Exercise 9.5.

20. The reader may check generally from (9.44)–(9.45) that the expense-preference firm will always find cost-minimising behaviour with respect to capital and labour to be optimal whenever $s = \beta$ or $\mu_3 = 0$. Intuitively this follows because the utility function has arguments S and Π, and with $\Pi = 0$, S will be maximising only if the other components of cost are minimised.

21. The reader may be a little surprised at our use of the traditional welfare function in evaluating policies involving different demand curves corresponding to different levels of advertising. For a partial justification of this, see Crew and Kleindorfer (1977). The benefits measured by the traditional welfare function give not wholly intuitive results, however, as can be seen, for example, in Table 9.2, where for $s = 10.2$, the expense-preference firm's behaviour is indicated to be socially more desirable than the profit-maximiser's behaviour, and this in spite of the fact that it entails lower output at a higher price and

with larger costs. The difference, as measured by the traditional social-welfare function, is made up by consumer awareness (brought about by advertising) of the nature and possibly the quality of the product.

22. A recent attempt to reduce this lag is embodied in fuel adjustment clauses in electricity supply which allow changes in fuel costs to be passed on to consumers without a rate hearing (see also Chapter 10).

23. $R(s)$ is the intersection of the plane formed by the regulatory constraint and the profit hill. Thus interior points will violate the regulatory constraints and exterior ones will correspond to a rate of return less than the rate allowed, s.

24. Note that this also holds when $\Delta L \neq 0$.

25. The present value of a share is taken to be the discounted value of all future dividends.

26. See, for example, Kahn (1970) and Chapter 8 above.

CHAPTER 10

1. For example, *I.E.E.E. Transactions (Power Systems)* deals with this. Very few of these are very accessible to economists as few employ a methodology easily recognised by economists. For an exception, see Hicks (1960). For an introduction in system planning written for economists, see Berrie (1967) and Anderson (1972).

2. This is cited by Lewis (1941) from Hopkinson's *Original Papers*. For a survey of later developments of Hopkinson's approach, see Schiller (1945a, 1945b) and *Electric Utility Rate Design Study* (1977).

3. On the Continent, however, the situation has been totally different, the time-of-day tariffs of *Electricité de France* presenting a different approach. We will discuss this briefly later on in this chapter.

4. In the U.S. these are usually called 'customer', 'energy' and 'demand'.

5. Load factor is a means of measuring the extent to which capacity is utilised. Thus system load factor is the ratio, expressed as a percentage of (i) the units of electricity supplied through the system in a year to, (ii) the number which would have been supplied if maximum demand had been maintained for all 8760 hours of the year.

6. The calculation turns out to be a fairly routine one in view of the experience that the load factor of domestic consumers is not very sensitive to the size of the consumer's total consumption. For more details, see Crew (1966), De Salvia (1969) and Ineson (1963).

7. See Ineson (1963) for a brief explanation.

8. Although they are offered alongside other tariffs, time-of-day tariffs have not become widespread in their adoption by consumers. Indeed, only a small minority of consumers have opted for the white-meter tariff, which is the time-of-day tariff. One of the authors opted for the white meter and found that savings in the order of about 10 percent in quarterly bills could be achieved without inconvenience even on a relatively small annual consumption of about 4000 units. There are also maximum-demand tariffs with variations in the kW charge, and a unit charge according to season and time of day.

9. This is *Electricity Rate Design Study*, which is a nation-wide effort by the Electric Power Research Institute, the Edison Electric Institute, the American Public Power Association and the National Association of Regulatory Utility Commissioners. U.K. experiments and research began rather earlier, for example the Electricity Council's 'Domestic Tariff Experiment' of 1974.

10. This monstrous figure is taken from *Electricity Rate Design Study* (1977).

11. Equations (10.12) and (10.13) can be transformed with our notation by recalling that Wenders's running costs b' are 'the marginal and average energy cost of producing a kW for a year' (Wenders, 1976, p. 233). Thus for the equal-period case $b' = 3b$, where b is our notation for running costs. Thus (10.13) and (10.14) now read:

$$\beta_2 - \beta_3 = 1/3(3b_3 - 3b_2) \tag{10.13a}$$

$$\beta_1 - \beta_2 = 2/3(3b_2 - 3b_1). \tag{10.14a}$$

From (10.3a), by Lemma A, only plant 3 need be used. Thus only plants 1 and 3 need be used. The reader may verify, however, that the same actual values for optimal prices will emerge as in (10.12).

12. For this reason, rather than burden the text, we have left it to the interested reader to work through Exercise 10.4.

13. The total *was* substantial. As Munby (1959, p. 73) noted, 'Gross fixed capital formation of the nationalized industries (coal, gas, electricity, transport) is roughly of the same order of magnitude as the total for manufacturing industry representing expenditure of some £900 millions in 1957', and the electricity-supply industry was the biggest user of capital of these.

14. For an evaluation, see Bates (1966).

15. In November 1970 the Heath government announced that it

intended to abolish the board.

16. See Fells (1972) for a complete list and for an interesting evaluation of all aspects of the work of the N.B.P.I.

17. For a flavour of the reports and the level of analysis, see Turvey (1971).

18. See Crew (1966) for an extension of Bates's approach.

CHAPTER 11

1. We have addressed these issues in a previous paper (see Crew and Kleindorfer, 1975b).

2. These restrictions on $\partial P_i/\partial x_i$, $\partial P_i/\partial x_k$ will apply for any reasonable definition of interdependent peak and off-peak demands. Otherwise, the *peak demand curve* and the *off-peak demand curve* would shift in such a way that the off-peak demand curve was above the peak demand curve, so great was the interdependence. We think such situations are sufficiently perverse for us to exclude. The reader may also consult Exercise 11.1 for further consideration of such points in relation to the special case of independent demands.

3. The one-plant case is dealt with in Exercise 11.1.

4. We note from (11.25) that:

$$\overline{P} - \hat{P}_1 = \frac{c_2 - a}{c_1 + c_2 - 2a}(\hat{P}_2 - \hat{P}_1); \text{ and}$$

$$\overline{P} - \hat{P}_2 = \frac{c_1 - a}{c_1 + c_2 - 2a}(\hat{P}_1 - \hat{P}_2),$$

from which (11.31) follows. Some further arithmetic in (11.13) shows, in fact, that $\overline{x}_2 - \hat{x}_2 = \hat{x}_1 - \overline{x}_1$.

5. They are not very plausible. For example, in order that $\overline{x}_1 - \hat{x}_1 > 0$ and $\overline{x}_2 - \hat{x}_2 < 0$ it would be required that $\partial x_1/\partial p_2 < \partial x_2/\partial p_1 < 0$, and that these interdependencies are sufficiently strong. This would imply strong complementarity between peak and off-peak.

6. Acton, Manning and Mitchell (1978) give a detailed account of the effects of time-of-day pricing in Europe.

References

Acton, J. P., Manning, W. G. Jr and Mitchell, B. M. (1978), *Peak Load Pricing: European Lessons for U.S. Energy Policy* (Cambridge, Mass., Ballinger Publishing Co.).

Alchian, A. A. and Demsetz, H. (1972), 'Production, Information Costs, and Economic Organization', *American Economic Review*, **62**, 5 (Dec 1972) 777-95.

Anderson, D. (1972), 'Models for Determining Least-Cost Investments in Electricity Supply', *Bell Journal of Econ.* **3**, 2 (Spring 1972) 267-99.

Arrow, K. J. (1968), 'Applications of Control Theory to Economic Growth', in *Lectures in Applied Mathematics*: vol. 12, *Mathematics of Decision Sciences* (Providence, American Mathematical Society).

Arrow, K. J. and Kurz, M. (1970). *Public Investment, the Rate of Return, and Optimal Fiscal Policy* (Baltimore, Resources for the Future Inc./John Hopkins University Press).

Arrow, K. J. and Scitovsky, T. (1969), *Readings in Welfare Economics*, (Homewood, Irwin).

Averch, H. and Johnson, L. L. (1962), 'Behavior of the Firm under Regulatory Constraint', *American Economic Review*, **52**, (Dec 1962) 1052-69.

Bailey, E. E. (1972), 'Peak Load Pricing under Regulatory Constraint', *Journal of Political Economy*, **80**, (July/Aug 1972) 662-79.

Bailey, E. E. (1973), *Economic Theory of Regulatory Constraint* Lexington, D. C. Heath).

Bailey, E. E. and Coleman, R. D. (1971), 'The Effect of Lagged Regulation in an Averch–Johnson Model', *Bell Journal of Economics* (Spring 1971) 278-92.

Bailey, E. E. and White, L. J. (1974), 'Reversals in Peak and Off-Peak Prices', *Bell Journal of Economics*, **5**, 1 (Spring 1974) 75-92.

Bates, R. W. (1963), 'Capital Costs and the Peak Problem in Electricity Supply', *Manchester School of Economics and Social Studies*, **31**, (May 1963) 149-70.

Bates, R. W. (1966), 'Stabilization Policy and Public Investment 1950–60 with Special Reference to Electricity Supply', *Yorkshire Bulletin* **18** (May 1966) 3–19.

Bator, F. M. (1957), 'The Simple Analysis of Welfare Maximization', *American Economic Review*, **47** (Mar 1957) 22–59.

Baumol, W. J. (1967), 'Reasonable Rules for Rate Regulation: Plausible Policies for an Imperfect World', in Phillips and Williamson (1967).

Baumol, W. J. (1972), Economic Theory and Operations Analysis (Englewood Cliffs, N.J., Prentice-Hall).

Baumol, W. J. (1977), 'On the Proper Tests for Natural Monopoly in a Multiproduct Industry', *American Economic Review*, **67**, 5 (Dec 1977) 809–22.

Baumol, W. J. and Bradford, D. (1970), 'Optimal Departures from Marginal Cost Pricing', *American Economic Review*, **60** (June 1970) 265–83.

Baumol, W. J. and Klevorick, A. K. (1970), 'Input Choices and Rate of Return Regulation: An Overview of the Discussion', *Bell Journal of Economics*, **1** (Autumn 1970) 162–90.

Bergson, A. (1938), 'A Reformulation of Certain Aspects of Welfare Economics', *Quarterly Journal of Economics*, **52** (Feb 1938) 310–34.

Berrie, T. W. (1967), 'The Economics of System Planning in Bulk Electricity Supply', *Electrical Reveiw*, **181** (Sep 1967).

Billingsley, P. (1968), *Convergence of Probability Measures* (New York, Wiley).

Boiteux, M. (1949), 'La tarification des demandes en point: application de la théorie de la vente au coût marginal', *Revue Generale de l'électricité*, **58** (Aug 1949) 321–40; translated as 'Peak Load Pricing', *Journal of Business*, **33** (Apr 1960) 157–79.

Boiteux, M. (1956), 'Sur la gestion des monopoles publics astrients a l'équilibre budgetaire', *Econometrica*, **24** (Jan 1956) 22–40; translated as 'On the Management of Public Monopolies Subject to Budgetary Constraints', *Journal of Economic Theory*, **3**, 3 (Sep 1971) 219–40.

Boyes, W. J. (1976), 'An Empirical Examination of the Averch–Johnson Effect', *Economic Inquiry*, **14** (Mar 1976) 25–35.

Brown, G. Jr and Johnson, M. B. (1969), 'Public Utility Pricing and Output under Risk', *American Economic Review*, **59** (Mar 1969) 119–29.

Buchanan, J. M. and Tulloch, G. (1962), *The Calculus of Consent* (Ann Arbor, Michigan University Press).

Carlton, D. W. (1977), 'Peak Load Pricing with Stochastic Demand', *American Economic Review*, 67, 5 (Dec 1977) 1006-10.

Chang, Hong-Chang (1978), *Dynamic Peak Load Pricing and Investment of a Nationalized Electric Utility in a Developing Country*, Ph.D. thesis submitted to University of Pennsylvania.

Coase, R. (1946), 'The Marginal Cost Controversy', *Economica*, 13 (Aug 1946) 169-82.

Comanor, W. and Leibenstein, H. (1969), 'Allocative Efficiency, X-Efficiency, and the Measurement of Welfare Losses', *Economica*, 36 (Aug 1969) 304-9.

Coombes, D. (1971), *State Enterprise: Business or Politics* (London, Allen and Unwin).

Courville, L. (1974), 'Regulation and Efficiency in the Electric Utility Industry', *Bell Journal of Economics*, 5 (Spring 1974) 53-74.

Crew M. A. (1966), 'Pennine Electricity Board', in Kempner and Willis (1966); also reprinted in Turvey (1968a).

Crew, M. A. (1967), 'Capital Costs and the Peak Problem in Electricity Supply: Comment, *Manchester School of Economics and Social Studies*, 35 (Sep 1967) 289-92.

Crew, M. A. (1975), *Theory of the Firm* (London, Longmans).

Crew, M. A. and Kleindorfer, P. R. (1971), 'Marshall and Turvey on Peak Loads or Joint Product Pricing', *Journal of Political Economy*, 79, 6 (Nov/Dec 1971) 1369-77.

Crew, M. A. and Kleindorfer, P. R. (1975a), 'On Off-Peak Pricing: An Alternative Technological Solution', *Kyklos*, 28, 1, 80-93.

Crew, M. A. and Kleindorfer, P. R. (1975b), 'Optimal Plant Mix in Peak Load Pricing', *Scottish Journal of Political Economy*, 22, 3 (Nov 1975) 277-91.

Crew, M. A. and Kleindorfer, P. R. (1976), 'Peak Load Pricing with a Diverse Technology', *Bell Journal of Economics*, 7, 1 (Spring 1976) 207-31.

Crew, M. A. and Kleindorfer, P. R. (1977), 'Managerial Discretion and Public Utility Regulation', unpublished manuscript (Oct 1977).

Crew, M. A. and Kleindorfer, P. R. (1978), 'Reliability and Public Utility Pricing', *American Economic Review*, 68 (Mar 1978) 31-40.

Dansby, R. E. (1976), 'Capacity Constrained Peak Load Pricing', *Bell Laboratories Economic Discussion Paper No. 62* (July 1976).

Dansby, R. E. (1977), 'Multi-Period Pricing with Stochastic Demand', *Bell Laboratories Economic Discussion Paper No. 111* (Oct 1977).

Davis, Blaine E. (1970), 'Investment and Rate of Return for the Regulated Firm', *Bell Journal of Economics*, **1**, 2 (Autumn 1970) 245-71.

Davis, O. A. and Whinston, A. B. (1965), 'Welfare Economics and the Theory of Second Best', *Review of Economic Studies*, **32** (Jan 1965) 1-14.

De Salvia, D. N. (1969), 'An Application of Peak Load Pricing', *Journal of Business*, **42**, 4 (Oct 1969) 458-76.

Demsetz, H. (1968), 'Why Regulate Utilities', *Journal of Law and Economics*, **11** (Apr 1968) 55-65.

Domestic Tariffs Experiment (1974), (London, Electricity Council).

Downs, A. K. (1957), *An Economic Theory of Democracy* (New York, Harper).

Drèze, J. (1964), 'Some Postwar Contributions of French Economists to Theory and Public Policy, with Special Emphasis on Problems of Resource Allocation', *American Economic Review*, **54**, supplement (June 1964) 1-64.

Dupuit, J. (1844), 'De la Mesure de l'Utilitié des Travaux publics', *Annales des Ponts et Chaussées*, **8**; reprinted in Arrow and Scitovsky (1969).

Edwards, F. R. (1977), 'Managerial Objectives in Regulated Industries: Expense Preference Behavior in Banking', *Journal of Political Economy*, **85** (Feb 1977) 147-62.

Edwards, F. R. and Stevens, B. J. (1976), 'Relative Efficiency of Alternative Institutional Arrangements for Collecting Refuse: Collective Action vs. the Free Market', Research Paper No. 151, Columbia University, Graduate School of Business (Oct 1976).

El Hodiri, M. and Takayama, A. (1973), 'Behavior of the Firm under Regulatory Constraint: Clarifications', *American Economic Review*, **63** (Mar 1973) 235-7.

Electric Utility Rate Design Study (1977), 'Analysis of Electricity Pricing in France and Great Britain', Topic 1.2 (25 Jan 1977).

Farrell, M. J. (1958), 'In Defense of Public Utility Price Theory', *Oxford Economic Papers*, **10** (Feb 1958) 109-23.

Feldstein, M. S. (1972), 'Equity and Efficiency in Public Pricing', *Quarterly Journal of Economics*, **86** (May 1972) 175-87.

Feller, W. (1966), *An Introduction to Probability Theory and Its Applications*, (New York, Wiley) vol. II.

Feller, W. (1968), *Introduction to Probability Theory and Its Applications*, 3rd edn (New York, Wiley).

Fells, A. (1972), *The British Prices and Incomes Board* (Cambridge University Press).

Ferguson, C. E. and Gould, J. P. (1975), *Microeconomic Theory* (Homewood, Irwin).

Galatin, M. (1968), *Economies of Scale and Technological Change in Thermal Generation* (Amsterdam, North-Holland).

Goldberg, V. P. (1976), 'Regulation and Administered Contracts', *Bell Journal of Economics*, 7, 2 (Autumn 1976) 426-48.

Gravelle, H. (1976), 'The Peak Load Problem with Feasible Storage', *Economic Journal*, 86 (June 1976) 256-77.

Harris, M. and Raviv, A. (1976), 'Optimal Incentive Contracts with Imperfect Information', unpublished manuscript (Carnegie-Mellon University).

Harris, M. and Raviv, A. (1978), 'Some Results on Incentive Contracts with Applications to Education and Employment, Health Insurance, and Law Enforcement', *American Economic Review*, 68, 1 (Mar 1978) 20-30.

Hayashi, P. M. and Trapani, J. M. (1976), 'Rate-of-Return Regulation and the Firm's Equilibrium Capital–Labor Ratio: Further Empirical Evidence of the Averch–Johnson Hypothesis', *Southern Economic Journal*, 42 (Jan 1976) 384-98.

Henderson, A. M. (1948), 'Prices and Profits in State Enterprise', *Review of Economic Studies*, 16, 13-24.

Henderson, A. M. and Quandt, R. E. (1971), *Microeconomic Theory* (New York, McGraw-Hill).

Hicks, J. R. (1941), 'The Rehabilitation of Consumer's Surplus', *Review of Economic Studies*, 8 (Feb 1941) 108-16.

Hicks, J. R. (1956), *A Revision of Demand Theory* (Oxford, Clarendon Press).

Hicks, K. L. (1960), 'Theory of Economic Selection of Generating Units', *A.I.E.E.E. Transactions*, 79 (Feb 1960) 1794-800.

Hirshleifer, J. (1958), 'Peak Loads and Efficient Pricing: Comment', *Quarterly Journal of Economics*, 72 (Aug 1958) 451-62.

Hotelling, H. (1932), 'Edgeworth's Taxation Paradox and the Nature of Demand and Supply Functions', *Journal of Political Economy*, 40, 5 (Oct 1932) 577-616.

Hotelling, H. (1935), 'Demand Functions with Limited Budgets', *Econo-*

metrica, 3 (Jan 1935) 66-78.

Hotelling, H. (1938), 'The General Welfare in Relation to Problems of Taxation and of Railway and Utility Rates', *Econometrica*, 6 (July 1938) 242-69.

Ineson, J. L. (1963), 'Fixing Electricity Tariffs', *Electrical Power Engineer* (June-Aug 1963) 1-11.

Jensen, M. C. and Meckling, W. H. (1976), 'Theory of the Firm: Managerial Behavior, Agency Costs and Ownership Structure', 3 (Oct 1976) 305-60.

Joskow, P. L. (1972), 'The Determination of the Allowed Rate of Return in a Formal Regulatory Hearing', *Bell Journal of Economics*, 3, 2 (Autumn 1972) 632-44.

Joskow, P. L. (1976), 'Contributions to the Theory of Marginal Cost Pricing', *Bell Journal of Economics*, 7, 1 (Spring 1976) 197-206.

Kafoglis, M. Z. (1969), 'Output of the Restrained Firm', *American Economic Review*, 59 (Sep 1969) 553-9.

Kahn, A. E. (1970), *The Economics of Regulation* (New York, Wiley).

Kaldor, N. (1939), 'Welfare Propositions in Economics and Interpersonal Comparisons of Utility', *Economic Journal*, 49 (Sep 1939) 549-52.

Katzner, D. (1970), *Static Demand Theory* (New York, Macmillan).

Kelf-Cohen, R. (1961), *Nationalisation in Britain* (London, Macmillan).

Kelf-Cohen, R. (1969), *Twenty Years of Nationalisation* (London, Macmillan).

Kempner, T. and Wills, G. (1966), *Bradford Exercises in Management* (London, Nelson).

Kleindorfer, P. R. and Glover, K. (1973), 'Linear Convex Stochastic Optimal Control with Application in Production Planning', *I.E.E.E. Transactions on Automatic Control*, 18, 1 (Feb 1973) 56-9.

Klevorick, A. K. (1971), 'The "Optimal" Fair Rate of Return', *Bell Journal of Economics*, 2 (Spring 1971) 122-53.

Lebowitz, J. L., Lee, C. O. and Linhart, P. B. (1976), 'Some Effects of Inflation on a Regulated Firm with Original-Cost Depreciation', *Bell Journal of Economics*, (Autumn 1976) 463-77.

Lehmann, E. L. (1959), *Testing Statistical Hypotheses* (New York, Wiley).

Leibenstein, H. (1966), 'Allocative Efficiency versus X-Efficiency', *American Economic Review*, 56 (June 1966) 392-415.

Leland, H. A. and Meyer, R. A. (1976), 'Monopoly Pricing Structures with Imperfect Discrimination', *Bell Journal of Economics*, **7**, 2 (Autumn 1976) 449-62.

Lewis, W. A. (1941), 'The Two-Part Tariff', *Economica*, **8** (Aug 1941) 249-70.

Lipsey, R. E. and Lancaster, K. M. (1956), 'The General Theory of Second Best', *Review of Economic Studies*, **24**, 1, 11-32.

Little, I. M. D. (1953), *The Price of Fuel* (Oxford, Clarendon Press).

Little, I. M. D. (1957), *Critique of Welfare Economics* (Oxford University Press).

Marchand, M. G. (1973), 'The Economic Principles of Telephone Rates Under a Budgetary Constraint', *Review of Economic Studies*, **40** (Oct 1973) 507-15.

Marshall, A. (1890), *Principles of Economics* (London, Macmillan).

Meek, R. L. (1963), 'The Bulk Supply Tariff for Electricity', *Oxford Economic Papers*, **15** (July 1963) 107-23.

Meyer, R. A. (1975), 'Monopoly Pricing and Capacity Choice under Uncertainty', *American Economic Review*, **65** (June 1975) 426-37.

Mishan, E. J. (1971), *Cost-Benefit Analysis* (London, Allen & Unwin).

Mohring, H. (1970), 'The Peak Load Pricing Problem with Increasing Returns and Pricing Constraints', *American Economic Review*, **60**, 4 (Sep 1970) 693-705.

Morrison, H. (1933), *Socialisation and Transport* (London, Constable).

Munby, D. L. (1959), 'Finance of the Nationalized Industries', *Bulletin of the Oxford Institute of Statistics*, **21** (May 1959) 73-84.

Nelson, J. R. (1964), *Marginal Cost Pricing in Practice* (Englewood Cliffs, N.J., Prentice-Hall).

Nerlove, M. (1974), 'Estimation of a Cost Function: Returns to Scale in Electricity Generation', in de Neufville, R. and Marks, D. H. (eds) (1974), *System Planning and Design* (Englewood Cliffs, N.J., Prentice-Hall).

Ng, T. K. and Weisser, M. (1974), 'Optimal Pricing with a Balanced Budget Constraint - the Case of the Two-Part Tariff', *Review of Economic Studies*, **41** (July 1974) 337-45.

Nguyen, D. T. (1976), 'The Problems of Peak Loads and Inventories', *Bell Journal of Economics*, **7**, 1 (Spring 1976) 232-41.

Niskanen, W. A. (1973), *Bureaucracy, Servant or Master* (London, Institute of Economic Affairs).

Oi, W. Y. (1971), 'A Disneyland Dilemma: Two-Part Tariffs for a Mickey Mouse Monopoly', *Quarterly Journal of Economics*, **85**,

1 (Feb 1971) 77-96.

Olson, M. Jr (1965), The Logic of Collective Action (Cambridge, Mass., Harvard University Press).

Panzar, J. C. (1976), 'A Neoclassical Approach to Peak Load Pricing', *Bell Journal of Economics*, 7, 2 (Autumn 1976) 521-30.

Peck, S. C. (1977), 'A Note Concerning the Effect of Reserve Margins and Regulatory Policy on New Turbogenerator Size', *Bell Journal of Economics*, 8, 1 (Spring 1977) 262-9.

Peles, T. C. and Stein, J. L. (1976), 'The Effect of Rate of Return Regulation is Highly Sensitive to the Nature of Uncertainty', *American Economic Review*, 66 (June 1976) 278-89.

Petersen, H. C. (1975), 'An Empirical Test of Regulatory Effects', *Bell Journal of Economics*, 6 (Spring 1975) 111-26.

Phillips, A. and Williamson, O. E. (eds) (1967), *Prices: Issues in Theory, Practice, and Public Policy* (Philadelphia, University of Pennsylvania Press).

Phillips, C. F. Jr (1969), *The Economics of Regulation* (Homewood, Irwin).

Posner, R. A. (1974), 'Theories of Economic Regulation', *Bell Journal of Economics*, 5, 2 (Autumn 1974) 335-58.

Pressman, I. (1970), 'A Mathematical Formulation of the Peak Load Pricing', *Bell Journal of Economics*, 1, 2 (Autumn 1970) 304-26.

Rees, R. (1974), 'A Reconsideration of the Expense Preference Theory of the Firm', *Economica*, 41 (Aug 1974) 295-307.

Robson, W. A. (1962), *Nationalized Industry and Public Ownership* (London, Allen & Unwin).

Ross, S. A. (1973), 'The Economic Theory of Agency: The Principal's Problem', *American Economic Review*, 63 (May 1973) 134-9.

Ruggles, N. (1949), 'The Welfare Basis of the Marginal Cost Pricing Principle', *Review of Economics Studies*, 17, 29-46.

Salkever, D. S. (1970), 'Public Utility Pricing and Output under Risk: Comment', *American Economic Review*, 60 (June 1970) 487-8.

Samuelson, P. A. (1947), *Foundations of Economic Analysis* (Harvard University Press).

Scherer, F. M. (1970), *Market Structure and Economic Performance* (Chicago, Rand McNally).

Schiller, P. (1945a), *Technical Report R/7106: Methods of Allocating to Classes of Consumers or Load the Demand Related Portion of the Standing Costs of Electricity Supply* (London, British Electrical and Allied Industries).

Schiller, P. (1945b), *Technical Report K/T109: An Improved Method for Allocating the Demand Related Portion of the Standing Cost of Electricity Supply* (London, British Electrical and Allied Industries).

Scitovsky, T. (1941), 'A Note on Welfare Propositions in Economics', *Review of Economic Studies*, 9 (Nov 1941) 77-88.

Sherman, R. (1972), 'The Rate of Return Regulated Public Utility Firm is Schizophrenic', *Applied Economics*, 4, 1 (Mar 1972) 23-32.

Sherman, R. (1974), *The Economics of Industry* (Boston, Little, Brown).

Sherman, R. (1977), 'Financial Aspects of Rate-of-Return Regulation', *Southern Economic Journal*, 44, 2 (Oct 1977) 240-8.

Sherman, R. and Visscher, M. L. (1978), 'Second Best Pricing with Stochastic Demand', *American Economic Review*, 68, 1 (Mar 1978) 41-53.

Sheshinski, E. (1971), 'Welfare Aspects of a Regulatory Constraint: Note', *American Economic Review*, 61 (Mar 1971) 175-8.

Simon, H. A. (1961), *Administrative Behavior* (New York, Macmillan).

Smithson, C. W. (1978), 'The Degree of Regulation and the Monopoly Firm. Further Empirical Evidence', *Southern Economic Journal*, 44, 3 (Jan 1978) 568-80.

Spann, R. M. (1974), 'Rate of Return Regulation and Efficiency in Production: An Empirical Test of the Averch-Johnson Thesis', *Bell Journal of Economics*, 5 (Spring 1974) 38-52.

Steiner, P. O. (1957), 'Peak Loads and Efficient Pricing', *Quarterly Journal of Economics*, 71 (Nov 1957) 585-610.

Stigler, G. J. (1971), 'The Economic Theory of Regulation', *Bell Journal of Economics*, 2, 1 (Spring 1971) 3-21.

Takayama, A. (1969), 'Behavior of the Firm under Regulatory Constraint', *American Economic Review*, 59 (June 1969) 255-60.

Takayama, A. (1974), *Mathematical Economics* (New York, Holt, Rinehart & Winston).

Telson, M. (1975), 'The Economics of Alternative Levels of Reliability for Electric Power Generation Systems', *Bell Journal of Economics*, 6, 2 (Autumn 1975) 679-94.

Turvey, R. (ed.) (1968a), *Public Enterprise* (Harmondsworth, Penguin).

Turvey, R. (1968b), *Optimal Pricing and Investment in Electricity Supply: An Essay in Applied Welfare Economics*, (London, Allen & Unwin).

Turvey, R. (1969), 'Marginal Cost', *Economic Journal*, 79 (June 1969) 282-99.

Turvey, R. (1970), 'Peak Load Pricing and Output Under Risk: Comment', *American Economic Review*, **60** (June 1970) 485-6.

Turvey, R. (1971), *Economic Analysis and Public Enterprises* (London, Allen & Unwin).

Tyndall, D. G. (1951), 'The Relative Merits of Average Cost Pricing, Marginal Cost Pricing, and Price Discrimination', *Quarterly Journal of Economics*, **56** (Aug 1951) 342-72.

Visscher, M. L. (1973), 'Welfare-Maximizing Price and Output with Stochastic Demand: Comment', *American Economic Review*, **63** (Mar 1973) 224-9.

Webb, M. G. (1973), *The Economics of the Nationalized Industries* (London, Nelson).

Wellisz, S. H. (1963), 'Regulation of Natural Gas Pipeline Companies: An Economic Analysis', *Journal of Political Economy*, **71** Feb 1963) 30-43.

Wenders, J. T. (1976), 'Peak Load Pricing in the Electricity Industry', *Bell Journal of Economics*, **7**, 1 (Spring 1976) 232-41.

Wenders, J. T. and Taylor, L. D. (1976), 'Experiments in Seasonal-Time-of-Day Pricing of Electricity to Residential Users', *Bell Journal of Economics*, **7**, 2 (Autumn 1976) 531-52.

Westfield, F. M. (1965), 'Conspiracy and Regulation', *American Economic Review*, **55** (June 1965) 424-43.

Wilcox, C. (1966), *Public Policies Toward Business* (Homewood, Irwin).

Williamson, O. E. (1964), *The Economics of Discretionary Behavior: Managerial Objectives in a Theory of the Firm* (Englewood Cliffs, N.J., Prentice-Hall).

Williamson, O. E. (1966), 'Peak Load Pricing and Optimal Capacity under Indivisibility Constraints', *American Economic Review*, **56** (Sep 1966) 810-27.

Williamson, O. E. (1975), *Markets and Hierarchies: Analysis and Antitrust Implications* (New York, Free Press).

Williamson, O. E. (1976), 'Franchise Bidding for Natural Monopolies – In General and with Respect to CATV', *Bell Journal of Economics*, **7**, 1 (Spring 1976) 73-104.

Willig, R. D. (1973), *Welfare Analysis of Policies Affecting Prices and Products*, Memorandum No. 153 (Center for Research in Economic Growth, Stanford, California).

Willig, R. D. (1976), 'Consumer's Surplus Without Apology', *American Economic Review*, **66**, 4 (Sep 1966) 589-97.

Wilson, G. W. (1972), 'The Theory of Peak Load Pricing: A Final Note', *Bell Journal of Economics*, **3**, 2 (Spring 1972) 307-10.

Wiseman, J. (1957), 'The Theory of Public Utility Price: An Empty Box', *Oxford Economic Papers*, **9** (Feb 1957) 56-74.

Zajac, E. E. (1970), 'A Geometric Treatment of the Averch-Johnson's Behavior of the Firm Model', *American Economic Review*, **60** (Mar 1970) 117-25.

Zajac, E. E. (1972), 'A Note on "Gold Plating" or "Rate Base Padding"', *Bell Journal of Economics*, **3** (Spring 1972), 311-15.

Zajac, E. E. (1977), 'More on Consumer's Surplus Without Apology', *Bell Laboratories Economic Discussion Paper No. 112* (Oct 1977).

Zangwill, W. I. (1969), *Nonlinear Programming: A Unified Approach* (Englewood Cliffs, N.J., Prentice-Hall).

Index

243